AFRICAN STUDIES SERIES

The African Studies Series is a collection of monographs and general studies
that reflect the interdisciplinary interests of the African Studies Centre at
Cambridge. Volumes to date have combined historical, anthropological,
economic, political, and other perspectives. Each contribution has assumed
that such broad approaches can contribute much to our understanding of
Africa, and that this may in turn be of advantage to specific disciplines.

AFRICAN STUDIES SERIES

1 *City Politics: A Study of Léopoldville, 1962–63*   J. S. La Fontaine
2 *Studies in Rural Capitalism in West Africa*   Polly Hill
3 *Land Policy in Buganda*   Henry W. West
4 *The Nigerian Military: A Sociological Analysis of Authority and Revolt, 1960–67*   Robin Luckham
5 *The Ghanaian Factory Worker: Industrial Man in Africa*   Margaret Peil
6 *Labour in the South African Gold Mines, 1911–1969*   Francis Wilson
7 *The Price of Liberty: Personality and Politics in Colonial Nigeria*
   Kenneth W. J. Post and George D. Jenkins
8 *Subsistence to Commercial Farming in Present Day Buganda: An Economic and Anthropological Survey*   Audrey I. Richards, Ford Sturrock and Jean M. Fortt (eds)
9 *Dependence and Opportunity: Political Change in Ahafo*   John Dunn and A. F. Robertson
10 *African Railwaymen: Solidarity and Opposition in an East African Labour Force*   R. D. Grillo
11 *Islam and Tribal Art in West Africa*   René A. Bravmann
12 *Modern and Traditional Elites in the Politics of Lagos*   P. D. Cole
13 *Asante in the Nineteenth Century: The Structure and Evolution of a Political Order*   Ivor Wilks
14 *Culture, Tradition and Society in the West African Novel*
   Emmanuel N. Obiechina
15 *Saints and Politicians: Essays in the Organisation of a Senegalese Peasant Society*   Donal B. Cruise O'Brien
16 *The Lions of Dagbon: Political Change in Northern Ghana*   Martin Staniland
17 *Politics of Decolonisation: Kenya Europeans and the Land Issue 1960 to 1965*   Gary B. Wasserman
18 *Muslim Brotherhoods in Nineteenth-century Africa*   B. G. Martin
19 *Warfare in the Sokoto Caliphate*   Joseph P. Smaldone
20 *Liberia and Sierra Leone. An Essay In Comparative Politics*
   Christopher Clapham
21 *Adam Kok's Griquas: A Study in the Development of Stratification in South Africa*   R. Ross
22 *Class, Power and Ideology in Ghana: The Railwaymen of Sekondi–Takoradi*
   Richard Jeffries

WEST AFRICAN STATES: FAILURE AND PROMISE

A study in comparative politics

Edited by
JOHN DUNN

Fellow of Kings College and
Reader in Politics in the University of Cambridge

CAMBRIDGE UNIVERSITY PRESS

CAMBRIDGE

LONDON · NEW YORK · MELBOURNE

Published by the Syndics of the Cambridge University Press
The Pitt Building, Trumpington Street, Cambridge CB2 1RP
Bentley House, 200 Euston Road, London NW1 2DB
32 East 57th Street, New York, NY 10022, USA
296 Beaconsfield Parade, Middle Park, Melbourne 3206, Australia

First published 1978

Phototypeset by Western Printing Services Ltd
Printed in Great Britain at the
University Press, Cambridge

Library of Congress cataloguing in publication data
Main entry under title:
West African states.
(African studies series; 23)
Includes index.
1. Africa, West – Politics and government – Addresses,
essays, lectures. I. Dunn, John, 1940–   II. Series.
DT476.5.W47   320.3'0966   77-80832

ISBN 0 521 21801 2 hard covers
ISBN 0 521 29283 2 paperback

Contents

		page
List of contributors		vi
Preface		vii
Map of West Africa		viii
1	Comparing West African states JOHN DUNN	1
2	Ghana RICHARD RATHBONE	22
3	Guinea R. W. JOHNSON	36
4	Ivory Coast BONNIE CAMPBELL	66
5	Liberia CHRISTOPHER CLAPHAM	117
6	Nigeria GAVIN WILLIAMS and TERISA TURNER	132
7	Senegal DONAL B. CRUISE O'BRIEN	173
8	Sierra Leone CHRISTOPHER ALLEN	189
9	Conclusion JOHN DUNN	211
Notes		217
Index		253

List of contributors

Christopher Allen, Department of Politics, University of Edinburgh

Dr Bonnie Campbell, Department of Political Science, University of Quebec at Montreal

Dr Christopher Clapham, Department of Politics, University of Lancaster

John Dunn, King's College, Cambridge

R. W. Johnson, Magdalen College, Oxford

Dr Donal Cruise O'Brien, Department of Economic and Political Studies, School of Oriental and African Studies, University of London

Dr Richard Rathbone, Department of History, School of Oriental and African Studies, University of London

Dr Terisa Turner, London School of Economics

Gavin Williams, St Peter's College, Oxford

Preface

All but one of the chapters in this volume originated in a series of public lectures given in Cambridge under the auspices of the University's Centre for African Studies. The contributors are beholden to the Centre's Committee of Management and especially to its Director, Dr A. F. Robertson, both for this initial sponsorship and for the continuing assistance which has made it possible to produce the present volume.

Anyone who finds the volume of any interest or value should also be aware that its production has owed at least as much to the patience, the diplomatic charm and the efficiency of the Centre's secretary, Louise Speed, as it has to any of the authors concerned.

Cambridge, April 1977

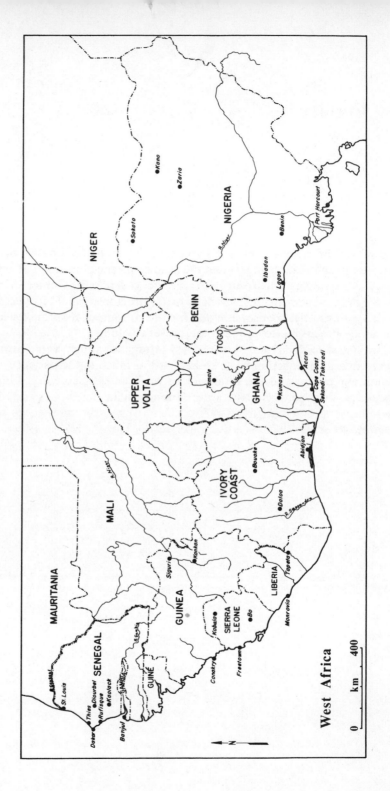

West Africa

0   km   400

1

Comparing West African states

JOHN DUNN

Even at best comparative politics is a shaky trade, uneasy as to its intellectual ambitions and fickle in its criteria of analytical achievement. There are many reasons for this disarray, by no means all of them ills for which there is any obvious remedy even in principle. One of the main difficulties facing the student of comparative politics is the simple question of which units it is appropriate to select for comparison. Persons may be compared to summer's days and leaders of the British Tory Party to medieval implements of torture. Comparison can be as much a discerning of similarity as a savouring of contrast. It is certainly not difficult to find differences between historical experiences. But if one hopes to learn anything very clear or instructive from the activity of comparing, it is essential to select as units for comparison items which resemble each other in a great many ways. For the most part this problem of selection is resolved in professional practice in political science by the adoption of conventional institutional or ideological boundaries. Institutions which share a common descriptive label are compared systematically: political parties, public bureaucracies, educational systems, institutions of local government, armies, trade unions, multinational corporations. At the level of the state itself the units of comparison are often more overtly ideological (communist states or capitalist democracies), though the direct contrast between the favoured and the disfavoured naturally does not preclude being equally ideologically explicit.[1] Such comparisons may serve well enough to evoke anxiety or to reassure. But they are better calculated to define the differences between sets of polities than to explain the characteristics of any particular polity. The implicit or explicit ideological specification of the units of comparison also frequently means that it is the ideologically focused aspects of these polities which are most clearly defined, a feature which renders the comparison a trifle circular as political analysis. Few, by contrast, are likely to dispute the intellectual viability and the potential illumination of the comparative study of distinct subordinate institutions. Studies of both trade unions and armies in African states have proliferated in the last decade and a half and, if the best of the resulting works thus far have been monographs on particular countries rather than extended comparative studies,[2] their analytical approach has frequently been explicitly comparative.

At the state level the potential illumination of comparative studies remains more open to dispute. There have been valuable studies of West African states governed by a single party[3] and an illuminating early sketch by Ken Post of *The New States of West Africa* as a whole.[4] Now that the novelty of these states has worn off and many of their governing parties have succumbed along with it, there have in turn been a number of studies of military regimes.[5] But ideological and constitutional classifications of West African states by now evoke little credence either inside or outside West Africa itself. Except within the frame of a more or less Marxist political economy there is little residual conviction in the comparative study of West African states as such. It is not clear, however, that this diffidence is particularly well-advised. States are bounded institutions just as much as armies or civil bureaucracies. Without succumbing to the solemnities of reference group theory, it is plain enough in the modern world, too, that states are political entities peculiarly concerned to characterize themselves in a reassuring manner and peculiarly apt to couch their self-characterizations in explicit comparison with other states. Even if their novelty has now worn off, it is also true that the states of West Africa inhabit a more homogeneously common historical time than most sets of states selected as objects of comparison by political scientists. By contrast with Seymour Martin Lipset's comparison of all states in the world over a given time span on the basis of political and economic indicators in the quest for the preconditions of stable democracy,[6] a comparative focus on states in West Africa posits a temporal frame which has historical substance and is not a mere chronological stipulation. Both the physical boundaries of these states and their organizational cores are products of the phase of European imperialism in the second half of the nineteenth century. With the single exception of Liberia every state in West Africa today was a colonial administrative unit a mere three decades ago, though in the case of the former French territories these units were in their turn incorporated into other larger units which have not survived as such into the present day. The economies and social structures of every West African country have been overwhelmingly modified by their incorporation into a capitalist world trading system. No modern state in West Africa, despite one or two titular pretensions (Ghana, Mali, Benin) is a legitimate inheritor of an African state formation which existed in 1800 or earlier. Again with the single exception

2

of Liberia, no present West African state existed as an independent nation state in 1956, while in the entire area south of Mauretania and north of Rhodesia and Namibia there remain today no further direct relicts of colonial rule. If we add one further restriction, in this case ecological rather than historical, we will be left with a frame for political comparison as promising as can reasonably be expected, at least at the state level. The states of the interior, the southern fringe of the Sahara, the *Bilād al-Sūdān* of medieval Islam, are highly distinctive political formations. Some of the least viable states in the world, weakly integrated into the world market because endowed with so few resources worth exploiting, they have also endured in the last decade an ecological trauma in the shape of drought and famine of a highly distinctive character. The most placid and optimistic observer of post-colonial political capabilities will hardly escape a measure of dismay in the face of this experience, though the detailed assignment of causal responsibility for past disaster remains understandably contentious. But issues of culpability aside, it takes today a real ideologue, whether of the right or of the left, to see with any confidence a happy political future for the Sahel. Some of the interior states possess political organizations as distinctive as they are apparently simple. Marshal Bokassa, for example, in the Central African Republic for a time united with his posts of life-president, president of the government and secretary-general of the single governing party, the portfolios of the Minister of Justice, the Minister of National Defence, War Veterans and Victims, the Minister of Public Functions and Social Security, the Minister of Information, along with responsibility for the armed forces as a whole.[7] Beneath the burden of these responsibilities the Marshal plainly has better grounds than even Louis XIV for identifying the state with himself; and we need not be excessively surprised that he has now drawn the logical conclusion and taken the imperial purple. Little in the politics of the Guinea Coast has quite this grand simplicity of outline, though there are national units whose demographic insufficiency and material resource base make them as implausible candidates for lasting autonomy and statehood as any sovereign segment of the interior. In the days when ideological or constitutional categories appeared the most promising basis for analysing West Africa's new states, the evanescent contrast between multi-party and one-party states or the slightly more protracted contrasts in the intensity of the socialist rhetoric employed in governmental publicity provided frames of comparison which cut across the geographical division between coast and interior. One need not in retrospect feel surprised that geography should have proved more durable than public rhetorical preferences or constitutional law.

The states of the West African littoral from the northern border of

Senegal with Mauretania to the south eastern border of the Federation of Nigeria with the Cameroons are not of course wholly homogeneous in ecology. The distance from north to south in this range is some nine hundred miles. The true rain forest stretches north only as far as Guinea and the internal extension of the coastal countries varies substantially. Senegal, for example, a predominantly savannah country, was heavily affected by the Sahel drought, while Ghana or the Ivory Coast were scarcely touched by it. When set against Nigeria or Ghana, the ecological problems of Senegal, even the threat of desertification, are undoubtedly extremely urgent. Such ecological variations are politically important. But they are distinctly less important than the fact that (with the possible but probably not very long-lasting exception of Guiné-Bissau[8]) the majority of agrarian producers – and in all these countries a substantial majority of the adult population still consists of agrarian producers – is engaged today, as it was in 1956, partly in the production of foodstuffs or raw materials for the world market. This state of affairs is today actively deplored by many. But it is now clear, as it perhaps was not in 1951 or 1957, that it is a pattern of production which it is by no means easy to change for the better. There are many structural similarities between these states: in geographical patterns of uneven development, in the powerful impact of the state as such on internal patterns of social stratification, in rates of population growth unmatched by the expansion of employment opportunities. Even if one does not deploy utopian standards or culturally exotic norms (as analysts in the period of decolonization were understandably apt to do), it seems reasonable to identify a fair measure of failure in the performance of this set of state powers as a whole. Nor is this a verdict which their own subject populations are likely to have much motive to dispute. But if failure is a relatively objective, even uncontentious, judgement, promise lies more squarely in the eye of the beholder. Optimism of the will is a fine thing (and the populations of these countries, as perhaps of our own, plainly need all the optimism they can muster); but for the moment there remains ample room for pessimism of the intelligence.

At the level of structural classification, then, and still more at the level of serious political judgement, there seems good reason for attempting a direct comparison between the political experiences of these states over the last two decades and more – and at least some grounds for optimism in hoping for a measure of progress in the explanation of homologies in and disparities between these experiences. A number of qualifications, however, must be acknowledged from the outset. Although the states of the West African littoral do share many historical and geographical features (and decidedly more of such features than are common to most sets of

4

states selected by political scientists for comparative study), several of them nevertheless stand out extremely sharply from the remainder in ways which could easily vitiate the analytical interest of comparison. Most of them, for example, are clearly in geopolitical terms states of no importance – the Gambia or Dahomey/Benin for instance at present meeting the severest standards of geopolitical triviality. But one of them, the Federation of Nigeria, as a result of its large if numerically disputed population and its OPEC-assisted oil wealth, is now the most powerful black state in sub-Saharan Africa, a cynosure for anxious British bankers and (more impressively) for an American secretary of state. There are many respects in which a political comparison between the Gambia and Nigeria might prove deeply uninstructive. Two other littoral states, Guiné-Bissau and Liberia, also stand out from their fellows in ways which may well be thought highly significant. It is a matter of the greatest consequence that the modern state powers in every other country in West Africa are direct continuations of the colonial state power, an external apparatus of control created for the express purpose of dominating the local society as a whole and keeping it firmly subordinate to the purposes of those beyond its borders. Liberia has at no time been a formal colony of another state and its governmental machinery and apparatus of coercion were consequently local creations, though of course creations in which foreign assistance always was and has plainly always remained of major consequence. How much eventual difference this idiosyncratic history has meant for Liberian political structures and relations today is an interesting question. It has certainly given post-war Liberian history a different and rather less hectic rhythm than that of most of its neighbours. The distinctiveness of Guiné-Bissau, potentially perhaps equally instructive, lies in the scale and duration of the struggle which it was obliged to undergo in order to win its escape from colonial domination. Liberia is a neocolonial state, without formally being a post-colonial state. Guiné-Bissau, by contrast, is indubitably a post-colonial state; but it is a more interesting question whether it is now in any danger of becoming a neocolonial state. By the standards of some other zones of European colonial rule, the populations of West Africa won their freedom with remarkable ease in the aftermath of the Second World War, benefiting at second hand from the struggles of the fellow colonial subjects of their colonial masters in South East Asia and in the Maghreb. Only those whose colonial overlords were themselves the most backward economically and politically[9] met really protracted military resistance once any significant level of mass struggle had been developed. The consequences of the Portuguese obduracy in the small enclave state of Guiné-Bissau were striking. The national liberation movement, the PAIGC (Partido

5

Africano da Independência da Guiné e Cabo Verde), blessed with a leader of great political talent in Amilcar Cabral, were obliged to attempt the construction of a complete counter-state in the zones of the country which they controlled and they proved fully capable of doing so through the years of protracted struggle. Such patterns of construction of organizations of effective popular leadership and control in the face of incumbent state power have been the most distinctive twentieth-century innovation in revolutionary process.[10] In China and Vietnam, as perhaps in Yugoslavia and Algeria, they have created state powers with a formidable executive capacity in the most unpromising of historical contexts. Unsuccessful attempts have been made to emulate this pattern in some areas of sub-Saharan Africa, notably in what is now Zaire.[11] Some aspects of it have now been implemented in the other and geopolitically far more consequential ex-colonies of Portugal, Mozambique and (more raggedly) Angola. But in Guiné-Bissau the balance between the slow and careful establishing of political consent and the construction of an effective war machine has been uniquely favourable. The PAIGC has not lacked its western propagandists and it has not always been easy to discern where their direct observation or reliable information ends and political optimism begins to take over. But the broad outlines of their judgement have weathered very well.[12] Though the same can perhaps not be said of its ocean consort, the Cape Verde Islands, Guiné-Bissau is geopolitically about as trivial as a state could well be. But in political terms its distinctive history plausibly holds as much promise as any single residual outcome of the process of decolonization in West Africa. For present purposes, however, such hopes are mere surmises, involving as they do a more or less confident comparison between the future of Guiné-Bissau and the post-colonial past of its West African neighbours. The tardiness of the Portuguese decolonization, itself a product of Portugal's own failure fully to inhabit the historical time of post-war Western Europe, has excluded Guiné-Bissau until very recently from the post-war history of independent statehood in West Africa, the experience of which is being considered here. It is easy enough to see now that there may prove to be very handsome advantages in such backwardness. But since the comparisons which we seek to draw here are comparisons between the political experiences of independent states, Guiné-Bissau must make its presence felt largely off-stage, as a persisting contrast, explicit or implicit, and not through a full dress appearance *in propria persona.*

For the present we may use the case of Guiné-Bissau simply to sharpen one of the key questions of West African political development. If to be a neocolonial state is to be involved in a certain pattern of trading and producing relations on the world market, to be largely an exporter of

primary commodities on what are necessarily largely externally determined terms of trade, then there is some evidence that Guiné-Bissau is
currently attempting to *become* a neocolonial state. If, on the other hand,
to be a neocolonial state is to be a state whose state power was fashioned
by a colonial ruler to preside over this pattern of producing and trading in
such a way as to advantage the national economic interests of the colonial
metropolis itself and which was finely enough tuned to this task to find
itself carrying on in much the same fashion after independence had come,
if the *idea* of the neocolonial state is an emphasis on a readily intelligible
historical continuity in this sense, then Guiné-Bissau is very plainly *not* a
neocolonial state in the sense in which the Ivory Coast, for example, is a
paradigm neocolonial state. Not being over-refined, it seems reasonable
in the first instance to explain how the officials of the Ivory Coast state run
the Ivory Coast economy by pointing out that this was roughly the way in
which the French *taught* them to run it and by indicating that the French
(along with some of their foreign friends) have by no means abandoned
their instructional efforts in the period since independence and that they
have little difficulty in making it broadly to the advantage of these
officials to continue to run it in much the same way. Leaving aside for the
moment the question of how this pattern has benefited or damaged the
different groups who make up the remainder of the Ivorian population,
and supposing that the government of Guiné-Bissau opts not for a rigid
autarky but for a pattern of economic development in which the export of
agricultural products remains of central importance, we can at least be
sure in the case of Guiné that the explanation of this trading pattern is not
the success of Portuguese colonial political engineering and post-colonial
ideological blandishment.

The state apparatus of Guiné-Bissau is the *political* product (however
much it may have taken over logistically from the departing Portuguese)
of a lengthy war of independence, of an alternative road. It was not a road
selected gratuitously by Guiné's nationalist party, the PAIGC, but rather
one forced upon them by the archaic economic and political posture of
Portugal as a colonial power. But once the PAIGC had undertaken this
path, it compelled them to learn how the consent of the population could
be won and held and to grasp the realities of the social and economic
situations of the majority of the population.

From the point of view of political judgement the most important issue
in analysing the post-independence politics of the West African littoral is
simple to pose (though like most serious political questions it is a good
deal less simple to answer confidently than it is merely to formulate).
Given the judgement that the political and economic predicament of
West African populations in 1977 is not on the whole enviable and given

the perception (an evident enough one) that there is an intimate link between this predicament and the situation of these populations as trading on (and largely producing for) a capitalist world market which is far from being a charitable institution, whose fault precisely is it that this predicament, group by group, individual by individual, is so dire? Is it the recalcitrant reality of the world economy which generates these patterns? (And if it is this recalcitrant economic reality, how exactly should this be conceived? As politically and militarily generated inequalities of power which could in principle (if not as yet in practice) be politically and militarily reversed? As a simple function of relative factor endowments (in part, to be sure, historically generated, but nonetheless at present historically *real* for that)? On what terms precisely would historically and economically unequal nations trade within a world the economic relations of which were no longer capitalist in character? Or are these patterns generated, rather, by the derelictions of the political authorities of these societies who accept *as* recalcitrant realities (for their own sinister reasons: greed, cowardice, stupidity) what are merely humanly generated practices which it is perfectly open to men, braver, more vigorous, more austere and more imaginative, to alter decisively for the better?

This may appear a pretty simple sort of question to answer; and so at one level it is. But since the answer is not *either* the one (objective economic reality) *or* the other (the weakness, folly and vice of political leaders) but instead a fair measure of both, the answer can be pronounced with confidence only at a rather evasive level. Neither comprehensive social determinisms nor comprehensive political voluntarisms offer coherent and veridical political perspectives. The key question is always the proportions between external constraint and the opportunity for creative agency. It remains, moreover, conceptually unclear how far these proportions can even be thought of as a potential item of *knowledge* while they are still in the future. For what will determine them includes what men will in fact *choose* to do. There are none so uncreative as those that do not try.

These, then, are the types of question which we need to bear in mind as we settle down to compare the political experience of these seven states. But what, more simple-mindedly, ought we to be attempting to compare? To compare at the state level implies the selection of some particular political dimensions as appropriate objects of comparison and a corresponding neglect of others. We may assume the presence of some pattern of factional conflict in many if not in most village communities in the countries of West Africa and we may also safely presume a pervasive presence in personal social relations of the lop-sided amities of patrons and clients.[13] Such patterns may well be of dominating existential import in the political lives of individuals, families and communities. But they will appear here, if they appear at all, because of their direct impact at the state level, in the manner in which the state apparatuses in these countries carry out the political tasks which history has assigned to them. What we seek to assess and to explain are the different levels of success and failure which these apparatuses have exhibited in the performance of their tasks. It is not overwhelmingly difficult to identify some aspects of the performance of these apparatuses and it is possible, consequently, if one possesses confident and univocal criteria of political achievement, to attempt an assessment of their performance. But it is distinctly less easy to be certain (partly because it is necessarily politically more contentious) precisely how it is appropriate to seek to explain the variations between these performances. The intellectual tradition which possesses the strongest answer to the question of how to explain the performance of state powers as such is, of course, Marxism. But even this tradition, if it has lost nothing recently in the assurance of its answers, has perhaps wilted a little when it comes to specifying precisely what its answers now are. The resolute rejection of economism[14] (what most non-Marxists suppose and one suspects the great majority of Marxists also until fairly recently supposed to *constitute* Marxism) and the causal recrudescence of the class struggle and even of ideology in the works in particular of Professor Poulantzas offer various intellectual and political felicities – shifting for example Marxist theory of the capitalist state from the status of splendidly clear but sadly contingently false to that of the hopelessly vague and very possibly necessarily true (and thus vacuous). Simplifying ruthlessly and recklessly incurring the risk of major distortions, Poulantzas seems above all anxious to conceive the state as a relation, the means (whatever they may be) by which the dominant class (or fraction of a class) in a given social formation contrives to reproduce a particular pattern of the organization of production within the territory occupied by this social formation. What such a theory selects as its explicandum plainly has much in common with the political outcomes which we are here seeking to understand. Whatever direct clarification it can contribute may thus be received with gratitude. (It would be nice to be as sure of anything in the human sciences as Professor Poulantzas seems of almost everything.) In particular it is easy enough to accept the political appropriateness of selecting as the persistent focus of inquiry the means by which a particular pattern of socio-economic power contrives to (or fails to) sustain itself in being. There is some felicity too in Poulantzas's stalwart repudiation of two other fundamental theoretical modes of

9

conceiving of state power, the state as a thing (a discrete and docile implement of an external social group – as it might be, the strong right arm of the bourgeoisie) or the state as subject ('the rationalizing instance of civil society' as Galbraith allegedly conceived the governing organizations of all modern industrial states and as the rulers of the Soviet Union no doubt prefer to envisage themselves).[15] But although there are advantages, even for those who do not share all (or indeed most) of Poulantzas's political opinions, in his selection of the appropriate object for explanation in the theory of the state and although there are evident analytical merits in his criticisms of competing traditions in the analysis of state power, there are also unfortunately severe limitations for our purposes which follow from this approach. The most important of these is simple enough. In the days when the state of the bourgeoisie was envisaged as a passive and discrete instrument, it was relatively easy to know where in society to look and what to look for if one wished to see how the bourgeoisie did its sinister work. Today the means of the bourgeoisie and its ends are less neatly distinguished and the greater potential ingenuity and complexity now permitted to its agency within the theory has left it substantially harder for the analyst to know just where to direct his gaze. One of the main analytical conveniences of the idea of the state in non-Marxist political theory is its comparatively clear institutional boundaries: the gaps, juridical or organizational, between government and governed or between public and private institutions (the latter a distinction particularly scorned by Poulantzas).[16] The far greater emphasis which Poulantzas places on the causal importance of ideology in the class struggle has led to a clear recognition that the bourgeoisie not only would be well advised to deploy but has in fact had the prudence to deploy means for maintaining its political dominance which are firmly outside the legally conceived boundaries of the public sector. Poulantzas identifies, for example, the existence of a mass social democratic party of the working class (apparently even when such a party has at no point held a formal share in government) as a component of the ideological state apparatuses.[17] Anyone who has had the opportunity to watch the British Labour Party's strenuous efforts in government to rescue the residue of British capitalism will be well prepared to see that there is something in this general line of thought. But as the acknowledged ingenuity of the bourgeoisie's means is increasingly extended, so the analytical convenience of a simple focus on governmental apparatus and the determinants of its performance is progressively sacrificed. Heuristically, for those who are not themselves Marxists, the merits of recent Marxist theory of the state, in its firm selection of a politically crucial explicandum, are not as yet matched by any equivalent provision of clear facilities

10

for constructing the explanations themselves. Moreover (and this perhaps will be more widely acknowledged) such explanatory facilities as Marxist theory of the state does proffer in the context of North American or Western European capitalism are in very short supply in relation to the societies of West Africa. Class analysis at the territorial level remains in all West African societies in an exceedingly confused and inconclusive condition, while even experienced practitioners acknowledge that it will hardly do for a Marxist political analysis simply to ship Professor Poulantzas out to West Africa and set him promptly to work in the new environment as best he may.[18]

All of these states, even Guiné-Bissau at a political extreme and Nigeria at an economic extreme, still display a pattern of economic development organized around the export of primary products. All were constituted organizationally as export economies and, although the restrictions imposed by this pattern are now more readily apparent than they were in the early nineteen-fifties, it is still difficult for most observers (except Professor Samir Amin)[19] to identify any clear and plausible alternative pattern. But, if they operate within essentially the same frame of economic activity, it is of course very far from being true that these states have displayed throughout their independent history at all the same orientation towards this common frame. It would probably only be fruitful to study the development of national economic policies within the individual countries, case by case, with careful attention to the international market opportunities and constraints specific at different times to their major products. Mining iron ore or bauxite, smelting alumina or establishing a major oil industry involves much more elaborate and potentially inelastic international economic integration than simply vending cocoa or groundnuts. But at the same time, plainly, the enjoyment of substantial oil wealth has permitted a far wider range of economic choice on the part of the Nigerian government, at least since 1973, than has been open to the government of any West African state since the independence of Ghana in 1957. Neither of the first two broad strategies of economic development essayed by these countries since independence, those centred on the attraction of foreign private capital investment or those centred on import-substitutive industrialization directed by the state itself and financed by government foreign exchange reserves, eked out by international loans and later patched up by suppliers' credits,[20] offers a very convincing way forward for most states, particularly in the aftermath of October 1973. But there is sharp disagreement as to whether either strategy can yet be said to have failed in every case in which it has been tried, the rulers of the Ivory Coast for example retaining evident faith in the merits of the first[21] and those of Nigeria (who can afford to back more than a single horse) at present essaying both at once. A common recent motif in the policy of all these states, with the partial exception of the Ivory Coast,[22] has been a sustained effort at the indigenization of more lucrative employment opportunities in the modern sector, of equity capital in privately owned local firms in the commercial or industrial sectors (including local branches of multinational corporations), and of entrepreneurial access where this does not require very large initial supplies of capital or technical expertise. Indigenization of the share capital of local subsidiaries of multinational corporations may aptly be seen, through the eyes of Henry Ireton,[23] as the giving to those whose task it is to maintain the nation state in its present form of a firm stake in the country as defined by this present form. At the same time in the public sector a persistent preoccupation with restricting the outward flow of profits on foreign capital investment has led to a much greater extension of state ownership over the extractive industries. It is not difficult to see the political and economic advantages of this drift towards indigenization, either for those employed within the formal state apparatus or for those inside the societies to whom they are most effectively responsible. Nor is it thus far particularly difficult to see that the interests which have suffered directly as a result of this drift are on the whole less those of metropolitan capital than they are those of the alien entrepreneurial communities of the coast, more particularly the Lebanese.[24] Though the details vary, it is thus not very difficult either politically or economically to explain the broad outlines of this pattern. What is less clear and what one may reasonably hope to ascertain from a closer comparison between the experiences of the different states is precisely what serves to explain not merely the disparities between the current levels of economic development within the different territories but the determinants of the changing orientations of their rulers to a relatively constant set of objective external economic constraints. Economic comparisons between particular West African states have thus far mostly been made with a view to disclosing their common economic impasse[25] or else with a view to celebrating the just rewards of the superior ideological virtue shown by the rulers of one state as against those of another.[26] The contrast between Ghana and the Ivory Coast, one of the more favoured, would require a more intricate level of treatment than it has thus far received to establish any very clear set of conclusions about the strictly economic issues concerned, and at the political level has as yet scarcely transcended the level of praise and obloquy directed at individual leaders.[27] But it remains difficult to believe that there are not more substantial historical explanations, at the level of political and socio-economic structure, for these divergencies than the

12

firm realization that Nkrumah was the paladin of national liberation and Houphouët-Boigny a lackey of international (or perhaps simply of Gallic) capitalism, or Houphouët-Boigny a paragon of pragmatic rationality and Nkrumah a vain and histrionic fool, allegations between which there is in any case perhaps less analytical distance than there might with advantage be.

A second issue of orientation for which comparison between these states could reasonably be expected to provide some illumination is the attitudes to economic ownership and control exhibited not in the formal economic policies of the state apparatuses but throughout their populations. There have been a number of very illuminating studies of the prevalence of capitalist forms of organization and of corresponding economic attitudes among rural producers [28] and there is good reason to believe that the attitudes extend (at the level of individual economic aspiration, if not of mass action within the workplace) into the most modern sectors of the urban industrial workforce (railwaymen, miners, factory workers).[29] From the viewpoint of the longer-term future of the capitalist mode of production in West Africa the extent of such attitudes among the populace at large is of great significance and neither their present scope nor their prospective political implications have as yet been very convincingly analysed. But in seeking to explain the development of national economic policies in the face of a relatively homogeneous international economic environment, it is less the penetration of capitalist economic attitudes among the population at large which is significant than the more direct personal linkages across the formal boundaries of the state apparatus between those in positions of power within it and those who possess social and economic power and who seek entrepreneurial opportunities or still better monopolistic privileges from outside it. Sometimes these relations are conducted in a singularly open manner, as for example in Ghana in the period of Dr Busia's Progress Party government. At other times they appear in a more dramatic chiaroscuro as in Nigeria in the later years of General Gowon. But it does not seem likely that anywhere in independent West Africa (except perhaps once again Guiné-Bissau) they have failed to thrive with more or less discretion. The post-1973 Nigerian boom saw a veritable explosion of capitalist zest at the federal and state levels, a phenomenon which would have required the pen of Brecht – or perhaps better of a Ben Jonson or John Gay to do it justice. The part played by the state apparatus in the distribution of monopolistic economic opportunities was as direct and arbitrary as in the great days of Lionel Cranfield or Robert Walpole. *Business and Politics under James I* or the ferocious techniques of social control deployed by the Whigs in the aftermath of the South Sea Bubble[30]

13

may well cast a sharper light on the political role of the Nigerian government in recent years than the solemn abstract conceptualization of the role of the state within the neocolonial version of capitalist production.

Conditions for the systematic study of such relations cannot in principle be particularly favourable whilst they are still in progress. Even those at the centre of government do not find it easy to keep themselves very amply informed on the subject (although they certainly devote much energy to the attempt to do so). Police and above all Special Branch files probably contain as systematic a record of such flows at all but the very highest levels as could readily be pieced together. If these files were to survive in any quantity and to become thrown open to scholars they would no doubt furnish rich rewards to Nigerian Tawneys or Thompsons. But, with the startling if perhaps transient exception of the United States of America, states are not on the whole in the habit of providing much access to such files to their own or (voluntarily at least) to foreign citizens. Only the shifts between regimes in West African states have so far provided much data on these relations; and, although the information which has emerged in the course of governmental inquiries is probably accurate enough as far as it goes, the narrowly accusatory and punitive intention behind its gathering and presentation has made it relatively unhelpful for purposes of systematic analysis.[31] Studies of public bureaucracy in the tradition of organizational sociology have contributed some additional diffuse light.[32] But attempts to apply such approaches to particular West African countries have not as yet proved particularly illuminating.[33]

It is not obvious quite how these vigorous if murky activities relate to the unitary worldwide drama of 'the class struggle'. It is indisputable that there are going on in West African countries not only severe struggles between the state apparatuses of the countries and their foreign trading partners over the proportion of wealth produced within their borders which is retained within them, but also the most drastic struggles between different groups within these societies themselves over the distribution of the proportion which is in fact retained within their borders. Precisely who is struggling against whom, however, is very much less clear, except at the weary level of a *bellum omnium contra omnes*.

Leaving aside the more vexed theological issues such as where precisely surplus labour ends and true surplus value begins to be extracted,[34] there does seem clear merit to the Marxist insistence that what matters for purposes of class analysis is the reproduction of patterns of social relations through time.[35] If it proves to be the case, for example, that the disparities between incomes of higher civil servants and more prosperous entrepreneurs and the majority of agrarian producers in the populations

14

of West African countries are roughly similar to those enjoyed on average by the children of each in thirty years' time, and so too by their children in turn, then this will represent a central political characteristic of these societies, irrespective of the formal divisions between public or private ownership of the means of production. It is appreciably easier to see how large a part the state will play in future decades in determining the structure of production and distribution than it is to forecast the precise pattern of social stratification and the distinctive institutional order which will result from this state action. If, for example, the children of office-holders can solve their employment problems in the public service by the possession of skills and qualifications which in turn have been generated from an education which has been financed publicly as well as privately, their effective economic inheritance may be secured more cheaply and almost as reliably as, if less formally than, used to be the case with the *vénalité des offices* under the Ancien Régime. The distribution of income or even of life chances is a somewhat less vulgar (and less dynamic) index of exploitation than the approved Marxist panoply. But it will serve clearly enough to mark one of the major political issues in the near future of these countries. To refer to the present beneficiaries of these positions as an elite or a bourgeoisie sheds little analytical light on their situation. But, whatever we choose to call them, we may readily agree that the internal political futures of these countries for coming decades will turn largely on the question of how far these present beneficiaries contrive to preserve and to transmit the current scale of their privileges and their effective lien on the national income. None of this, of course, in itself illuminates the future, a topic on which the informative capabilities of political scientists should not be overestimated. But the attempt to compare the relative political fragility of the privileged groups in the different states of West Africa may at least serve as a focus for instructive assessment of their present.

Besides the two central issues of the relation of West African economies to the world economy and of the role of the state apparatus within these territories in the process of class formation, some light may reasonably be hoped for from a comparison of the scope and role of the state power within them. There is good reason to see all West African state powers (again with the exception at present of Guiné-Bissau) as firmly subordinate export–import agencies on externally determined terms of trade and good reason to see the degree of internal dominance of the state power as a product of the relative insubstantiality of civil society in these countries, the limited degree of viable and enduring institutionalization of local social forces outside the sphere of the state. A comparison

15

between the internal representative vigour of political and social agencies in, for example, Sri Lanka and the evanescence of all but a handful of local nodes of power and social organization in Ghana (or for that matter most other West African countries) is striking.[36] Localities as such, communities of residence and in the extended sense of kin affiliation, display considerable durability[37] (hence the political prevalence of what is loosely characterized as 'tribalism'); but neither political parties nor in most cases even trade unions have shown much capacity to reproduce themselves when deprived of the sustenance of the state. But, if the state power is intrinsically a colonial artefact with a role which is still largely externally assigned and if the self-organizing capabilities of West African societies in relation to their state powers have proved thus far fairly limited, it does not follow that West African societies do not as yet make their own history. It is by no means the case that the state apparatuses have had matters all their own way internally,[38] even if they have thus far had sufficient preponderance of force to win almost all of the pitched battles. Nor is it any more the case, as Henry Bretton's somewhat morose and uninflected work suggests,[39] that foreign economic interests have had matters all their own way either.

There are three further broad aspects of the situation of these state powers which comparative treatment must attempt to explain: firstly and least puzzlingly, the simple scale of the state apparatus and its formal agencies. The most important determinants of this scale are plausibly the population size and the pattern of economic integration of the countries into the world market in the colonial period, as modified by the sequence of political options which the rulers of the country have adopted since independence. The relation between the extent of agricultural commercialization and the scale of extractive industry in the colonies and the scope of the colonial state apparatus is apparent enough. But it is also very clear that the distance between the scale of the Ghanaian state sector when Nkrumah became Leader of Government Business in the early 1950s and its scale when he was discarded from the government employ in February 1966 reflected his personal selection of political goals (modified by those acceptable to his political associates) at least as much as it did the structure of production established in the colonial era. The major qualification to this pattern of explanation, plainly enough, must be the drastic changes in the nature of the Nigerian state apparatus and its role produced by the civil war and by the development, particularly since October 1973, of its oil industry. The sheer size of the Nigerian army and the real wealth which has been disbursed through the state apparatus in the course of the last three or four years dwarfs the scale of all previous West African state power, whatever one may think of the uses to which

16

this power has been put. It seems analytically appropriate to treat the Nigerian oilfields and their handsome OPEC price increment as acts of God in the context of explaining Nigerian political development. But it would be unimpressive, even by the standards of political science, to be obliged to treat the occurrence of a major civil war within a country solely by invoking ad hoc and extrinsic variables. By the same token, as noted earlier, it does not seem altogether adequate to attribute the diversities of political attitudes between the successor nationalist political movements within the different territories solely to dispositional characteristics or moral qualities of their respective leaders.

Neither the variations in internal national viability nor the differences in the ideological and political attitudes of the inheritor political movements have as yet been explained with much success. There have been valuable studies of some aspects of these themes: Crowder's treatment of West Africa as a whole in the later stages of colonial rule, Ruth Schachter Morgenthau's useful political history of party formation and development in the francophone states, Zolberg's briefer discussion of the one-party state as a form of regime.[40] There have also been many studies, some of outstanding quality, of the development of the nationalist movements within different territories. The limitations of the internal national viability of all post-colonial states in Africa as a whole or West Africa in particular have been extensively proclaimed;[41] and the internal political strains of particular territories have received some analysis, most importantly for obvious reasons in the case of Nigeria.[42] But little sustained effort has yet been made to compare these experiences and it can hardly as yet be said that many plausible ideas have been advanced on possible determinants of the variations between them. We do now possess an admirable synthetic treatment of the historical development of the West African economy as a whole.[43] But we have no study of the causes of the differentiation in colonial patterns of economic development to compare with Brett's discussion of the three British territories in East Africa[44] and no study of the role of the state in the development of the post-colonial economic order within a single country with the systematic qualities of Colin Leys's *Underdevelopment in Kenya*.[45] In these deprived circumstances it is probably better not to speculate with too much vigour. But there seem two relatively certain explanatory categories on which to insist and one caveat which might usefully be added to them.

The first of the explanatory categories is universal enough and its analytical significance will today scarcely be disputed. The patterns of uneven economic development within all the West African territories can be explained in more than one way – as a reflection of geography, initial factor endowments and the doctrine of comparative advantage, or as a structural consequence of the colonial and neocolonial pattern of incorporation of the West African economies into the world capitalist system. But it is not clear that these really do represent alternative explanations and not merely politically preferred descriptions of a (phenomenally) identical process. The coastal focus of all these economies, their labour drain from interior to coast (with the partial exception of Nigeria)[46] and the explicit part played by the colonial state in developing an infrastructure and even a labour force fully appropriate to their role as export economies,[47] added to the unevenness of missionary (and hence of educational) penetration during the period of colonial rule have endowed all of these states with formidable regional conflicts of economic interest. It is possible, if far from certain, that such conflicts might be mediated more comfortably in economies which were expanding dynamically, though the example of Nigeria since 1973 does little to confirm this expectation. But most of these countries in any case have economies which are very far from expanding dynamically and it is scarcely surprising that these should display sharp political strains between the representatives of different areas of the country within whatever political institutions political power is at the time being exerted. The recent history of the United Kingdom, a realm long united by the unevenness of its development, has perhaps made it easier for British social scientists to grasp how readily political conflicts can come to be conceived in terms of the interests of different geographical areas and not in terms of conflicts of class interest within an unthinkingly accepted national frame. In West African societies, where so many other categories of social identification compete with those of class for the attention of agents and where the consciousness of class at a national level is consequently so evanescent, it should hardly be a matter for surprise that the political categories of 'tribalism' should be so prominent in political perception and political action. The pattern of uneven development is obviously central in explaining the prevalence of such regional and ethnic political fissures in all the states of West Africa; and the variations in this pattern of uneven development may help to explain (though this has not as yet been shown at all convincingly) some of the variations in the extent to which these political fissures have been explored and formalized. It is certainly true that the independent political histories of these countries have varied greatly in the extent to which they have revolved around such regional struggles – Dahomey/Benin and Nigeria for example vary much more than Senegal or the Ivory Coast or even Ghana. In the case of Ghana such themes have become prominent whenever stable control over central political power has been disrupted and real opportunities to compete for its exercise have opened up, while

18

the relative lack of salience of such themes in Senegal and the Ivory Coast does appear to be a product of the extent to which an effective political monopoly was established at a fairly early stage of decolonization and the extent to which it has been sustained ever since.[48] This suggests that the political articulation of social forces within the period of anticolonial struggle by the nationalist movement may be one of the major determinants of the political stability of the post-colonial regimes, and that the political consequences of uneven development whilst the colonial regimes were still in existence may well be a more important factor in explaining variations in the national viability thus far of the post-colonial regimes than any direct variations in the subsequent impact of such unevenness on the post-colonial regimes themselves have proved.

Without adopting any definite theory of the dynamics of global economic process, we can see, as a simple historical perception, the pattern of uneven development in West Africa as a product of European imperialism and of the firm incorporation of West Africa into the global division of labour created by the development of capitalism. Seeing it in this light, it represents the product of a unitary process of singularly drastic restructuring. But if the powerful external logic to which the societies of West Africa have thus succumbed can be thought of as unitary, the precise manner of their political and social response to this experience can scarcely be so considered. The political response of different groups and societies in West Africa in the last century has been a differentiated and active response on the part of real historical actors. Precolonial West Africa had its own history and did not have to wait for its incorporation into the capitalist mode of production to be provided with that facility. Such formidable agencies for the engineering of unevenness in pre-colonial development as the kingdoms of Dahomey or Ashanti or the Hausa-Fulani emirates of Northern Nigeria have left their political imprint on colonial and post-colonial political and social development. The genesis of such states was, of course in part causally related to the creation of the world market;[49] but it was also causally related to many other more local factors. West African social, economic and political differentiation before colonial rule did much to determine both the pace and rhythm at which colonial rule was established. Furthermore, since colonial regimes were structures of political control and not merely of economic exploitation, such local patterns of differentiation at the inception of colonial rule and their creative adaptation throughout the colonial period served to dictate much of the form of colonial control.[50] As the study of colonial and post-colonial history becomes more local and more intensive, the extreme intricacy with which the political consequences of colonial rule were differentiated becomes steadily more apparent.[51] Once colonial rule was drawing towards its close this patch-work quilt of political exchanges necessarily served largely to determine the conditions within which competition for post-colonial political power must take place. Relations between the colonial rulers and, for example, the Mouride brotherhood in Senegal[52] or the Ashanti Confederacy in the Gold Coast (Ghana) had major consequences for what sorts of political forces were present to compete once electoral political articulation was to begin. Many of such political forces, of course, fell by the wayside soon enough. But even those who fall by the wayside often contribute their weight to political causality. In the post-colonial period, where politics is a relatively open (if rather rough) competitive game, quite minor features of colonial education or religious or administrative policy have continued to affect the outcome of the competition. The contrast between the educational backwardness of Northern Nigeria and its demographic weight and the educational backwardness of Northern Ghana and its democratic paucity remains one of the central axes in comparing the politics of these two countries.[53] It is still unclear, historiographically and analytically, quite how one should seek to periodize the development of political and social forces in West African states. But even these superficial considerations suggest the dangers of presuming on the incon-sequentiality of any phase in recent centuries. In West Africa, as else-where, history happens all the time.

It seems proper to close with a caveat. In some respects the history of modern West Africa and the understanding of its recent politics have progressed greatly in the last dozen years. But there is one respect in which, for the best of motives, they are now in some danger of regressing. Although it was a convenience and in some cases even an aesthetic delight for colonial administrators that effective agencies of political articulation in African territories should often take the form of 'traditional' political units, it has proved something of a trial for post-colonial analysts that this should to such a degree have continued to be the case. 'Tribalism' is a term with the political sneer carefully built into it and there have been anxious efforts, understandably enough, to launder it out and to find more euphemistic terms. 'Tribalist' politics are the politics of those appropriately organized in tribes, the politics of savages. 'The role of ethnicity in determining political allegiance' is undeniably a more polite formula. Ethnicity plainly does continue to play a major role in deter-mining political allegiance in many (if not indeed in all) African countries. As noted earlier, this is not a phenomenon which need surprise a British subject and citizen of the United Kingdom. Recently, however, there has been increasing unease among scholars writing on African politics about discussing the very substantial part which ethnicity does still play in determining political allegiance within these societies. Some of this unease is well enough judged: tribe (or for that matter ethnos) is certainly not a category given by nature. But it is important not to confuse external political disapproval with a judgement of lack of political weight.[54] Political allegiance is a social reality, though not necessarily of course a very enduring one. As long as 'tribalism' remains a major axis of political allegiance it will be important to distinguish assessments of the desirability of its effects from those of its prospective durability. It would no doubt be edifying (as well as reassuring for ourselves) to be able to change this state of affairs; but in the meantime an analyst can hardly be permitted to shirk the responsibility of explaining it. And in seeking to explain it, one can hardly rest content with seeing it simply as the deplorable effect of the efforts of small groups of politically motivated men at home and abroad. If this is *the* way above all others in which political followings can be mustered in most West African states today, then the explanation of why they can be mustered in this way and cannot (or cannot yet) be mustered in other ways, must be at the centre of the account we offer of West African politics.

2

Ghana

RICHARD RATHBONE

The Ghanaian Studies industry has made any extended survey of the main events in Ghanaian political history since March 1957 largely and mercifully redundant. The last twenty years of Ghana's story are copiously if (perhaps) unevenly dealt with in a large number of recent works.[1] In brief, then, Ghana was destined to be the first sub-Saharan African colony to go beyond the initial step of internal self-government when it was granted independence by the United Kingdom government in 1957. The former Gold Coast became Ghana under the same Convention People's Party government which had won the colony's first general election in 1951. Kwame Nkrumah was its prime minister, a position he had held *de facto* since that same general election and one he was to hold until his election as president of Ghana in 1960.

In each of the three pre-independence elections the Convention People's Party (CPP) had gained a plurality of votes cast although, as has often been noted, that vote never constituted more than the support of about 35 per cent of the enfranchised electorate.[2] Until the hotly contested election of 1956, the competition for power had been a profoundly unequal one in terms of moral power, immoral power and sheer sophistication. The CPP had been first at the post with the acceptably populistic brand of nationalism which had wide appeal; any attempt to outflank the CPP by using the same or a watered-down version of that ideology was doomed to failure. What is often described as the 'right' in Ghanaian politics, a complex set of frequently antagonistic interests rooted in traditional politics, modern business and sometimes simply hostile to the personnel of the CPP, suffered a decisive set-back in 1951. The CPP's acute reading of the radicalization of the politically active population, as well as its active encouragement of it, was unstoppable by a group of politicians with a marked leaning to patrician inertia and personal hostility. Similarly the 'left', in particular the militant elements in the labour unions and the more radical members of the CPP itself, were pro-

22

gressively crushed, illegalized or bought-out by the CPP and its partner in dyarchy, the colonial administration.

In short, no other grouping in the Gold Coast of the early 1950s had the command or understanding of the modern political skills which the CPP developed, not least of which was the ear of the colonial administration. Once the CPP *was* the government it could utilize that position of privilege to direct funds, minds and people in its direction. Its very possession of power was used, not always subtly, to attract support from those who realized that the CPP was the new pay-master. But this position did not insulate the CPP from challenge altogether. From late 1954 the excluded, with the exception of most of the ideological left, patched together a loose alliance they called the National Liberation Movement.

Rather than challenging radical nationalism, the NLM shrewdly accepted the notion of rapid decolonization, but questioned the shape of the inherited state. They advocated federalism both as a means of welding together a disparate collection of dissident political fragments and as a mode for creating a series of smaller pork-barrels to challenge the CPP's central control of resources. The challenge of the NLM became sufficiently grave to compel the CPP to accept a third general election in 1956 despite the British government's prior assurance that the 1954 election would be, *de facto,* the independence election. In the event the election proved little; the CPP again won a plurality of the votes cast. The NLM, however, won a significant degree of support outside the south, the CPP heartland. The unbalanced regional distribution of votes enabled the NLM to dignify a last ditch stand against the CPP's inheriting the colonial state and encouraged them to make wild separatist demands. In an attempt, amongst many other tie-breakers, to solve the impasse, the British Secretary of State for the Colonies sold both the CPP and the NLM a constitution with ornate and bureaucratic fine print. It provided for regionally devolved decision-making in limited spheres through the agency of regional assemblies. As the earlier government enquiries had concluded that regionalism for so small and poor a country as Ghana was wasteful, the constitutional solution must be seen as somewhat cynical. In the event it allowed the NLM to climb down from their more extreme hobby-horses with a measure of dignity. The CPP's early abandonment of most of that constitution in its early years as an independent government was undoubtedly the fruit of a growing tendency to politically cavalier behaviour, but it can also be seen simply as practical.[3]

Independence in CPP packaging was achieved, then, over the grumbling of a politically disaffected minority who had little love for the CPP. The clash between the NLM and the CPP had at its worst been violent and passions were hardly cooled by independence. The CPP rapidly outlawed the methods of the NLM by banning the operation of parties deemed to be regional or ethnic in ideology. (The NLM had of course, combined both elements in its appeal.) The opposition accordingly regrouped into a weakened national opposition party called the United Party. The UP was unable, at least openly, to articulate the old NLM's vote winning formulae of playing on perceptions of regional deprivation and ethnically based particularisms. Deprived of this opportunity and in the face of continuing harassment and temptations to cross the floor the UP drifted inexorably into the shadows. Indeed much of its residual substance was provided gratuitously by the CPP's unrelenting insistence on the UP's responsibility for every vestige of oppositional activity in Ghana. There is much in its activists' comportment to suggest that they would like to have been puppet-masters of a grand and effective conspiracy against the government of Ghana between 1957 and 1966. There is equally much in their track-records to suggest that few if any of them had the ability or resources to mount anything so grandiose. By the time of the coup which toppled Nkrumah in 1966 most of its leading members were in exile, in prison, had crossed the floor or had retired from politics. While there are excellent reasons for supposing the 1960 presidential election fell short of the standards of perfectly fair competition, there seems little reason to doubt that the low poll of the UP's veteran candidate, Dr Danquah, was a fair measure of the proper esteem in which his party was by this time held.

The CPP continued in office with a variety of challenges to its hegemony. There were attempts on Nkrumah's life including a frightening near-miss. There were severe labour reactions to the declining standards of living suffered by most wage earners from 1959 onwards. Most labour action was outlawed by the restrictive Industrial Conciliation Act of 1957 which marked a further stage in the CPP's campaign against the emergence of an organized 'left' in Ghanaian politics. This failed to contain the vivid and courageous stand taken by the railway and harbour workers of Sekondi-Takoradi in 1961 against, amongst many things, a compulsory savings scheme and the gradual centralization of union control in Accra under the CPP's thumb.[4] In addition there was rioting in Accra fomented by the Ga Standfast Association or Ga Shifimo Kpee against the perceived exclusion of the indigenous population of Accra, the Ga, from good jobs in the capital. There was revolt within the CPP which Nkrumah and the Central Committee solved by purges, promotions and demotions. Despite all these significant discomforts there was little in the fabric of CPP rule itself, other than its failure along with most other governments of the underdeveloped world, to control the declining economic situation, which made military intervention either

24

obvious or necessary. Indeed few of the authorities on Ghana even mention this possibility in work published before 1966. While there were real differences between the enthusiastic support the party had enjoyed in its youth and the hold it had assumed over a largely indifferent population by the early 1960s there were no obvious predisposing causes for the 1966 coup other than the most general and those which related immediately to the autonomy and power of the military itself.

But the military did intervene decisively in 1966 while the president was out of the country. The military regime, the National Liberation Council it called itself, took power largely without bloodshed and against little overt popular opposition. The military regime's legitimacy appeared to depend in large measure upon their proof of the illegitimacy of the regime they had replaced. The spirit of Enquiry stalked the land and self-righteousness as well as political astuteness led to commission after commission of enquiry. These examined, with a degree of rigour governed closely by the sensitivity of the subject (who he knew and who he could implicate), the affairs of individuals, corporations and ministries under the old regime. Their revelations showed an unsurprising catalogue of corruption both major and minor and fell short of exposing much which was universally and in many cases no doubt correctly believed in Ghana at the time. It seems that the limits of such enquiry were set early on. Root and branch examination would have discredited just about everyone with public office and many of these were vital to the NLC's maintenance. The commissions were directed with some political care against the old CPP and those of its clients who were dispensable or in the way.

The NLC recognized its weaknesses early on in its career. In the immediate post-coup period, when some essential civil servants showed signs of distaste for their duties, they were forcefully reminded that the Special Branch files, which one of the major figures in the NLC, John Harlley, had overseen for some years, contained material that could send many of them to jail for years. The agreement of many of those who chose to work closely with the NLC during its first weeks was occasioned by calculations such as this. In this sense then the campaign of vilification of Nkrumah and the CPP regime was politically instrumental. It was also political in that the new regime in seeking internal and external support as well as listening to the conservative conscience of most of the senior military men was markedly more right-wing in expressed ideology than its predecessor.

Although expression of ideology in Ghana, as perhaps elsewhere, is less important than watchers overseas make it, this bias to the right was reinforced by the civilian support the NLC was forced to retain. It was

25

clear that few if any of the old CPP stalwarts would be suitable bedmates in an inquisitorial period. Thus the NLC recruited its Political Committee for the most part from the old UP and many of those who were to be prominent on that committee had begun their political careers in the NLM, some ten years previously. Their failure to secure any chance of cracking the whip in the 1956 election was ironically redressed by the military. The new regime gave them a base in its virtual selling-off of state-controlled enterprises, its reallocations of local contracts and other economic options to its new clients. This was barely policy; it was rather an acquiescent line taken by a somewhat naive military regime, cautiously sweetening opportunistic civil collaborators who had been denied opportunity for many years. The NLC despite its strong-man ethos constantly gave the impression of bemusement. The takeover had been simplicity itself but the realities of running a complex state apparatus revealed, not least to the NLC themselves, their shortcomings. They were manipulated by their civil colleagues but were prey in addition to those elements within the military itself who had adapted in more subtly political fashion to the new situation.

Although there were politically ambitious men in the NLC, the urge to civilianize was rapidly obvious. There was no fast turnabout in the economy which in the everyday terms of the Ghanaian consumer continued to show a disturbing capacity to increase the cost of living year in and year out. The myth that de-socializing the economy, based in part upon the false assumption that the Ghanaian economy between 1957 and 1966 had been socialist, would immediately improve Ghana's economic prospects was rapidly exploded. The NLC was no more master of the malign features of the world economy which had progressively reduced Ghana's economic power than had been the CPP. The NLC was fearful of becoming internally discredited; throughout its brief career it had been rather charmingly approval-oriented. It was moreover fearful of internal dissent breaking up the solidarity of the military; one of the earliest threats to military hegemony had, indeed, arisen from an ill-conceived counter-coup led by an army lieutenant which had, *inter alia*, killed one of the 1966 coupistes (after whom Accra's airport is now named). By the end of the period of army rule, the NLC was itself dangerously divided.

Eager though the NLC might have been to return to barracks, the Council wished to be assured that any successor regime would be of a style within which they could work without frustration. In some senses they had already ensured that it would be by outlawing the CPP *ab initio*. The UP/NLM Political Committee-men had been given a flying start in the electoral stakes. Indeed the first faction forming occurred only weeks after the formation of the Political Committee. That factions would form was inevitable. The UP had been monolithic largely because in opposition it had been small and beleaguered. The prospect of power, the limited number of offices open to the victor and the emergence of some new faces – and some very old like Komla Gbedemah – ensured that there would be hot competition in the 1969 election. Indeed of the 104 constituencies at that election only two were uncontested.

The election was of course significantly different from the colonial elections although the 'referee' function once fulfilled by the colonial regime had been interestingly replaced by a similarly partisan military. As before the percentage of the enfranchized who voted was low, almost precisely 50 per cent and again the majority party, like the CPP in 1951, 1954 and 1956, could not boast that it had the votes of the majority of the country. The 58 per cent who voted for Dr Busia and his Progress Party matched almost exactly the 57 per cent who had voted for the CPP in the last colonial election. But thirteen years had passed since that election and the discovery of resonances is little more than to play with numbers.[5]

That Busia won was not perhaps because of anything decisive about the programme the Progress Party professed. Partly the PP won because many Ghanaians had bought the vilification programme against the CPP and felt that the dignified 'Prof' Busia and his supporters betokened a real change in the older corrupt style of Ghanaian politics. But they also won because many believed that Busia was meant to win by the military. Busia had been propelled, after all, into an unparalleled prominence throughout the NLC's regime. He had enjoyed more column inches and more air-time than his competitors. He and his followers were, in addition, freed from the old embargo on ethnic politics and played on such susceptibilities in the electorate. In this they were fortunate that their main competition came from the National Alliance of Liberals led by the somewhat discredited Komla Gbedemah. Gbedemah, a founding father of the CPP, had not only been sufficiently weak to be chased from office by Nkrumah four years after independence; he also had a dubious track-record which included an over close relationship with the infamous Dr Savundra. As important was the fact that Gbedemah was an Ewe; partly because of the ethnic attentions of Dr Busia *et alii* and partly because of the bogey-man image of his fellow Ewe and NLC strong-man John Harlley who had been instrumental in ensuring that Gbedemah returned to Ghana unscathed in 1966, being an Ewe became something of a political liability outside the Volta region.

This tension is not easy to comprehend for there is little evidence of anti-Ewe sentiment before the late 1960s in Ghana. The Ewe are a latently suspicious sort of people; their language is the one, main southern language that very few non-native speakers ever master. Their social-

27

ization has tended to take place within the melange of the three cultures open to them on both sides of the Togo border. Some Ghanaian Ewe had been historically irredentist. Lastly the relative poverty of their area of domicile coupled with the rather intensive mission activity in the area from early times has tended to make the Ewe the 'Ibo' of Ghana. They are active in 'modern' roles, are forced to sell their skills outside the Volta region and are socially salient because of their language. They had been something of a non-factor in colonial electoral politics because they had been so divided. At one time the Ewe were to be found in the irredentist Togoland Congress, the conservative and particularist Anlo Youth Association as well as in other, national parties. Thus their votes went to a variety of candidates in 1954 and 1956. In 1969 the allegedly Ewe-based National Alliance of Liberals won fourteen out of the sixteen seats in the predominantly Ewe areas. There was a touch of the Ewe 'menace' in Progress Party propaganda and a consequently defensive Ewe response. Akan exclusiveness so divided in the 1950s between the Asante (NLM) and Fante (CPP) at its crudest, was amplified and to some extent created by the propaganda of external threat.

NAL's programme may have been a trifle closer to that of the deposed CPP than the Progress Party's programme was, though even this might be disputed. What is certain is that it was one of Progress's planks to suggest forcefully that NAL aimed at recreating something of the CPP *ancien régime* if returned to power. This was a potent smear on two counts; first the CPP was discredited enough to make anything uttering even remotely similar noises immediately suspicious; secondly it was clear that any party steering close to the CPP's wind was a likely candidate for another military intervention.

Busia's honeymoon with the electorate was to prove short-lived. Busia himself had two identities. The first is that of the international statesman, a universally acceptable reasonable man. His easy, articulate style is readily accepted in the outside world. His writings are clearly for just such an audience. But as a stump-speaker in Twi he is much closer to what has become a trenchant Ghanaian political style, strident, somewhat defamatory and, above all, tough. His career in Ghanaian politics is at least as devious as that of any other Ghanaian politician as anyone looking at his NLM/UP record would be forced to conclude. Despite his long attempts to present himself as Simon Pure, amongst his earliest actions as prime minister was an involved yet crude constitutional gerrymander which removed the leader of the opposition – Gbedemah – from his seat. Later the Busia government enacted legislation which exiled a large number of non-nationals who had traditionally worked and lived in Ghana. In 1970 over 550 civil servants were dismissed on the grounds of

28

inefficiency though the briefest of examinations of the people involved shows that in some cases the most efficient were sacked whilst in others the optimally inefficient were retained if they had friends at court. When one of the dismissed civil servants, E. K. Sallah, quondam manager of the Ghana National Trading Corporation, challenged the decision in the High Court there were state objections to four of the five judges of the Supreme Court who constituted the tribunal; when a three to one decision in Sallah's favour emerged, Busia denounced the judges and their decision in a poorly argued and hysterical speech on the Ghana Broadcasting Service.

The Progress Party government was, then, like its CPP predecessor profoundly intolerant of opposition. It was ruthless in suppressing rural discontent, most markedly to be found once again amongst the highly taxed and poorly rewarded cocoa-farmers. It hit labour dissent sternly. Like its predecessors it did no better with the economy. Import costs rose, cocoa prices fell and after the rainy season of 1971 draconian economic measures were introduced including a devaluation of the Cedi by 45 per cent. Against this background the army struck once again in 1972 in a bloodless fashion reminiscent of their first innings in 1966. But the actors had changed largely because the surviving coupistes of 1966 were now for the most part civilians engaged in the pursuit of happiness and cash.

The population responded as mutely as it had done in 1966. Busia's government was certainly as unpopular as had been that of Nkrumah in its last years. The modern elite had been seared by their experience of Busia whom they regarded as 'their man'. Many prominent figures had lost office and opportunity between 1969 and 1972. The business interest had seen the economy driven even more solidly onto the rocks, to the accompaniment of soaring taxation, import controls and the rest. The rocketing cost of living spared almost no-one. All sectors of Ghanaian society from senior civil servants and judges to primary school teachers and cocoa-farmers had manifest grievances. These, while for the most part caused by Ghana's economy and its relationship to the wider world, were conveniently laid at Busia's feet.

Acheampong's National Redemption Council, like its military precursor, had no elaborate need for the establishment of legitimacy. Essentially a younger generation of officers, they have judged, correctly, that the period 1957–66 was an infinitely brighter chapter in Ghanaian history than the years that followed the first military coup. Since 1966 Ghana had after all suffered a positive and frightening decline in its international importance and respect. Economically Ghana had never been worse off. Thus not the least important act of the NRC has been the gradual rehabilitation of the CPP era. In keeping with this the NRC has followed a

29

centrist, ascetic policy with socialist pretensions. The image, through moderately successful efforts like 'Operation feed yourself', has been that of a boy-scoutish CPP in army uniforms, a CPP without panache. It is a government which feels seriously threatened from within as the recent treason trials have shown. But the NRC has proceeded cautiously and has not lacked luck. They have had to deal with the malign effects of the oil-price hike of late 1973 alongside the highest cocoa prices in history for example. But they have lubricated luck with judgement. Selective import controls, a cautious policy of majority state share-holding in major enterprises have made for something of an improvement in the current balance of payments situation. At the same time the NRC has inherited an unenviable set of debt obligations from all its predecessors since 1957.

This brief narrative has no detectable thread other than the unimportance of the ideologies of each of Ghana's regimes since 1957. It is also a story in which the ordinary Ghanaian appears not to write his own history. Either of these propositions is possibly immediately challengeable at the level of micro-analysis, but at the level of the state one can see a history in which the state itself is relatively untroubled by apparent changes in political direction from the top, is relatively untouched by their differing touches on the tiller and has, in short, a trajectory of its own. In dramatic form it seems that formal, national politics in Ghana do not clearly reflect changes in social and economic structure; for this reason, and others, there is a widespread cynicism in Ghana about national politics and politicians; this is in no sense an ignorant or naive response for the Ghanaian electorate is an informed, sophisticated and aware group. The verities of the political economy are not arcane to those who participate daily in it. Those who benefit from it are unlikely to wish it challenged; those disadvantaged by it are either too poor, too weak or too spatially diffuse to make their voice of protest heard in any manner other than that of periodic and largely uncoordinated action of the sort put down by security forces rather than those leading to the formation of articulate, modern political institutions with constitutional muscle.

The reasons for this are complex. The history of Ghana is by no means unique. Like many other ex-colonial states in Africa, Ghana as presently constituted is scarcely more than seventy years old. The nine million or so people who live there were incorporated into a unitary state which, over time, has laid down the basic physical infrastructure of the modern Ghanaian economy. This took on force during what Tony Hopkins has called West Africa's 'transport revolution'.[6] This of course facilitated the growth of a mass market for goods and labour in Ghana. The colonial state encouraged the development of cash agriculture, in particular the growingly lucrative cocoa, and left that development in local, African hands. Cocoa and mineral revenues, and general taxation provided the funds for the physical development of Ghana and the remuneration of the growing numbers of civil servants and service personnel who governed and developed it. Urban wage labour was created by the gradual development of Ghana's mining industry, the employment of Africans by the big trading houses who handled the import–export business and by the employment of Africans in the public service. Additionally the state established a social infrastructure for the peaceful extraction of minerals and the growing of cash crops and a climate in which the market for British manufacture could be encouraged to grow. Compulsion was for the most part absent; plantations were rare, white settlement non-existent and cruel taxation the exception rather than the rule. The pre-colonial commitment of many Ghanaians, especially in the south, to commercial production and trade enabled them to opportunize upon, rather than having to be coerced into, the newly opening possibilities. Hence in a situation in which land hunger was rare, Ghana's urban population swelled from 5 per cent of the population in 1929 to 23 per cent in 1961.

As Keith Hart has effectively argued urbanization is a convenient peg on which to hang an important argument.[7] Urbanization clearly took place because the maximization of opportunity could be achieved in towns. In respect of this there is a linear history of Ghanaian urbanization which irrespective of the swings and roundabouts of the economy – boom from 1900–30, slump from 1930–45, boom from 1945–60 and slump from 1960 onwards – has altered the nature and location of Ghana's dominant socio-political segments. Those dominant elements are difficult to define in class terms, in ethnic terms or in any classificatory terminology which carries with it any predictive overtones. It nonetheless constitutes a selfish, ruling group which dominates the political economy irrespective of the character of the holders of power in the centre.

Until the Second World War the Ghanaian economy was a thin affair and the state's role encroached almost for the first time in the financial sphere from 1940 onwards. But from then onwards the state has acted as the prime mover in the massive transfer of income between the rural areas and the urban sector largely through the exploitation of the surplus earned by cocoa-farmers. Between 1950 and 1960 government expenditure increased by over 200 per cent, and in no sense has the earning power of the state kept abreast of its demands. Government expenditure exceeds revenue by a large margin and has done so for at least fifteen years. The indebtedness of the state has been facilitated by its control of

31

most significant areas of marketing, purchasing and banking in Ghana as well as by private trade and foreign aid.

This process has taken place outside the arena of political contest but has shaped the nature of Ghanaian politics far more certainly than Nkrumah's personality or Acheampong's class origins. In short the Ghanaian economy has increasingly become centralized since the first steps in that direction in the 1940s. The main avenues for government expenditure have all had profound implications for Ghanaian society. The educational programme, consistently the largest item in Ghanaian budgets, has continued to expand. The provision of social amenities such as medical provision, roads and sanitation has grown enormously. The civil service has been enormously expanded and has been remunerated at an increasingly high level relative to the majority of Ghanaians. Public service employment in the blue-collar sector has also expanded although the increase in numbers has been achieved whilst reducing their real wages. Last but not least the state itself has become not only the major employer but also the most significant capitalist in Ghana by its purchase of 51 per cent controlling interests in a large number of enterprises, most notably in the field of import substitution.

Most of this expenditure and hence most of the amenities and opportunities have clustered in towns. The dominant political class, the beneficiaries of the political economy are thus predominantly urban. They achieve their rewards by milking the rural areas of Ghana which constitute in very real terms the major areas of wealth creation. As the urban dwellers, and particularly the relatively comfortable urban dwellers, constitute a tiny minority of Ghana's population one must ask how it has been possible for them to get away with this under every political regime since 1951. Essentially it must be because Ghana has never really spawned an effective domestic opposition. The wholesale success of the urban minority under four flags has been essentially parasitic and has proceeded virtually unchecked. And it has been a success not because of their own organization, for they have no self-conscious organization, but rather because of the lack of organized interest groups in opposition to them.

Ghana's cocoa producers in particular, the aphids of the state-created bourgeoisie's ladybird, have not since the early 1950s combined in any serious fashion and shown themselves as anything but a self-aware class of capitalist farmers; they above all have had significant grievances against every regime that has ruled Ghana since the Second World War for rarely have they been allowed to retain more than a minute proportion of the market price for their product. Similarly industrial workers, although they have had their moments, are few in number, well-organized but in organizations which have little capital. Above all their clout is significantly reduced by the large and growing reserve army of unemployed or semi-employed people. In each regime's history the wage force has been hit by wage freezes, compulsory savings schemes and other measures which have, along with galloping inflation, reduced their real wages. Inflation, government action and the increase in the dependency rate, which has grown in Ghana as unemployment has grown, have all reduced most wage earners' standards of living. But industrial workers have not been able to resist this turn of events. If cocoa farmers and industrial workers have been incapable of mounting resistance to the predatory role of the state, and those who profit from its predation, then such weakness has been even more marked amongst the poor, both rural and urban, who have had to stand by while a succession of elite factions have fought over high office.

The power the urban dominant class have is in part domestically explained. But it is also the case, and this is harder to explain, that international agencies have consistently underwritten Ghana's bankruptcy. Ghana's relative openness as a consumer of developed world products and her unwillingness to act as a dog-in-the-manger as a producer has undoubtedly contributed to this. Ghana appears also to have some residual diplomatic power which cannot be discounted in this context.

Ironically their domestic sources of power lie essentially in the failure of capitalism proper to emerge in indigenous hands. The state and those who command it – the bureaucratic elite and influential businessmen rather than politicians or soldiers – under each or any banner are the nearest the population gets to capitalism. The state itself dominates all internal forms of capitalist relations and is both dependent upon and logically antagonistic to international business. There is little reason to expect this pattern to change in the short run. Indeed as growth occurs, albeit at a very slow rate, the state is likely to prove even more influential in the direction of the formation and location of internal capital formation.

This dominance has, of course, been reinforced by a rapid increase in the scale of the domestic market, stimulating, as Keith Hart has emphasized, petty commodity production but also, of course, increasing the dependence on imports. Such petty commodity production has failed to generate an independent capitalist class, since capital formation by petty commodity production does not promote direct investment or surplus in anything that could be seen as industry. Instead, because of the intimate links between this form of production and the older traditional economy, such capital has on the whole been redistributed rather than accumulated.

The strength of this traditional social economy owes much to the lack of disruption which it underwent in its period of development alongside and within the colonial economy. Simply expressed, the state in the Gold Coast and now in Ghana has not systematically or at all extensively alienated the traditional economy's key resource, namely land.

The political relationships which have stemmed from this political economy and have thrived upon it can of course be challenged from a number of directions. While radical pessimists predict stagnation, this cycle can – and probably will in time – be broken by a combination of such factors as population growth and the development of pressure on land. Similarly the immiseration of rural and urban poor could break the traditional economy and thus in turn revolutionize the attitudes of petty commodity producers by removing the constraints under which they operate, not least of which is the highly personalized nature of labour relations in this sector. A country in which the fall in the real value of the minimum wage over the last decade and half has been one of the steepest in the world – a full 50 per cent between 1963 and 1974 for example[8] – and in which the annual inflation rate at the beginning of 1977 was estimated at over 50 per cent[9] is subjecting its existing pattern of social relations to considerable strain. The survival of the traditional social economy has permitted Ghana a protracted process of social involution in response to governmental mismanagement of relations with the world economy. But even the most elastic modes of reproducing social relations can under some conditions simply snap. Nor is it clear that the process will even be permitted to continue indefinitely without external interruption. International capital might simply choose to annihilate the petty commodity producers by moving into the domestic market in a big way, though the incentives for it to do so at present are scarcely overwhelming. Lastly, it would in principle be possible for the state either to devote greater energy to fostering domestic capital investment or alternatively to collectivize and socialize the economy, each of which moves would break down traditional relationships relatively rapidly.

The gyrations at the centre of national political life in Ghana do not mirror these structural relationships with any clarity. The events of the last twenty years have, of course, a fascination of their own but on their own tell a misleading story. Dissection of the body politic remains a daunting task in any polity, but a great deal of the literature on Ghanaian politics gives to that body politic more autonomy than it warrants. That literature presupposes open choices for actors and dwells too much on the Great Man tradition of political analysis. The argument here is simply that political relationships in Ghana depend essentially upon other relationships. The primacy of economics is of course profoundly moderated by local social and political relationships which in some cases are independent of recent economic history. But essentially it remains true that Ghana has exhibited a degree of stability in such relationships over time. The toils at the centre have represented little more than political manoeuvres within an urban 'middle class' and have made for little, if any, significant structural change in Ghana.

3

Guinea

R. W. JOHNSON

A study of the political development of the Republic of Guinea since its independence in September 1958 is of special interest and importance to any comparative attempt to understand the evolution of post-independence politics in Africa in general. For Guinea is still ruled by a radical single party regime: the PDG (Parti Démocratique de Guinée),[1] led by Sekou Touré,[2] won power in May 1957 and in 1977 it – and he – are still in control. The fate of such regimes elsewhere in Africa suggests strongly that it is a vanishing species and there is no doubt that the isolation to which the Touré regime has, so to speak, condemned itself by virtue of its sheer durability is itself a major factor affecting Guinean development. In the early 1960s Touré was self-consciously a member of a radical cohort, flanked by Nkrumah of Ghana, Massemba-Débat of the Congo (Brazzaville), Modibo Keita of Mali, Nyerere of Tanzania, Ben Bella of Algeria, Lumumba of the Congo (Zaire), and Nasser of the U.A.R. These *compagnons de route* fell in a steady succession: Lumumba almost immediately, Ben Bella in 1965, Nkrumah in 1966, Massemba-Débat and Modibo Keita in 1968. Nasser, mortally stricken by the Six Day War of 1967, from which he never recovered either personally or politically, died in 1970 and it is already clear that his regime has not survived him.

For the Touré regime the demise of these radical analogues has provided a series of bitter and successive shocks. The regime sees itself as a lonely outpost of militant purity in a struggle against imperialist forces which will not rest until their writ runs in Conakry, as elsewhere. The other 'radical survivor', the TANU regime of Nyerere in Tanzania, is too distant to lend much comfort and is, in any case, of hardly comparable pedigree. TANU emerged virtually without challenge as the sole inheritor of power in Tanzania and its independence 'struggle' was fought largely in the corridors and committees of the UN. Nyerere, its leader, is a Christian pragmatist whose radicalism stems from the need to keep a balance with revolutionary Zanzibar, from Tanzania's position as virtually the poorest country in the world, and from his own position as the uncontested, if mild-mannered, philosopher-king of his country. The PDG, on the other hand, was for more than a decade before independence a party of radical opposition, hounded and opposed not only by the French colonial administration but by the indigenous chiefs and most of the educated *évolués* of the country. The party's struggle revolved around covert organization, insurrectionary strikes, and militant defiance of the chiefs and the French.

Not surprisingly the territory's exiguous middle class for the most part kept well clear of the PDG which fell back upon the support of trade unionists, peasants and petty *fonctionnaires* (Touré was one of the latter – older French *colons* can still remember being served by him in the Conakry post office). The party's militants led a precarious, embattled existence, in the towns the objects of harassment, in the countryside of straightforward persecution. Thrown into prolonged and intimate association with the forces of opposition within colonial society, the PDG leadership developed a strong trait of suspicious, truculent populism which heavily overlaid its earlier Marxist and Moslem inheritance. Touré himself had cut his political teeth in the ambience of the PCF and CGT[3] at the height of the Cold War, and though he moved clearly to the right in the mid-1950s after reaching a compromise 'understanding' with the French administration, he and the PDG as a whole bore for ever the scars of its long years in the wilderness.

Thus the Guinean regime acceded to independence with a depth of radical education and experience distinctly unusual in West Africa. The regime had captured world attention at independence by its dramatic and overwhelming 'No' vote to de Gaulle's new Community in September 1958. Since then it has repeatedly caught the imagination of those[4] hoping to find at least one African regime determined to carry through the radical promise of the nationalist struggle to an authentically popular and uncompromising conclusion.

In word and symbolic gesture, at least, the Guinean regime has not disappointed them. Even before independence it had removed not merely the chiefs but abolished the very institution of chieftaincy itself. Thereafter a continuing popular campaign was launched against other forms of traditionalist 'obscurantism' – against the witch-doctors and secret societies of the Forest, against beliefs in (and practitioners of) magic, and against *maraboutage*.[5] Parallel mass literacy drives were launched. Although the regime and the country remain predominantly Moslem a strong stand has been taken in favour of female emancipation. Women had played a notable role in the national struggle and frequently occupied leading positions in post-independence Guinean society. Nonetheless, the regime made it clear that it believed there was still far to go, and has, for example, waged a strong campaign against polygamy.

Within Guinea the regime has espoused a consistent cultural nationalism, attempting to connect itself with its purely African past, at the same time that it has espoused a radical pan-Africanism in the continent as a whole. These two strands achieved an eloquent symbiosis in 1968 when, with much pomp and circumstance, the government brought home (from Mauretania) and re-interred the remains of Alfa Yaya, commemorated as a hero of the pre-colonial resistance. The enormous funeral procession was led by Touré – and by Kwame Nkrumah, his titular co-president then living in exile in Guinea, and viewed by the regime as a victim of the same anti-imperialist struggle which had crushed Alfa Yaya.[6]

The regime has stressed self-reliance. It has sent few students abroad and has tried, instead, to produce a home-grown intellectual elite from its two polytechnics at Kankan and Conakry (named after Nyerere and Lumumba, respectively). Shortly after independence Guinea left the franc zone and launched its own currency; it carried through sweeping and comprehensive programmes of nationalization; and it launched large-scale 'human investment' programmes. This last was undoubtedly a Chinese inspiration – an important if indirect influence reflected also in the 'cultural revolution' launched by Touré in 1967 (the year after Mao's); in the universal attire of Mao-jackets; and in Touré's voluminous Works[7] (which run to over twenty volumes) as well as his occasional forays into poetry.

The Guinean regime has sharply differentiated itself from its neighbours. It espouses 'scientific socialism' and pours scorn upon creeds of 'African socialism', 'negritude', and the 'African personality' as, at best, reactionary mystifications, or, at worst, racism. Touré's own Works have become increasingly – and quite explicitly – Marxist–Leninist in tone, and the regime makes it clear that it regards toleration of capitalism as quite incompatible with opposition to imperialism. In foreign policy the regime has unswervingly aligned itself with the revolutionary left throughout the world.

Finally, and perhaps most strikingly, Guinea is still ruled by the PDG, which was certainly a mass party at independence and still claims to be one. Virtually the entire population belongs to the party (see pp. 50–2); every village, every neighbourhood, every factory, every office has its party committee; all the policies mentioned above have, formally, at least, flowed from the congresses, councils and conferences of the party and have been discussed at local level throughout the country.

Such have been, to put it crudely, the selling points of the Guinean regime. It is difficult, however, to conclude that the product is as good as the advertising. Indeed, there is an important sense in which Guinea under Touré has been too self-consciously responsive to some notional Third (or Second) World audience, has been only too willing to assert a combative, truculent purism. For the regime has shown a continuing penchant for taking up and maintaining awkward, embattled postures, proudly proclaiming its imperviousness to damage to the country's material interests. This often provides very good theatre (and Touré is the ultimately theatrical politician); the messages of international solidarity rain in and Guinean delegates at all manner of progressive gatherings and Communist Party congresses[8] throughout the world are able to accept bouquets and applause. Yet the fact is that Guinea is a weak, small and very poor country, despite its possession of considerable unexploited mineral wealth. Under Touré it has become weaker and poorer and more isolated. The regime can simply not afford to ignore the constraints imposed by such facts on their freedom of manoeuvre. Yet it has ignored them, and has, indeed, affected a sort of grandiose contempt for them. One result is that the famous Italian political judgement – that the situation 'is hopeless, but not serious' – often seems applicable to Guinea.

The parameters of Guinea's internal development have been determined quite heavily by the regime's self-conscious stands on principle. The origins of this stance lie in the manner of Guinea's accession to independence in 1958. The 'No' vote of 28 September is now celebrated annually as the birth of the 'Guinean Revolution' when the modern state emerged in a moment of glorious defiance and self-liberation. Such celebration, it must always be remembered, depends on an act of partial bad faith. When de Gaulle came to power in May 1958 neither Touré nor any other PDG leader had shown signs of wishing to jeopardize its compromise with the French authorities by pushing for independence. Indeed, in the preceding year Touré had gone to great lengths to crush and expel a PDG section which had embarrassed the leadership by raising the independence issue.[9] De Gaulle, however, was determined on a new constitutional settlement for France to give him the authority he needed to deal with Algeria. He coincidentally took the opportunity to head off any colonial distractions in French West Africa by offering a large degree of self-government to all the French colonies there. Once this perspective opened up radicals throughout francophone Africa naturally sought out a flanking position to the left of de Gaulle – which, in the circumstances, could only mean opting for independence. Touré and the PDG leadership, almost alone among established African politicians, enjoyed the respect of such radicals and were unwilling to sacrifice it by aligning themselves with Senghor and Houphouët behind a 'Yes' vote to de Gaulle (already depicted by the FEANF[10] radicals as an act of slavish obeisance to colonialism). So Touré attempted to take up a middle position in terms of which each colony entering the new Community would have the 'right of divorce' from it at will. That is, he would choose to refuse independence provided Guinea's future hypothetical right to independence was recognized. Like Giscard d'Estaing, Touré wanted to vote 'Yes, but . . .'. Since France could hardly rule out such a future hypothesis as impossible, the calculation was that de Gaulle could agree to this compromise but lose nothing by it. It was a grave miscalculation, rooted only too clearly in Touré's desire to retain his good name among a largely external radical audience. Just as the point was very largely that Touré and the PDG should be *seen* to be asserting their authority to determine their future status, so de Gaulle was determined, above all, that his authority should be *seen* and asserted as unchallengeable at this gravest juncture in French history since 1940. Hitherto Touré had dealt only with Fourth Republic politicians, men who always compromised in the end. De Gaulle wished precisely to prove that he was not such a man and so the Guinean compromise was publicly, even contemptuously dismissed. Touré, trapped in a corner of his own construction, sought instinctive salvation in playing to the gallery. To the general amazement[11] (and certainly to the General's amazement) Touré told the huge Conakry crowd which had turned out to greet de Gaulle that Guinea preferred 'poverty in freedom to prosperity in chains'. It is doubtful whether de Gaulle ever suffered an equally public insult in his whole career (he was standing next to Touré on the platform when the crowd erupted in cheers at this rhetorical rejection of France). He refused ever to see Touré again. Touré, perplexed and unhappy,[12] sought desperately to retrieve the situation and spent much time in the next few weeks attempting to see de Gaulle in order to retract and apologize. It was no good: the alternatives, after weeks of dithering, were a total and humiliating climb-down or a 'No' vote. Even after the resounding 'No' vote the Guinean government waited for months and in vain to hear that they were to be welcomed back into the French fold. Only at the end of 1958 did the regime embrace its independence as a positive fact. Guinean independence may be celebrated as a 'revolution', but it was won by a reluctant revolutionary in a state of psychological trauma brought on by compulsive resort to rhetoric.[13]

The Guinean regime has continued to exhibit the same schizophrenia since independence that it displayed in acceding to it. The regime has publicly, vehemently, and continuously attacked western imperialism, neo-colonialism and capitalism; Zionism, American imperialism, West German imperialism, French and Portuguese colonialism have been singled out for most particular attack. The regimes of most other African states have been depicted scathingly as mere artifices of neo-colonial puppetry. The regime portrays itself as aligned in word and spirit with the People's Democracies, Cuba and Vietnam as a non-metropolitan socialist state, ever watchful against the nefarious schemes of the imperialist powers to bring it down.

All this the regime has said, and said repeatedly. But it has frequently acted as if it did not really believe what it was saying and reacted with outraged surprise whenever any of its dire suspicions and predictions have seemed to materialize. From independence on the regime has expressed the warmest affection for France, mixed with bitter condemnation. In October 1962 Touré fiercely condemned American action over Cuba and offered air-landing services to the USSR to break the blockade. In the same month he met and was enchanted by President Kennedy and happily invited the Peace Corps into Guinea. Indeed, the regime sought close and friendly co-operation with all those it most condemned (saving only the Portuguese). It claimed to be independent and socialist; but it gave ambassadorial status to the West Germans and denied it to the East Germans. When the government determined to show how seriously it took its own independence, it was the Russian ambassador, Mr Solod, who was expelled in 1961.

Meanwhile, while still hoping for a rapprochement with France, Guinea had taken the fateful step in March 1960 of opting out of the franc zone, indignantly denouncing the currency area as a means for ensuring continuing colonial economic control. A month later Touré indignantly discovered and denounced a French colonial plot, in which Senegal and the Ivory Coast were also allegedly implicated. Six French *colons* were expelled and another condemned to twenty-five years hard labour.[14] Only in March 1961 did France name an ambassador to Conakry. In December, however, Touré announced the discovery of a (left-wing) 'teachers' plot', ejected Solod and accused the eastern bloc of wanting to turn Guinea into a Communist state. Two weeks later, however, he accused France, too, of having been involved in the plot.

A period of relative calm followed. Mikoyan visited Conakry and relations with the East improved. A similar rapprochement was attempted with France once it became clear that the Algerian War was ending. Touré fulsomely invited de Gaulle to re-visit Guinea. There was no response. In May 1965 Touré offered to compensate French concerns for losses incurred by their nationalization and asked for the resumption of French economic aid. In November 1965, however, Touré furiously denounced a 'traders' plot' and accused France, together with its Ivorian and Entente 'puppets', of having attempted to foment a plot against him (in company with Moïse Tshombe). Diplomatic relations between France and Guinea were broken off. From then on a state of cold war existed between Conakry and Paris, though the regime's bitter condemnations of the old metropole were always punctuated by professions of willingness for 'honest' co-operation with her.

The regime's by now quite morbid sense of embattled insecurity was given fresh impetus by Nkrumah's fall in 1966. When Touré invited Nkrumah to come to Guinea the Ghanaians retaliated by detaining a Guinean ministerial delegation in transit via Pan American Airways at Accra. Conakry drew the conclusion that the US was behind the Ghana coup. The US Cultural Centre was attacked and destroyed by the Conakry JDRA,[15] the Peace Corps given twelve hours to leave the country and the US ambassador placed under house arrest. In 1967, on hearing news of the outbreak of the Six Day War, Touré gave the Israelis twelve hours to leave the country. By this time Conakry had also become increasingly critical of the West Germans (who maintained a large aid and diplomatic presence in Guinea) over their application of the Hallstein doctrine.

The fall of Modibo Keita in Mali at the end of 1968 created a fresh shock-wave, with the normal round of panicky arrests. A few months later a fresh military plot was discovered, this time with the Portuguese, together with France and West Germany, getting much of the blame. At the same time (1969) Pompidou succeeded de Gaulle and Conakry sedulously wooed the new French leader[16] – who, however, maintained a frosty distance. Guinean denunciations of France redoubled.

In 1970 came the almost-successful invasion of Conakry by a seaborne Guinean exile force, set afoot by the Portuguese. In one sense this was nothing new – Guinea had been in a virtual state of war with Portugal for several years, owing to Conakry's total and unswerving support for the PAIGC of neighbouring Guiné-Bissau. Portuguese land and air raids across the Guinean frontier in the remote hinterland were almost a commonplace. But the November 1970 invasion was different. The capital was attacked; President Touré's residence was destroyed and he had to flee for his life into the shanty town area; there were grave question marks as to the loyalty of the Guinean army and air force. The regime survived by the narrowest of margins and furiously inveighed not only against Portugal and her alleged helpers in Senegal and the Ivory Coast, but against almost all the western powers, including Britain,[17] South Africa and, most of all, West Germany. The latter were, indeed, held chiefly responsible and were expelled lock, stock and barrel from the country. The pleasure of the East Germans at this turn of events was somewhat qualified by the arrest of one of their own mission on similar charges.

Arrests and political detentions were hardly new to the Guinean scene, but after the 1970 invasion there followed a purge of unequalled amplitude and severity, culminating in mass show trials a year later. Thousands of public denunciations were made and probably several thousands were actually arrested, including many foreigners and their families. La Voix de la Révolution (Conakry Radio) broadcast the trials and public confessions of 128 accused, including fourteen former members of the government and a considerable number of army officers, senior civil servants, former ambassadors, regional governors and top party officials. Party committees all over the country met to demand the death sentence and a considerable number of 'spontaneous' public hangings and lynchings took place. Most of the accused simply disappeared after their trials and many, perhaps all, were executed.

A tense and difficult situation continued thereafter. In January 1973 the PAIGC leader, Amilcar Cabral, was assassinated in Conakry, apparently at Portugal's behest, but the country returned gradually to a shell-shocked calm, punctuated by routine (if furious) denunciations of Senegal, Ivory Coast and other African 'traitors' and of the machinations of the *complot permanent* within Guinea. Interestingly, the chief accusation against Guinea's francophone neighbours was that they were preventing Conakry's reconciliation with Paris – a possibility again with Giscard's succession as president in 1974. Negotiation to this end continued through 1974 and in mid-1975 the resumption of diplomatic relations with both France and West Germany was announced, after ruptures of ten and five years respectively. A further major change of direction was signalled in 1975 by Guinea's signature of the Lomé Convention – the two preceding Yaoundé agreements had been denounced by Conakry as instruments of French and West German colonialism. Meanwhile the collapse of the Portuguese empire and the accession to power of the PAIGC had enormously relieved the pressures on Guinea. Not only was it a major vindication of her steadfast and self-sacrificing stand in favour of the PAIGC, but the Conakry regime now, at last, had a friendly, ideologically sympathetic – and grateful – neighbour. In July 1975 Touré actually felt secure enough to leave the country for two days – his first trip abroad in ten years.

In August 1976, however, a major new purge was launched after the discovery of another plot on President Touré's life. This time the chief victims were Telli Diallo, the former OAU secretary-general, Alioune Dramé, a former minister, and a number of senior military and civil service figures. This 'Foulah plot'[18] had also allegedly encompassed machinations by France, West Germany, Senegal, the Ivory Coast, and the US. (In the now routine broadcast public confessions Telli Diallo admitted to having CIA contacts in the US ambassador to Liberia and the US commercial attaché in Conakry.) A great campaign against Foulah 'racism' was launched. Conakry demanded the immediate extradition to Guinea of a long list of alleged conspirators in exile, a request refused even by the PAIGC government – which led to the immediate closure of Conakry's embassy in Bissau. Having half-emerged from her isolation, Guinea plunged back into it, making enemies on all sides. (Touré attempted to repair some of the damage done in Paris by sending a message to the new French premier, M. Barre, congratulating him on his succession to Chirac, who, Touré hinted, had been conniving with Diallo, Dramé and the rest.) Touré was keen, at all costs, not to jeopardize the visit to Guinea in 1977 of President Giscard d'Estaing.

In the eighteen years since independence there have, then, been at least six major internal convulsions in Guinea over alleged plots – and since 1970 Guinea has been living in the Kafka-esque era of the *'complot permanent'*. It is impossible to relegate these 'plots' to a matter of foreign policy. The atmosphere of fear, suspicion and insecurity on all sides engendered by the plots, the purges and the sudden turns of foreign policy has done more than provide the context within which domestic policy occurs. Rather, domestic policies have been merely the intervals between such turns and *éclatements*. For much of the period since independence Guinea has been at almost hysterical odds with her major neighbours and with the former metropole. This is a unique situation in Africa. The continuing importance of the metropolitan factor in most of francophone Africa is such that it is virtually impossible to consider the existence of governments in (for example) Abidjan or Dakar independently of the 'French factor'. De Gaulle warned Guinea in 1958 that if she voted 'No' she would have to 'reap the consequences'. Whatever judgement one reaches as to the credibility of the 'plots', there is not doubt that this, indeed, is, in good part, what has occurred.

It is very tempting to suspend all judgement as to the credibility of the 'plots'. The full facts are not, and may never be, known. There are no impartial sources.[19] One cannot take the public confessions of the plotters at face value any more than one can take at all lightly the allegations of torture in Guinean prisons. There can be no doubt that President Touré has become – if he was not always – a morbidly suspicious ruler who would rather err on the side of excess in security matters. His willingness (at least in the 1960s) to release detainees from prison and almost immediately promote them to high office – usually abroad[20] – was a virtual admission that his judgement had often been faulty and hasty, and the much more frequent recourse to capital punishment since the 1970 invasion suggests greater panic rather than better judgement. Equally, though, there is no doubt that the Guinean regime has been a thorn in the side of France, Guinea's francophone neighbours, and, to a lesser extent, of West Germany and the US,[21] as well as of pre-coup Portugal. Guinea's mineral wealth is potentially enormous and, under a different regime in Conakry, the opportunities for western multinationals in the country could be very considerable indeed. It is equally true that many of the regime's leading opponents in exile belong to formerly privileged social strata within Guinea, that their success would indeed constitute a victory for the 'forces of reaction' (in Touré's words). It is, finally, clear enough that no peaceful change in the present regime is possible and that, given the centralization of power in Touré's person, his assassination would constitute a merely logical objective for the regime's root and branch opponents.

Georges Chaffard, in a series of detailed articles in the *Nouvel Obser-vateur* in 1969,[22] states baldly that when the notorious Jacques Foccart became Secretary-General for Community Affairs in March 1960 he found that the SDECE[23] (which then fell under his control) had already given Guinea the benefits of its consideration: 'An operation seeking to provoke a coup d'état in Conakry and, ultimately, the physical liquidation of the Guinean president, had been under study since the beginning of 1959.'[24] This first project apparently got to an advanced stage, with Guinean exiles trained at Dakar by parachutists of the SDECE's 'Action' branch ready to go into service when a security leak reached the Quai d'Orsay, which leaked it further and thus killed the plan. Foccart constructed a second plan, involving a combined operation by guerrilla forces in the Fouta Djalon, in central Guinea, and French-officered commando raids across the Ivorian and Senegalese borders. According to Chaffard, Touré, suspecting some of the PDG leadership of plotting against him, chose this moment to conduct a minor purge; the French believed themselves discovered and news leaked to Houphouët who was furious to learn that his own territory had been used for the location of arms depots and as an 'Action' commando base. Houphouët's bitter complaint embarrassed and infuriated de Gaulle, for all that he had, claims Chaffard, given Foccart the go-ahead for the operation. De Gaulle apparently felt that he had narrowly avoided involvement in an almost exact replica of the Bay of Pigs dénouement and warned Foccart that he never again wished to hear talk of such projects. Thus, according to Chaffard, Foccart mounted no further operations against Touré after

1961 but bent his efforts, rather, to preventing the emergence of any parallel threat to the French Community.

However that may be, Touré, having learnt of these early plans, could hardly afford to take Foccart's post-1961 behaviour on trust – there was, after all, no halt to Foccart's activities elsewhere in Africa.[25] What is strange is that Touré should have blamed this 1961 plot on the Russians, the teachers' trade union, and a grotesquely unlikely collection of Guinean intellectuals. The alleged culprit of the 1965 plot – the unfortunate trader, 'Petit Touré', who had dared to announce his candidacy for the presidential election against his namesake – seems almost equally unlikely. On the other hand it is worth noting that *Le Monde*, with the benefit of four months' reflection on the 1965 plot, suggested that France might indeed have been involved.[26] It is also impossible to dismiss as fiction the 1969 plot – the chief alleged culprit, Col. Kaman Diabi, fled on discovery to take refuge with the Portuguese authorities in Bissau – providing circumstantial support for Touré's claim that he had been intriguing with them. The release of Portuguese documents since the Lisbon coup leaves no doubt whatsoever that the Touré version of the 1970 invasion plot was substantially correct. As for the 1976 'plot' of Telli Diallo and the Foulahs, it is simply too soon to make any judgement, apart from noting that Diallo has always been the chief candidate of the regime's opponents to succeed Touré. Such unwanted support has always gravely embarrassed Diallo, but Touré could not but regard him as a danger and a rival, for all the former's disavowals of his supporters in exile.

Enough evidence exists, then, to suggest that while Touré has certainly often struck out wildly, has imprisoned or executed many innocent people, and has often cried wolf – there have indeed been some real wolves at his door.

At independence Guinea's economy presented a fairly typical colonial mix with a large majority of its dominant peasantry involved in subsistence agriculture and pastoral farming, its commerce dominated by a few large foreign trading houses, a small mining enclave, a rickety transport and service sector (mostly state-run), and an export economy based overwhelmingly on bananas, coffee, palm kernels and groundnuts, in that order of importance. Guinea's apparent poverty was, however, in good measure the result of French under-investment – French colonialism did not exploit enough, it merely pillaged.[27] For Guinea is potentially a rich country. Its well-watered coastal plains could one day feed most of West Africa with rice, its extensive uplands pasture could support vast herds of cattle. The Forest area's potential for coffee production has hardly been touched. The country possesses prodigious reserves of high-grade bauxite, iron ore and various other minerals. There is some gold and diamonds. Many of West Africa's major rivers rise in the Fouta Djalon and, properly tapped, could provide abundant hydroelectric power. The problem – as the French realized only too well – is that very large quantities of skilled manpower and, above all, of capital would have to be mobilized for this potential to be realized.

This has not happened. The most important single export-earner at independence, the banana-crop, was heavily dependent on the activities of a few thousand European planters who left in droves at independence and in a steady trickle thereafter. Under other circumstances an African plantocracy might have emerged to replace them, but most African planters operated on a very small scale and with low productivity. Both the socialist policies and the sheer disorganization of the post-independence state were inimical to their expansion. The result was that while banana exports reached almost 100,000 tons in 1955, they fell to 35,000 tons in 1964 and have since levelled off at around 40,000 tons. The situation with the other cash-crops is not much better – only the pineapple export crop has shown any real growth since independence. While it is true that Guinean consumption of such crops has grown, leaving less for export, it is also true that absolute production levels are no higher than they were twenty years ago, and usually lower. Even this position is maintained thanks only to state subsidies and the staggeringly favourable terms of trade for such products offered by the Eastern European bloc.[28] There has been a clear fall in the absolute number of most forms of livestock over the period since 1958. Worst of all, Guinea has failed to achieve even self-sufficiency in food. For almost the whole of the post-1958 period Guinea has had to depend on supplies under the US PL480 programme of grain and rice – and rice is the basis of the Guinean diet. Each year Touré has issued dire warnings that these rice imports – which are as humiliating as they are financially debilitating – cannot be allowed to continue; each year they have been essential. There is, however, some sign that Guinea has turned the corner since 1970 with higher rice production and strict import controls producing a sharp and progressive drop in food imports.[29]

Since independence a small secondary industrial sector has been built up, almost all of it state owned. The state early on took over the import–export trade and has progressively taken over the country's domestic wholesale and retail trade as well. And the state still runs the extensive service sector – the railways, ports, airports, airline, telecommunications etc. Several state farms[30] exist and the state has also nationalized some of the less important mining concerns. In addition, the state is responsible for ambitious health, social welfare and educational programmes, plus such basics as the postal service, banking, insurance, water and electricity supply, all construction, and, of course, the sheer administration of the country. It goes almost without saying that the state is wholly unable to provide the number of reasonably trained, let alone honest, cadres required to run these concerns. The result is that virtually the whole of this extensive state sector is in a disastrous condition. There is, at every turn, wholesale under-utilization of capacity, chronic corruption and inefficiency, low quality and low quantity output. No critic of the state economic and administrative elite is more bitter and comprehensive in his attacks than President Touré.[31]

What saves the situation is bauxite and its semi-processed product, alumina. The giant foreign conglomerate at Fria (in which the dominant partner is the US Olin Mathieson corporation) commenced production in 1960 and within a year provided almost three-quarters of total exports by value and foreign exchange earnings. Dependence on bauxite increased further with the development of the huge deposits at Boké in the early 1970s (by Harveys of California in (theoretical) association with the Guinean state). By 1975 bauxite and alumina made up over 95 per cent of all exports, and Guinea was mining over 9 million tonnes of bauxite annually. It is impossible to over-estimate the importance of bauxite which provides the entire basis for the country's (and the regime's) economic survival.

After bauxite, the most important feature of the Guinean economy remains her exit from the franc zone in 1960. The Guinean franc – the *sily*[32] – is not convertible. As Guinean economic difficulties mounted in the early 1960s the regime ran up enormous foreign debts and simply printed money to meet its needs, producing run-away inflation which it refused to reflect in any alteration to the official exchange rate. The result is that Guinean currency is effectively worth nothing outside Guinea and very little inside Guinea given the paucity of real goods that it can buy. The paucity of goods is, in turn, quite largely the result of the valueless currency which has engendered smuggling and black-marketeering on a sustained scale quite possibly unique even in African history. Every producer or trader attempted to sell his goods across Guinea's extensive borders for hard currency and the goods it could buy. Traders found themselves quite inevitably involved in the black market to survive – including, of course, a huge black market in currency. PDG-run co-operatives fairly openly sold their entire production across the frontiers; shepherds herded their flocks across the border (hence the fall in live-stock numbers); and literally hundreds of thousands of Guineans emigrated by stealth to sell their labour abroad.[33]

The regime has reacted by erecting a complex network of external and internal customs and currency checks, political surveillance, an economic police force, continual symbolic punishments of the 'guilty' – and, inevitably, by turning a blind eye much of the time. The internal commercial network has always remained, throughout colonial times, largely in the hands of small African traders and transporters (chiefly the legendary *dioula*). Not surprisingly the regime has viewed such private traders as bourgeois traitors to the Guinean revolution, and has steadily and furiously denounced them since 1960. At the same time the gross corruption and inefficiency of the theoretically competitive state commercial agencies and shops made it impossible to do without the *dioulas* if any distribution network was to exist. So traders were denounced, sometimes jailed or executed, relied upon and treated as lepers. By the *loi-cadre* of 8 November 1964 office in the PDG was made incompatible with the exercise of trade. Guinea is, in Touré's words, a 'party-state', and exclusion from party office of any group has something like the force of the papal excommunication of the unfortunate Albigensians. In early 1975 the regime's campaign against the traders culminated in the complete suppression of all markets and all private trade; henceforward private trading was to be, in itself, a criminal act. Inevitably, it still exists, but severe dislocation of the rural economy has already resulted.

At the same time (early 1975) the regime decided to launch the full-scale collectivization of rural production. An earlier collectivization effort had been launched in 1960, allowing only small private plots to be retained. On the model of the famous Soviet MTS (Machine Tractor Stations) agricultural modernization centres were set up to provide loans, equipment, extension services etc. The whole scheme simply failed to get off the ground and had petered out everywhere by 1963 through lack of trained personnel and in the face of stolid peasant resistance. The loans given were generally found to be uncollectable, as was the equipment – producing only a tractor-bourgeoisie.[34] The 1975 effort is centred around Motorized Production Brigades and the sending of large numbers of students into the villages to spread new techniques and 'learn from the people' in the approved Chinese manner. It is far too soon to know whether this second attempt will succeed any further than the first, though there is no reason to believe that the peasantry will resist less now than then. Indeed, the real substance (if any) behind the 'Foulah plot' of 1976 lies in the refusal of the Fouta Djalon peasantry to see their beloved cattle collectivized. Quite certainly the regime, even if this new effort achieves a modicum of success, will for many years yet have to tolerate large-scale non-compliance with the collectivization decree. Meanwhile one must anticipate that this decree, together with the suppression of private trade, will, if taken at all seriously by the regime or its subjects, wreak utter havoc in the countryside with widespread starvation a clear possibility.

The analysis of Guinean political development since independence is clouded by the normal opaqueness of a single party state without competitive elections above the most purely grass-roots level. The PDG dominates every aspect of Guinean life in 1977 even more thoroughly than it did in 1958 and its continuing claim to be a true mass party has to be treated with some respect. Virtually every Guinean town-dweller is a member of the party and attends party meetings or gatherings at least occasionally. The situation in the countryside is more obscure and the party regional elites tend to constitute little clusters centred in the country towns and larger villages. There are word-of-mouth reports that the fall in popular sympathy with the PDG has been sufficient within the Fouta, at least, for the old chiefly families to regain some of their popular prestige. If so, there has been no formal reflection or repercussion from such developments and there is no suggestion that the previously influential *marabouts* have been able to conserve, let alone improve, their popular standing.[35]

Several elements are visible within the party. There are still a few remaining *'militants du premier heure'* – those who struggled against such heavy odds in the late 1940s and early 1950s. But this generation's importance had very greatly diminished even by the late 1960s. In many areas, indeed, such militants had become merely honorific elders or had simply dropped from view, to be replaced by a younger, better-educated and often socially more advantaged generation whose brashness frequently raised hackles among these 'elders'. In such an eventuality the latter would not be slow to evoke the party's populist ethic and complain bitterly and directly to the president – who did not dismiss such complaints at all lightly.

By the middle 1970s, however, these early militants had all but disappeared. Their younger successors – many of them of school age in the 1950s – had frequently joined the party at or even after independence. By this point the party's importance to career and social mobility had needed no emphasis and not a few attempted to satisfy their social ambitions via the party, often producing a schizophrenic blend of personal corruption and socialist militancy. Touré, for his part, has quite publicly placed his faith in the still-later post-independence generations, those who have grown up in and know only the life of the PDG party–state. The vast majority of this cohort have not travelled outside Guinea and are 'untainted' by experience of either a colonial past or the neo-colonial delights and pleasures of Dakar or Abidjan. A particular place within this group is occupied by the students of the country's two polytechnics. A lively suspicion is entertained of all those who have been educated abroad (even those who studied in the Eastern bloc after independence returned to Guinea under a shadow – hence the virtually universal fear of going home among Guinean students abroad). Entry to the polytechnics is highly competitive, with political criteria taken into account. Great stress is laid on the inculcation of political purity and militancy into the *poly-techniciens* – Touré himself attends and chairs the annual *séminaires de formation idéologique* held in both centres. Each *promotion* of students is named after a revolutionary hero (Ho Chi Minh, Fidel Castro, Mao, Cabral, Nkrumah etc.) and its members can expect rapid promotion within the state administration and enterprises virtually on graduation. A number of the first (Lenin) *promotion* of 1967 are already directors of major state enterprises and undoubtedly Touré's hopes for the success of the 1975 turn to the left rest quite heavily upon the *polytechniciens*. At a wider level the importance of this post-independence generation is also reflected in the greatly increased role and size (it probably outnumbers the party proper) of the JRDA, the 'shock-troops of the Guinean revolution' who routinely exercise extensive police, surveillance and organizational duties in the urban centres.

The JRDA's increased role is the more striking given the unmistakably diminished importance of the PDG's other two parallel organizations, the Women's Section and the Confédération Nationale des Travailleurs Guinéens. The Women's Section, large and powerful in the 1950s, gradually became a paper show-piece in the 1960s. The leading *militantes* acceded to major positions in the party proper or in the government but no younger feminine cohort emerged in their wake. Most of the older generation have now entered effective retirement as *grand-dames* of the revolution or have met their fate at the hands of jailers or executioners. While women undoubtedly exercised pressure to bring about the campaign against polygamy, there has been a relative absence of 'women's issues' beyond that.[36] It is possible that the energies of younger women are now devoted to the JRDA, but it also seems likely that the conditions of the party's struggle in the 1950s – particularly the key role often played by (feminine) small traders – were simply more favourable to the emergence of feminine activism, and have not been replicated. There is no doubt that the regime's pride in and support for feminine emancipation is sincere and strong, but the 'longest revolution' still has some way to go in Guinea, as elsewhere. At present the official ethic of total feminine emancipation runs considerably ahead of social practice.

The decline in significance of the trade union movement, though

51

paralleled almost everywhere else in post-independence Africa, is all the more striking in Guinea given the central role played by the unions in the colonial period. For years after independence Touré retained his position at the head of the CNTG and of UGTAN,[37] the breakaway pan-African federation which he had founded, attempting to depict himself as a trade unionist almost before he was a politician. (Well after he became head of state he commonly began replies to interviewing journalists with: 'Moi, je suis syndicaliste . . .'.)

The fact is, however, that the CNTG, with no freedom of action, became ever more clearly a mere arm of the PDG. Its major leaders were quickly promoted into high state or party positions. Bengaly Camara, the leading trade unionist after Touré, became Minister of Labour in the first independence government. (He was arrested in 1965, apparently, and died in jail of unspecified causes.) Any remaining illusions of trade union independence were thoroughly dashed by the crushing of the Teachers' Union and the arrest of its leadership in 1961 and by later, less-publicized show-downs with the only other notably independent group, the railway workers. When Touré relinquished the CNTG leadership he was careful to leave behind a central committee (under its new leader, Mamady Kaba) of men hand-picked for their loyalty to him. Such men, representing nothing, with no freedom of action, and with very little to do (strikes are illegal), simply echo their master's voice and rally to fresh efforts an apathetic and non-participant work-force.

Besides the parallel organizations of the trade unions, youth and women, there stands, since 1969, a fourth – the army. Shaken by the Mali coup of 1968 the regime attempted to head off possible military grievances by granting the soldiery full political rights, with party committees being elected within all the military camps. This arrangement potentially, though not actually, created a new authority structure within the army, alternative to the hierarchy of rank; helped emphasize political virtues as criteria for promotion, and increased political surveillance within the army. It also incorporated the military elite into the political establishment, with a place at the inner councils of the PDG. Concurrently the organization of the Milice Populaire, the para-military wing of the JRDA, received fresh impetus. The internal workings of the system do not allow for more detailed analysis but in the crudest sense (there has been no military coup) it seems to have worked. Undoubtedly, the regime continues to regard the army (and even the Milice[38]) with some suspicion. The army's popular standing is high, however – most of their time is taken up in economic activities (particularly road-building) and in parading at the innumerable public holidays of the revolution. They have a reputation for punctuality and efficiency quite unique among the arms of the state.

52

Political realities mirror the old French colonial pattern more closely than this formal structure might suggest. Until 1958 Guinea was ruled by a French governor with complete authority over the *commandants* of the thirty-odd *cercles* – the 'lords of the bush'. They, in turn, exercised entire authority over some 247 canton chiefs and, beneath them, some 4,200 village chiefs. The governor exercised authority through his cabinet, which was not responsible to the Territorial Assembly (parliament), and through occasional conferences of the *commandants*, called at his pleasure. At independence the regime attempted to break entirely with the old colonial pattern – symbolically enough, the statues of former governors were immediately despatched to the museum yard, there to face out to sea. The PDG (which had won fifty-six out of sixty Assembly seats in 1957) was to rule as a democratic party, with regular congresses and an elected central committee. The government was reorganized with the creation of four mighty ministries to cover the country's four regions (the coast, the Fouta, the Forest, and Upper Guinea). The number of *cercles* was increased to thirty-four and they were rechristened as regions, each with an appointed regional governor. The cantons, like the chieftaincy, were abolished and replaced by sixty-seven *arondissements*, run by elected municipalities. Elected village councils, instituted in May 1958, existed but were regarded as irrelevant from the first.

The governor's residence became the presidential palace and Touré moved in. . . . The Assembly remained impotent and, after the first year, seldom met. The president ruled through a nine-member Bureau Politique National (BPN). The four great regional ministries did not work and were eventually disbanded. The regional governors were visibly the successors of the *commandants* and moved into their residences. The elected municipalities were abolished and the number of *arondissements* raced up ineluctably over the 200 mark to approximate the old cantons. They were officered by appointed *chefs d'arondissement*, roughly equivalent to the old *adjoints* of the *commandants* – or, more nearly, the *chefs de canton*. . . . The secretaries-general of the party's village committees were, in function, exact replacements of the village chiefs. Six PDG national congresses were held between 1958 and 1967, when, however, they were made quinquennial. The void has been filled by regular sessions of the Conseil National de la Révolution (the thirty-seventh CNR session took place in November 1967). The CNR was the visible successor to the conference of *commandants*, attended by the regional governors and delegates of the party federations.

It is these party federations (one for each region) which are the true innovation of the post-independence system. For the party exists in parallel to the state structure, subsuming it at the lower levels. The bureaux of the party's regional federations constitute centres of power which had no equivalent under the colonial regime. The regional party secretaries are substantial rivals to the regional governors and frequently overshadow them. They have at least some local roots, whereas the governors are regularly transferred from region to region. The party structure stretching beneath the secretaries is hugely more extensive than the administrative network at the governor's command. A stranger arriving in a Guinean country town will have, as his first duty, to notify the party secretary of his presence; informing the governor is not thought essential. The Conakry government expects and demands that regional governors and party secretaries work together and take joint responsibility for the implementation of central government policy, but rivalry between these two pivotal groups is endemic.

Touré is the key arbiter between these groups, travelling endlessly around the country to inspect and address them, calling them continually in council, and publicly admonishing them in rabble-rousing speeches. Some degree of central control is secured by the continual promotions and transfers of the governors and the appointment of party secretaries to government office (frequently as governors, though never in their own region). On the other hand, although it is inconceivable that any party secretary could secure 'election' without Touré's support, governors and secretaries both are far from Conakry and their positions, regardless of personnel changes, guarantee them substantial power throughout the interior. The central control of Touré, the super-Governor of the independence era, is certainly greater than that of any of his French predecessors: (slightly) improved communications, Touré's staggeringly energetic touring, and the duality of secretary and governor (as opposed to the single *commandant de cercle*) guarantee that. But presidential control is not great enough for Touré to feel entirely secure, nor to achieve the socialist transformation he desires. His sense of frustration and insecurity are clear enough. He has attempted to respond to this situation in several ways, but always with a flood of exhortation, instruction and condemnation, and always by fresh organizational initiatives. The most important of these was inaugurated in 1967 with the announcement that Guinea would henceforth tread the path of the Socialist Cultural Revolution. Only at this juncture was Guinea's socialist option made explicit and official – the preceding period being termed one of 'national democracy', again using the Chinese terminology. Henceforth Marxism–Leninism, or Touré's idiosyncratic interpretation of it, was to be the philosophy of the revolution.

Touré, clearly doubting that the existing state and party structures were adequate for the tasks ahead, announced that the fundamental unit of the party–state was henceforth to be the Pouvoir Révolutionnaire Locale.

There are some 8,000 PRLs, one for every village and urban *quartier*. The ever-continuing process of peasant resettlement (and rapid population growth – from about 2·75 million in 1958 to perhaps 4 million now) means that there are now about 6,000 villages. The other 2,000 PRLs are based in *quartiers* – a pretty fair index of Guinea's urban growth since independence – Conakry alone is reckoned to have some 300,000 inhabitants. Ever since 1967 the regime has laid continuous stress on the primordial role of the PRLs. As in the Chinese Cultural Revolution, the national leadership made it clear that it had lost confidence in the generation which had inherited the revolution and which now constituted a swollen, opportunist, conservative and deeply-entrenched bureaucracy. The solution was to 'return power to the people'. What this entailed in practice was the revitalization of the old village councils to the detriment of both regional governors and federal party secretaries. The revolutionary national leadership would deal direct with the (revolutionary) mass in their PRLs. The PRLs were encouraged to denounce and unveil all intermediaries whose loss of touch with the people was evidenced by corruption, inefficiency or lack of revolutionary zeal. There was no way of guaranteeing that party or state cadres might not be corrupt – indeed, Touré continually warned that 'the fifth column is everywhere' – but the people as a whole could not be corrupt. 'The people', in Touré's dictum, 'is never wrong'. The PRL thus constitute both the theoretical and the practical base of the Guinean Socialist Cultural Revolution.

In fact, of course, the regional apparatus of the Party–State cannot be so easily disregarded. In order to set the PRLs on foot and keep them active and co-ordinated Conakry must rely upon these same intermediaries. In any case, the simple devolution of duties to the PRLs in no way makes those duties easier to carry out. Thus the regime is in the position of proudly proclaiming that the PRLs alone are the true basis of the Party–State – but effectively holding the regional authorities responsible for the successful functioning of the PRLs. This contradiction has become especially pointed since the leftward turn of early 1975, which is clearly meeting effective resistance precisely at the level of the PRLs. The measures of agricultural collectivization are meeting stubborn peasant resistance, particularly in the Fouta, it seems clear. The thirty-seventh CNR in November 1976 set agricultural production and delivery targets for the PRLs for 1977, threatening dire sanctions if the PDG Sections and Federations are unable to report the successful completion of these tasks by 14 May 1977 – the thirtieth anniversary of the PRG's foundation. But it is clear that the regime does not expect these targets to be met and can console itself that even in the USSR it took many years before a collectivization began to produce anything like its hoped-for results. A much more serious and immediate situation has been created by the abolition of private commerce, taxes on which have provided a large element in the state's revenue receipts. If the state shops fail to work properly; if collectivization not only does not work but actually produces losses (slaughter or herding away of cattle, for example); or if collectivization and the nationalization of internal commerce simply lead to sufficient disorganization to immiserate the rural economy – then taxes will be harder to collect.

This is precisely what has already happened – in 1976 there was a very large short-fall in tax receipts and Conakry has made it clear that, though taxes are collected by the PRLs in the first instance, it is the party federations and their bureaux who are held responsible by the national leadership. The governors and federations have been warned that in 1977 they must collect not merely the full tax revenue from each of their regions, but all the back taxes still owing. If one reads Touré's speech to the thirty-seventh CNR[39] one could without difficulty imagine oneself to be listening to any of Guinea's French governors twenty, thirty or fifty years ago, haranguing their *commandants de cercle* on how to manage their village and canton chiefs in the desperate business of tax-collection. Then, however, failures simply resulted in large-scale de-stoolings of the unfortunate chiefs. Touré, on the other hand, has made it clear now that it is the regional authorities who must carry the blame – and the sanctions. Having drawn up the production and tax-collection targets of each region, Touré drew up the following schedule:

(i) In all regions where more than 80 per cent of the allotted tasks are carried out the party cadres concerned will not have to submit to re-election for as long as they achieve 100 per cent results or better in years after 1977.

(ii) Those who achieve only 40 per cent to 60 per cent of their tasks must be regarded as mediocre. They must lose all their party offices for at least the remainder of their present term of office.

(iii) 'From 0 per cent to 40 per cent, well these are the culprits, the saboteurs of the People's work. In the future such saboteurs must not merely lose their positions of responsibility to others, but must be arrested and tried for sabotage.'[40]

'Henceforth', Touré announced, 'each session of the CNR must be a veritable tribunal, verifying the fidelity of cadres as reflected by concrete results.'[41]

It will already be clear that Guinea is not a place in which such threats may be taken lightly. That the revolution is capable of consuming its own is nowhere clearer than at the level of the national leadership itself. In the purges of the 1960s most prominent among the casualties were the former opposition leaders such as Ibrahima Barry and Diawandou Barry, who had dissolved their parties to join the PDG in 1958, but whom Touré had never really trusted. But old PDG militants like Bengaly Camara also fell. Fodéba Keita, the founder of the famous Ballets Africains, administered these purges as Minister of Defence and Security. He is alleged by the exile opposition to be responsible for the installation of the full-blown apparatus of secret police, prisons, and modern forms of torture. If the allegations are true he was able to sample his own handiwork after the 1969 plot, when he disappeared into jail, never to re-emerge.

The fall of Fodéba Keita was a clear turning-point. He had been part of the innermost ruling group, consisting of his closest associate, Ismael Touré, the president's notoriously corrupt brother, Sekou Touré himself, Lansana Béavogui, and Saifoulaye Diallo. So close was Ismael to Fodéba Keita that many believed that his survival proved that it was beyond even the president's power to remove him. The 1971 purges removed all the remaining figures whose pasts included any history of activity in opposition parties in the 1940s and 1950s, but it also cut a considerable swathe through old PDG militants. In the following year Saifoulaye Diallo was dropped from the BPN. Although no further sanction against him followed, it was a striking move – he had always been publicly regarded as – indeed, publicly announced by the president to be – the number two man, the president's successor in case of mishap, and he was certainly the leading Foulah within the PDG. Lansana Béavogui, always regarded as the president's most pliant supporter, became prime minister. Touré had clearly lost all confidence in his governmental colleagues by this point – in the wake of the 1970 invasion no less than sixteen of the government's 24 ministers had been arrested. The 1976 purge, as we have seen, brought about the downfall of Telli Diallo and Alioune Dramé, the latter having served in the government continuously since 1958. Few now have such a pedigree – of the seventeen BPN members who led the country to independence in 1958 only six still survive. It is reported that it was only with difficulty that the president was dissuaded from arresting a further two of these – Béavogui and N'Famara Keita – in the 1976 purge.[42] Moreover, suspicion again fell upon Ismael Touré. Many of his supporters and associates have now been arrested and he was a notable absentee from the thirty-seventh CNR.

Two trends are discernible amongst the carnage. First, virtually the whole of the national political elite now comes from the ethnic group of the president, the Malinkés (who constitute one-third of the total population). This gradually creeping process of Malinké-ization is visible at all levels of the party and administration,[43] and undoubtedly contributes to resentment against the regime among the Foulahs (a further one-third of the population). Secondly, many of the inner ruling circle (Moussa Diakité, Mamadi Keita, and Seydou Keita, for example) are related to Touré by marriage, and one (Ismael) is a direct relative.[44] Touré's wife, Andrée, plays a leading role in the PDG Women's Section. Few of the leadership have any sort of genuine popular or local base – those who did have mainly disappeared now. At present this hardly matters in that there are no competitive elections and the real jostling for power is conducted in the intrigues inside and around the presidential palace.

For, as will by now be obvious, the concentration of power in the person of the president is one of the most striking trends of the independence period. The presidentialist trend is so strong elsewhere in Africa that this might have been expected to occur in Guinea even if Touré was not such a remarkable, and in many ways attractive man, and even if he did not enjoy a very considerable and continuing popular rapport. He is an auto-didact of impressive intellectual calibre, a fact which is sometimes obscured by the grotesque over-exposure of his views on every subject under the sun. He is immensely strong physically – indeed his dynamism and energy are legendary within Guinea and have played no small part in his long political survival. No man in Guinea works harder than he, no potential opponent is conceivably more alert or suspicious. He was, in 1977, still only fifty-five. He criss-crosses the country continuously and is personally familiar with every corner of it and with literally thousands of militants. His working schedule on such tours (and he always drives his own car at high speed) is such that those who accompany him are exhausted within a day or two. Until 1970 it was his practice, when in Conakry, to receive all who wished to see him every morning. Long queues of the old, the poor, those seeking redress for grievances, those with simply personal difficulties – always waited at the presidential palace. Each would in turn receive his private audience with the president and few with any reasonable grievance or human problem would go away empty-handed. This practice ceased abruptly after the 1970 invasion, as did the president's former habit of driving himself around Conakry in an open car. Instead, like Nkrumah after the first assassination plots, he has sealed himself off in the presidential palace and great power has devolved upon those palace officials able to secure audiences with him. The presumably greater security which this arrangement ought to provide does not appear to have diminished Touré's penchant for wild surmise and comprehensive suspicion. When the leading Guinean football club was defeated by their Algerian opponents in

the December 1976 final of the African Champions Cup, Touré immediately dismissed the Minister for Youth, Culture and Sport – by no
means a junior figure – for 'betraying the Guinean revolution', and has
intervened to suspend two of the team's actual players as well.[45] Such
megalomania need not be funny: during the 1976 'Foulah plot' Touré
introduced certain evidence against the culprits which he had gained
'thanks to information directly received from God'. The Almighty is
doubtless a reliable source but divine revelation leading to the passage of
death sentences would seem to set some awkward precedents.

For all such possible errors of judgement – or communication – the
personal cult of Touré has advanced strongly since the late 1960s. From
1967 on his normal appellation became 'Responsable Suprême de la
Révolution'. More recently he has become 'The Eminent Strategist', 'The
Commander in Chief of the Revolutionary Popular Armed Forces', 'The
Father of Guinea' or simply 'Our Prestigious Guide'. PDG sections and
federations vote resolutions vowing their undying affection for Touré,
their concern for his health and long life and the Conakry second PDG
federation has adopted as its motto the slogan

> It is of small account to give one's life to preserve that of Ahmed
> Sekou Touré.[46]

However eccentric – and now visibly ageing – he may be, Sekou Touré
remains a magnetic, awesome figure. He will dominate Guinea while he
lives. Even after he departs, however, it will probably still be difficult to
characterize his regime. Guinea is in many respects a nightmarish place, a
police state, but in no other African country can one gain such a strong
sense of wholly African self-determination and self-emancipation. The
economy has gone back but many of the social advances in practice and in
attitudes are real and impressive. It may be that Guinea can only con-
struct a socialist society through the good offices of the multinational
aluminium corporations. The country may possess as much as two-thirds
of the entire planet's reserves of bauxite – it is reckoned to have some
eight billion tonnes. The world commodity boom has seen the bauxite
price almost treble between 1973 and 1976. As a result the normal
chronic Guinean balance of payments deficit has been transformed into a
growing surplus since 1974 with some 9 million tonnes of bauxite being
exported each year. Current plans allow this figure to rise by 1982 to 22
million tonnes. Under such circumstances the country can afford even a
prolonged period of disorganized socialist experiment elsewhere in the
economy. And Guinea's other mineral wealth has not begun to be
tapped, providing an almost infinite safety valve for the regime if it wishes
to auction off concessions to generate extra revenue. Its obvious

development strategy has always been to attract such capital imports, either to East or West, but thus far the regime has been unwilling to accept the degree of *de facto* external dependence which such a policy implies. The present compromise allows Guinea to acquire considerable western investment but, effectively, to be a member of the socialist bloc, the balancing act producing a very real degree of independence.

It remains to be seen how viable this course is. Its credibility is, of course, likely to be dismissed out of hand by those who find the co-existence of a Marxist regime with giant capitalist corporations a surreal and inevitably temporary situation. They may be right, but the fact that Libya, Algeria, Angola and Jamaica have all moved towards this same curious symbiosis suggests that this option may well be viable as a general strategy for third world states lucky enough to have large oil or mineral wealth.

There is another sense, too, in which Guinea represents a challenge to the influential neo-marxist school associated with the theories of under-development and 'dependence'. The oddity of this school, of course, is that while many of its proponents would have taken the side of socialist internationalism, their critique of neocolonial development policies effectively put the highest premium on a nineteenth-century conception of national sovereignty.

Guinea's development strategy ought, presumably, to gain considerable favour with theorists of this school. Not only has Guinea broken the economic hold of the old metropole more decisively than any other developing state.[47] She has also diversified her sources of aid and investment to the extent that a large part of the bauxite mined by American corporate investment is mortgaged directly to the Soviet Union in repayment of Guinea's debts to her. The country has received substantial aid from China, the US, the USSR, East Germany and West Germany, with smaller contributions from the World Bank, Cuba, the UAR, Yugoslavia, Mongolia, Britain and every state in Eastern Europe. The result of this elaborate set of compromises is that Guinea, though a small, poor and weak state, has been able to live to the full the life of moral and political independence. The regime has, indeed, taken an almost self-indulgent pleasure in not sullying itself. It has used its independence, as we have seen, to expel at various times the French, the Russians, the British, the Israelis, the American Peace Corps, the West Germans, the Ghanaians, the Senegalese, the Ivorians and a few more besides. The country has enjoyed playing David to Goliath, though this has not prevented it from registering shock and horror when Goliath has (immorally) hit back, as in the 1970 invasion.

The cost of this independence has been very high. The regime has had to endure isolation, invasion, and negative economic growth (outside the mining sector). The fine gesture of monetary independence has brought economic ruin and unmanageable corruption. The regime has lost prestige abroad and popularity at home. The country lives in a state of tension, distrust and fear. It is, perhaps, a party–state but it is also a police state. While it is possible that by no means all of the country's difficulties flow inevitably from the premium set on absolute national independence, there is no doubt that this option has, at the least, greatly exacerbated them. These difficulties have helped to produce an extreme and personalized concentration of power within Guinea sufficient to create severe doubt as to the regime's ability to survive Touré. Theorists of underdevelopment base their critique of 'dependence' and its concomitant, neocolonial control, on the implied preferred alternative of national independence plus socialism. If the Guinean symbiosis is to be criticized as offering an unsatisfactory or chimerical escape route from the problems of third world development, then it should be realized that this critique implies a more all-or-nothing choice than is generally posited. That is, if Guinea wishes both to preserve its socialist option and to generate the huge amounts of foreign capital it will require for its successful future development, it must clearly accept a degree of dependence on the Communist bloc at least equal to Cuba's. At present it would simply be irrational for either western investors or the Soviet Union to make available capital and manpower on such an order of magnitude unless they have a far greater degree of confidence than is possible at present in Guinea's unalterable future attachment to either the capitalist or the socialist road. Even were they foolish enough to risk their capital it is most unclear that Guinea could accept aid on such a scale without losing much of its real independence. It might be added, finally, that even should Guinea ultimately choose the 'Cuban road', it is hardly possible to recommend this model as a general prescription for the third world – even if the USSR were willing to subsidize more Cubas, its sheer financial capacity to do so is very limited.

One reason why it is impossible for either the West or the East to feel any confident security about Guinea's future development is that it is very difficult to categorize the Guinean regime in sociological terms. Guinea is not clearly a 'workers' state', but nor is the middle class established in power as it so evidently is in most of Africa. Impressionistic or descriptive accounts based on Dumont's[48] notion of a 'bureaucratic bourgeoisie' would leave unanswered the question of why this group, such as it is, has behaved so differently in Guinea than it has elsewhere in Africa. Similar problems beset any attempt to view Guinea's problems as the antenatal pains of a Guinean national bourgeoisie struggling to be born. It would be

61

possible to analyse the regime's (i.e. Touré's) ideology in the manner in which Sartre[49] once examined Lumumba's and to conclude, in similar vein, that Guinea represents a species of petit-bourgeois radicalism. But such a literary approach is superficial – it looks only at speeches – and in any case the regime's official ideology is now Marxism–Leninism. . . . Perhaps the best way of understanding the nature of the elite which commands the Guinean state is provided by First's analogous analysis of Libya where, she suggests, the post-colonial state

> is, after independence, not the instrument of any single indigenous ruling class. . . . Under an army regime like Libya's it is not the petit-bourgeoisie which rules directly – and a national bourgeoisie is virtually non-existent – but a military–bureaucratic faction which directly commands the power of the state. The army acts as a ruling class in charge of a statist economy. . . . economic power as much as political proceeded to accrue in the hands of a state which claimed to mediate the interests of all classes but which in fact was relatively autonomous of them all.[50]

In Guinea the military constitute a lesser fraction of the ruling group and play a less significant role than in Libya. In Guinea it would clearly make sense to assign to the PDG the role which First assigns to the Libyan army. The main feature of the Guinean ruling group is its party base – and the party does constitute a definite social reality, with still considerable popular social roots and functions. It is political virtue (defined by the party) which determines the allocation of jobs and resources amongst the bureaucratic and military elements of the state. The party lacks the quite straightforward strength and security which the army's monopoly of armed force gives it. Instead, the party elite is chronically insecure and unstable. Moreover, it has a pronounced tendency to devour itself. Not only can the political elite not be said to represent other classes in any readily understood way, but it is difficult to see it as an incipient ruling class itself. What is one to say of a ruling class which is almost the principal victim of its own rule? For a clearly preponderant part of Guinea's post-independence elite has now either lost its position or is in jail or is dead.

Touré's exiled opponents have frequently qualified the regime as 'Stalinist' and it is, perhaps, worth taking this more seriously than polemically. The Bolshevik Revolution, after all, showed that it was possible for a radical revolutionary elite, under special circumstances, to gain power in an underdeveloped country for which it was wholly 'inappropriate' in sociological terms. Without the World War it was inconceivable that the most radical wing of the working class movement could have taken power in Russia. It was equally unlikely that the PDG's motley collection of trade unionists and petit-bourgeois radicals could have taken power in Guinea except for the special conditions of the anti-colonial struggle. Such an 'inappropriate' ruling group can retain power by compromising its basic principles (NEP in Russia, the 'national democracy' of 1958–67 in Guinea). Thereafter it may attempt to transform the social structure and economy to create a sort of *post-facto* 'fit'. Since it lacks a majoritarian social base from which to launch such a transformation, the regime must needs do it by administrative coercion backed up by police and military 'terror'. The terrible strains of such a process, together with the in-securities engendered by 'capitalist encirclement' tend to produce the phenomenon of the continous purge within and against the revolutionary elite itself, directed by the supreme personal leader around whom a personality cult is woven.

The analogy, in fact, suits rather well. The position in Guinea is complicated, however, by the regime's strong populist streak and its (connected) admiration for the Chinese model. Faced by the procrustean social and economic realities of the as yet untransformed society, the Guinean leadership has – like the Russian and the Chinese – found that its own crucial intermediate level cadres tend quite inevitably to become a conservative, bureaucratic and even corrupt force, deforming the nature of the transformation which they are entrusted to implement. It becomes necessary, accordingly, to displace such cadres at regular intervals, thus opening up career opportunities to newer generations of *apparatchiks* who, for that very reason, are likely to provide strong support for the regime, until they too succumb to the forces which 'corrupted' their predecessors. But whereas Stalin sought to deal with this problem by continual and bloody purges, Mao attempted a somewhat different solu-tion – the Great Proletarian Cultural Revolution. Touré, who is deeply influenced by the Chinese example, launched his own Socialist Cultural Revolution the following year. His emulation of Stalin's 'plots' and purges is probably less conscious and deliberate.

The dangers of the Stalinist road to the leadership are obvious enough: it may destroy the party, create opportunities for usurpation by the all-powerful police and army, and engender a climate of desperation and violence in which the leader himself becomes vulnerable to assassination attempts. The dangers of the 'cultural revolution' strategy, for all that it is a clearly milder alternative, are actually greater still. For it cannot, of course, work. Mao's Cultural Revolution could not dispense with the functions of the Chinese bureaucracy, nor dissolve its power. It could weaken it, threaten it, demote its personnel, and temporarily un-nerve it to the point of a self-effacing invisibility. But society cannot function without intermediaries and the price of even trying to do so – of 'returning power to the people' – is in Guinea, as in China, disastrous. The regime's cadres are demoralized and become unwilling to act or take responsibility. A spreading wave of chaos results. The national leadership finds itself more, not less dependent on its despised intermediaries, for it must now rely upon them to re-assert some measure of control in the face of the confused popular pressure whose eruption it has encouraged. In China the regime had, by 1969, to turn to the army to bring a halt to the Cultural Revolution after three years. This is a lesson which it is possible Touré has learnt – at least the Guinean regime is celebrating the tenth year of its cultural revolution in 1977, which it is only able to do because it has in fact retained tight control over the 'return of power to the people'. Indeed, the thirty-seventh CNR decided to appoint political commissars, directly responsible to the BPN (i.e. to Touré), to oversee the work of all the party sections. These all-powerful envoys of the president are to be placed within the army, trade unions, women's and youth sections and will stand ready to correct and expose any failings of the regional party secretaries and governors.[51]

As yet, then, the Guinean leadership shows no disposition to treat very seriously its intentions of 'returning power to the people', though it remains possible that it will proceed further down the Chinese cul-de-sac. For once a revolutionary leadership embarks fully on the path of 'cultural revolution' the questions which have to be faced are what tactical or strategic compromises it will make to prevent anarchy (*which* cadres will it trust); and how, when anarchy does result, will it stage its retreat from 'giving power back to the people'? Revolutionary populists who, like Mao, take this path court their own total dénouement. If events are allowed to run their full course (as in China) there will be nothing left to the leadership save to retreat into a salving monastic isolation, leaving the stage to the intriguers and praetorians who are crowding in the palace yard. Only if the party or state bureaucracy is quite exceptionally resilient and united will the alternatives of military or dynastic rule – or even civil war – be avoided. Even Touré's admiration of Mao is probably not sufficient for him not to realize that this is indeed a cul-de-sac. Nonetheless, Touré may well have done sufficient damage to the party elite already to make his own succession a contest between the military and dynastic elements already jockeying for position in Conakry. Guinea may not find its Hua Kuo-Feng – indeed, it is perfectly likely that the PDG regime *in toto* will not survive Touré.

These analogies from Russia and China are, in an important sense, far-fetched. Stalin not only purged the elite but physically eliminated whole social classes. This Touré has not done and his regime is almost certainly too rickety and fragile for him to attempt such measures against the kulaks of the Fouta Djalon. In any case, in Russia Stalin had the resources for Stalinism to work – the economy and society were transformed, and at breakneck pace. This has hardly happened in Guinea where, if Stalinism exists, it is in a highly inefficient, makeshift, and ineffectual form. Similarly, the PDG was certainly forged in more testing circumstances than most African nationalist movements, but it hardly compares with the utterly formidable party-army coalition which emerged from two decades of guerrilla struggle in China. If these revolutionary analogues have to be considered seriously in the Guinean case it is because Touré's stated intentions *make* them relevant. To the visitor to Conakry it still seems as if the writings of Conrad and Graham Greene have more to offer then those of Stalin and Mao, but the Touré regime will be a determinedly revolutionary one while it lasts. The emergence of revolutionary regimes in Mozambique, Angola and Guiné-Bissau in 1974–5 make this the more certain. Not only does the triumph of the left in these states apparently vindicate Touré, it puts him on his mettle before the imaginary gallery to which he still plays. He will never happily suffer being outflanked on the left in Africa – indeed, the sharp leftward turn in Guinea in 1975 is quite possibly influenced by events in ex-Portuguese Africa. It is, perhaps, this trait which still gives the clue to the Touré regime: it has failed to learn that applause is not enough. It is this failing which makes it likely that Touré's ultimate obituary will read less like Stalin's or Mao's and more like that of Nasser or Sukarno – that all his regime will have provided is a vainglorious radical interlude.

4

The Ivory Coast

BONNIE CAMPBELL

What is the class character of the Ivorian state? What are the class interests of the Ivorian ruling class and why and in what manner has the post-colonial state intervened in order to reproduce a pattern of social rela-tions compatible with the class character of this state? Since there does not exist an accepted 'theory of the post-colonial capitalist state', the analysis of the Ivorian class structure and of the class character of the state raises problems for which at present one can offer only solutions which are at best provisional. Consequently, the concepts which will be used are advanced with a view of putting forward working hypotheses and raising questions which point to the need for a great deal more empirical research before these concepts be used with any rigour.

Since the perspective adopted here and the questions which it raises differ so widely from those which official documents (and more par-ticularly official statistics) are devised to answer, it is important to rec-ognize the difficulties raised even by the question of documentation. The absence of documentation concerning the distribution of national income: the percentage distribution of national income to the highest and lowest quintile, the distribution of access to piped water and electricity, the distribution of land ownership particularly in the plantation sector – the absence of such figures is as central a feature of official Ivorian statistics as it is a problem central to the critical analysis of Ivorian society.

The use of a broad framework of analysis not only indicates the inadequacy of many existing empirical studies. It also suggests the urgent need for a great deal of further research, research which ought preferably to be undertaken by Ivorians themselves since they are the only ones who can in practice transform the Ivorian image into reality.

Three propositions are central to the following analysis:

(1) The important characteristics of the Ivorian social formation, its productive process and consequently the nature of the post-colonial state, can only be understood through the historical analysis of changes in the

former metropolitan power and in the Ivory Coast itself, the interaction of which explains the political economy of that country in the post-independence period.

(2) Within this historical perspective, we must ask *how*, *under what conditions* and *in what historically determined structures* the process of surplus appropriation has taken and continues to take place in the Ivory Coast. In this way we may begin to define the essential characteristics of the Ivorian social formation and more particularly the nature of the post-colonial state.

(3) The *form* and *manner* of disposal of the economic surplus in the Ivory Coast equally defines the essentials of its productive process.

Within this perspective we can go beyond such questions as that of the relative freedom of manoeuvre conferred on the Ivory Coast state by its comparative wealth and seek to understand the basis, scale and scope of this state and the ideological rationalizations for its action, in other words *how* and *why* the Ivorian state succeeds in reproducing the pattern of social relations on which it is based.

Although one may have certain reservations concerning the methodological approach adopted by Poulantzas, one can nevertheless accept his definition of the state as a relation, the means (whatever they may be) by which the dominant class (or fraction of a class) in a given social formation contrives to reproduce a particular pattern of organization of production within the territory occupied by this social formation. By this focus on the state's role within the organization of the disposal of economic surplus we enquire directly into the identity of the interests on whose behalf the state defines and performs its tasks, and thus clarify the class character of the state.

It is the particular colonial past of the Ivory Coast which explains the original basis in the metropole of the state apparatus inherited by the post-colonial society. The same colonial heritage helps to explain the constancy and durability of the orientation adopted by the Ivorian ruling class in the face of a relatively fixed set of objective external economic constraints. The structures and orientation inherited from the colonial period have had a determining effect on the group which assumed power at political independence, and more fundamentally, on the manner and terms on which political independence was 'negotiated'. The perpetuation of this orientation has been crucial in determining the class character of the Ivorian state; the relationship between the dominant class and the state bureaucracy; the scale of the apparatus; its scope for intervention which perpetuates and reproduces existing social relations and finally, the ideology which rationalizes this intervention.

As will be seen, the role of the ideology of the dominant class has been

67

particularly important in masking the contradictions inherent in Ivorian post-independence 'development' policies. Consequently it would be difficult to analyse the role of the state in the Ivory Coast in terms of a simple dichotomy of failure and promise. For the promise or image and the effectiveness with which the Ivorian state intervenes and so maintains the very basis of its own power is inextricably linked to the reality or degree of success or failure of Ivorian post-colonial policies, whether these be internal or external. Failure or promise are therefore inextricably linked mirror images of one another.

We shall begin therefore by considering the nature of colonial penetration and the redefinition of the social and economic basis of production. In the following section, we shall examine the Ivorian political economy and in particular the framework within which political independence was to be negotiated. The third section analyses the nature of the post-colonial state. In the case of the Ivory Coast, it is in large part in the historical origins and the conditions surrounding the emergence of the ruling class that one must find an explanation for the capacity of this group to mobilize social forces in such a way as to maintain political control during the post-independence period. Finally, we discuss the nature and implications of state intervention and the political implications of this intervention.

HISTORICAL PERSPECTIVE

The establishment of a permanent European presence and the beginning of the production of export crops for the colonial market came relatively late to the Ivory Coast. From 1893 on, the area was administered as an autonomous colony, with a governor accountable directly to the minister of the colonies in Paris. Between 1895 and 1904 a series of French decrees resulted in the inclusion of the Ivory Coast along with other colonies in a larger unit, the federation of Afrique Occidentale Française (AOF). The fact, however, that the interior of the Ivory Coast remained outside French administrative and military control at the beginning of the twentieth century explains the lack of early colonial trade in this area and the relatively belated introduction of cash crops. The drop in world market prices for palm oil at first discouraged many Africans from processing this crop for export. In response the governor introduced coercive methods to induce Africans to engage in commercial agriculture. But, apart from an experimental coffee plantation at Elima, other attempts to diversify crops for export at the turn of the century were unsuccessful. Altogether only twenty-nine tons of coffee were produced in 1905 and only six tons of cocoa in 1910.[1]

The completion of French military 'pacification' in 1917 coincided with the increased commercial interest which characterized French colonial policy after the First World War. The development in this period, which was to have the most profound effect on all facets of the country's future, was the introduction of new cash crops. Until about 1925, the Ivory Coast's main contribution to the French economy continued to be timber and palm oil.[2] Unlike Senegal, European *colons* had been encouraged to settle in the Ivory Coast after the First World War.[3] These *colons* who were mostly French, and the African planters, notably those living in the southeast, produced about 1,000 tons of coffee by 1920. During the next decade cocoa production remained far more substantial than that of coffee. By 1930, however, the Ivory Coast and other colonies produced more cocoa than France could absorb. But since France imported most of its coffee from other monetary zones, coffee growing was encouraged by means of premiums and preferential prices.[4] Under the intervention of the colonial administration, at the end of the Second World War the production of coffee exceeded that of cocoa and it continued to expand rapidly. Not only did the colonial administration finance improvements in transport; above all it assumed much of the responsibility for labour recruitment.

When the French colonial administration first assumed control in West Africa, it instituted a system of unpaid labour services which served instead of tax collection and thus permitted public works such as the building of roads. During the period European plantation owners were able to recruit sufficient agricultural labour by making arrangements with traditional chiefs whereby the latter singled out teams of workers in return for a 'gift'. This system worked until about 1925 when increasing commercial interest on the part of the Europeans and Africans led to problems over the recruitment of labour which drew the administration closely into export crop production, resulting in an elaborated system of discriminatory privileges in favour of the French planters. By 1943 African planters had been debarred from any recruited labour, which from then on was reserved exclusively for work on European plantations. In some cases Africans were even removed from their own plantations to be recruited for European enterprises. Other administrative and commercial policies worked, if not explicitly to discourage African planters, at least to privilege the Europeans. The latter, for example, succeeded in securing higher prices than the African planters, through the collaboration of the administration with the trading companies.

The long-term importance of these discriminatory privileges can hardly be over-estimated. Because the consequences of forced labour were felt

69

so pervasively by the entire population, it was around this issue that the anti-colonialist movement began to form:

> One effect of this policy of economic discrimination in the countryside, reinforced by rigorous social discrimination in the towns, was to throw the vast majority of Africans involved in the exchange economy into determined opposition to the administration, cementing relations between African planters, labourers, traders, civil servants and chiefs.[5]

African planters, like the rest of African society, suffered from the effects of forced labour and from racial discrimination formalized in the *Code de l'indigénat*. Moreover, African planters, and particularly the owners of the largest plantations who stood to benefit greatly from the abolition of colonial recruitment policies, had strong reasons to struggle against certain aspects of French colonialism, more especially as labour became still scarcer with the outbreak of the Second World War.

It was the African planters, with their additional and very immediate interest in the struggle against the discriminatory effects of colonialism, who were to supply the political leadership of the anti-colonialist movement. The mixture of particularistic and nationalist interests in their leadership had far-reaching implications for the outcome of the movement and for the orientation of political and economic changes in the Ivory Coast after political independence. The dissatisfaction of African planters with the discriminatory privileges of the colonial administration led them to withdraw from the only existing planter organization, the European dominated Syndicat Agricole de la Côte d'Ivoire, and to form, in September 1944, their own countervailing African organization, the Syndicat Agricole Africain. The 20,000 African planters who became members of the SAA were not subject to administrative labour recruitment. However, since only those planters owning two hectares of coffee or three hectares of cocoa could be members of the organization, many smaller African planters remained subject to forced labour. The SAA challenged not only the European planters but also the European middlemen by signing contracts directly with the big trading firms, and its members began to compete more belligerently with the European planters in the recruitment of labour. At first, the SAA simply favoured the more equitable distribution of labourers between the two groups of planters. Soon, however, the SAA took a stand against the very principle of forced labour.[6]

This stand explains the popularity of the SAA and the support which it was able to mobilize in the campaign for the abolition of forced labour. But the breadth of popular support attracted in this way, although it did

70

serve to provide the basis for a mass party, certainly did not imply that the objectives of the SAA were in any sense 'popular'. The Syndicat had been created at the initiative of the largest planters, who stood to gain most handsomely from the abolition of forced labour. It was constituted from the top down. Its eight co-founders appointed agents at the level of every subdivision, usually leading planters who were also county-chiefs and literate in French. One of these co-founders was Felix Houphouët-Boigny, whose tribe, the Baoulé, formed the largest group of members. Consequently he was easily elected president of the SAA when elections were held at the first congress in September 1944. At this congress, held to define the aims of the organization, the most important resolutions adopted were: to secure premiums for African producers; to organize co-operative sales in order to eliminate middlemen; to obtain a quota of imported cloth and agricultural implements; to secure a more equitable allocation of manpower for its members.[7] The evident narrowness of the economic interests on which the SAA had been founded was to play a crucial role in the outcome of the anti-colonialist struggle.

The suppression of forced labour voted by the law of 5 April 1946, the abolition of the discriminatory legal code (the *régime de l'indigénat*), and the extension of equal rights of citizenship to the former 'subjects' of the French Union, formed in 1946 to replace the federation of AOF, all undoubtedly coincided with the popular aspirations of the African population. But the logic and timing of decolonization was determined by metropolitan preoccupations and according to a metropolitan time-table. At the same time the removal of certain discriminatory aspects of colonialism reinforced the position of relatively privileged social groups, notably the larger African planters. In the process of political decolonization, the political concessions conceded particularly after 1946 may be seen as the result of the interaction of changes taking place in both the metropolitan and the colonial areas.[8] After the Second World War economic and social changes in metropolitan France necessitated a re-definition of colonial relations to permit an evolved mode of colonial exploitation with more highly elaborated economic planning in the form of development plans, with greater investments, and with the decentralization of responsibilities and powers previously concentrated in metropolitan France.

To this end, the emergence of a local group whose economic interests were closely linked to metropolitan France and the perpetuation of close relations and who, consequently, could be vested with certain powers, may be seen as a prerequisite for the stability and continuation of metropolitan economic interests in the former colonial area. In this sense

71

'independence' constituted a transition from political dependence on the metropolitan state, to more clearly defined economic dependence on private economic interest whose importance in local economic activities, and for the Ivorian economy as a whole, gave them the ability to influence and restrict political decisions in a manner comparable to the situation which had existed before independence. While the continuation of internal political authority and legitimacy of the group which assumed power at independence depended above all on the continuation of a pattern of extraverted economic relations and the transfer of resources in a manner very similar to that which had existed in the colonial period, the nature and the constraints of the political power they exercised internally were to have very profound social, political and economic implications for changes within the Ivory Coast. What were the origins and the interests of this group?

Although in the 1930s the number of Africans who became planters and needed workers was not very large and the average yield per person during this early period was quite small, their methods of cultivation enabled them quickly to outstrip the production of the European planters.[9] In 1942, European planters produced approximately 55 per cent of the coffee and 8 per cent of the cocoa. In spite of the extensive and persisting discrimination in their favour, by 1952 the European planters produced 6 per cent of coffee and 4 per cent of cocoa.[10] By 1947, Africans produced 90 per cent or more of the coffee and cocoa exported from the Ivory Coast.

This African planter group grew both in size and importance particularly after the abolition of forced labour. Rising coffee and cocoa prices after 1946 encouraged an increase both in the total output (see Table 1) and in the land area cultivated of these two crops. This expansion involved not only the increase in the number of the planters but also increasing differentiation amongst African planters. By 1965

TABLE 1[11] *Acreage of African plantations*
(in thousands of hectares)

Year	Cocoa	Coffee	Total
1946	115	158	273
1950	153	158	311
1953	177	212	389
1956	222	318	540
1959	230	503	733
1960	240	525	765

72

there had emerged a group of about 20,000 wealthy planters, a landless proletariat of about 120,000 plantation workers, and about 200,000 small or medium plantation owners.[12] By 1965 the wealthy planter group represented 10 per cent of cash crop producers, controlled about one quarter of cultivated land, employed two-thirds of salaried labour and received an average 40,000 francs CFA yearly income which permitted luxury consumption, or urban investment in real estate, trucks or taxis, etc.[13] (1,000 francs CFA = 20 French francs = 4 US dollars). The interests of this group, as Morgenthau put it: 'became those of employers, as they shared activities with European entrepreneurs and with the wealthier traders and transporters'.[14]

The origins of this 'véritable bourgeoisie de planteurs', as a distinct class[15] lay in the traditional élite, which used its powers during the colonial regime to appropriate land for private use.[16] From the creation of the SAA many of its local agents in the plantation belt were official chiefs. This made it easier for SAA delegates to reach agreements with the northern chiefs who supplied workers, incorrectly described as 'voluntary' labour.[17]

The growth of the Ivorian planter class from several hundred families in 1950 coincided and in fact is largely explained by the *de facto* end of forced labour, abolished officially in 1946 but perpetuated in various ways by the administration for the benefit of French planters until the end of the decade. In spite of the narrowness of the economic interests on which it was founded, the importance of the SAA grew beyond the confines of its membership. After the war its membership lists were used to draw up electoral registers and during the first political campaign it served as an admirable machine to promote the candidacy of its president, Houphouët-Boigny, by this time one of the richest planters in the country. He not only symbolized the achievements of the emerging planter bourgeoisie, but personally possessed the means to finance a political campaign.

The role which the planter bourgeoisie was to play in Ivory Coast politics is especially clear in relation to the ruling party. The Ivorian branch of the territorial Rassemblement Démocratique Africain (RDA), the Parti Démocratique de la Côte-d'Ivoire (PDCI) founded by Houphouët-Boigny in 1946, had begun as a 'comité d'action politique du Syndicat des planteurs' (SAA).[18] Later the same year about one-third of the party's 80,000 estimated members and supporters belonged to the SAA.

The formation of local parties in French West Africa, the end of forced labour, the extension of French citizenship and legal rights, were preliminary changes in the process of political decolonization.[19] But they did little to increase local autonomy. Political relations within the French Union were not redefined for at least another decade, and, like most significant changes affecting the colonies, were determined according to a French rather than an African political time-table.

The constitutional settlement over the French Union of the October 1946 Constitution, which restricted the competence of the local assemblies, had the ambiguous effect of 'constitutionalizing' the powers of the colonial administration, until the *Loi-cadre* of 1956 resolved this ambiguity.

During the intervening period, although Africans secured certain political powers within their territories, the apparatus of the government and the administration and control of all important economic decisions remained in the hands of Europeans. This arrangement and the repressive policies of the administration in 1949–50 (formerly sympathetic to the Vichy government) were of great importance during the crucial period of 'transition'.[20] The structure of the local party was seriously weakened by mass arrests of 'militants', reinforcing its hierarchical nature and particularly the powers of its leader Houphouët-Boigny. The repression also generated and intensified internal conflicts, among ethnic groups and between *originaires* and strangers. Finally, and only in part because of the repression, the African leadership's policy of collaboration and reconciliation with the colonial administration meant in practice a close working alliance with the French business community. During the 1950s flows of public and private capital into the territory and the stimulus of the Korean war enriched the emerging Ivorian bourgeoisie and consolidated relations with the metropolitan power.

On the other hand, Ivorian economic success during this period placed the country ahead of Senegal by 1956 as the largest exporter of French West Africa. The wealth of the Ivory Coast, which implied making a larger contribution to federal revenue without commensurate return, stimulated anti-federalist and particularist attitudes which resulted in the dissolution of the RDA and have obstructed a greater degree of regional integration to this day. The emergence and consolidation during the decade 1946–56 of a wealthy planter class benefiting from the past orientation of growth perpetuated close relations with the metropolitan power and ensured the continued presence and importance of French economic interest. It is important to understand precisely how this political and economic orientation was maintained.

THE IVORY COAST POLITICAL ECONOMY

The social and economic interests of the Ivorian planter class who

74

favoured the continuation of close economic ties with the metropolitan power can only be analysed within the broader context of the redefinition of French colonial interests. This redefinition was accompanied by the drawing up of colonial development plans which reflected both the economic difficulties of the metropolitan power and its deteriorating commercial relations with the colonies before and during the war, and changes in the mode of exploitation within the colonies which led to the abolition of forced labour.[21]

The allocation of funds from the Fonds d'Investissement pour le Développement Économique et Social (FIDES), and the Caisse Centrale de France d'Outre-Mer (CCFOM), created to finance the post-war overseas French development plans, was to be crucial for latter developments.[22] Metropolitan support of the colonial development plans, together with the institutions created to serve the needs of the French economy during this period, established a pattern of economic activity and of distribution which persisted throughout the period of 'decolonization' and after political independence also. After the war French economic interests shifted away from extensive cultivation based on recruited labour towards more intensive modes of exploitation dependent on metropolitan financial aid. This re-orientation was evident in each area of economic activity, whether concerned with agriculture, commerce or the beginning of light industry,[23] and its reflections are easy to trace. The law of 30 April 1946, which was to become the charter of future development activity, authorized the minister of overseas France to create specialized agencies in support of private economic interests (Article 2.2a). To this end financial assistance was allocated to public bodies such as railway boards, chambers of commerce and state corporations, and the creation was authorized of semi-public bodies in which the public sector and private interests overseas would work together.

Significantly the most important of these public and semi-public bodies were concerned with the development of overseas energy and resources, through prospecting, research in agriculture, forestry or real estate development.[24] The creation of these bodies was very much in keeping with the conscious attempt of the French government to orient its funds in support of private interests, on whose success development of the overseas territories was believed to depend. Most of the funds authorized by the FIDES programme took the form of loans administered on favourable terms directly by the CCFOM. These funds during the period 1946–56 were directed to private enterprises particularly in public works, agriculture and food industries, forestry and extractive industries.[25] Before 1956 private investment was responsible for only a minor portion of the capital invested in French West Africa. The relative importance of

75

public financing enabled the metropolitan power to influence the pattern of development during this crucial transitional period. Moreover, private metropolitan interests benefited from the very substantial portion of public investments (65 per cent) devoted to the building of an economic infrastructure. This infrastructure, while of advantage to commercial and extractive interests, was of far less immediate and direct benefit to the overwhelming majority of the population whose welfare depended on improved agricultural production and the establishment of basic industries. The serious neglect of directly productive investment is illustrated by the fact that of the funds made available in 1946 for French West Africa, only 12 per cent went to agricultural production, 11 per cent to mining and industrial activities while 49 per cent, by far the largest allocation, was channelled into the financing of an economic infrastructure.[26]

Although some funds were allocated to improving agricultural production, such projects as the 'Office du Niger' proved to have little impact. Far more important in its long-term implications was the creation during this transitional period of bodies funded from the metropolis to promote the production of individual agricultural products or the development of specific economic sectors. Among the organizations created were Institute de Recherches du Coton et des Textiles Exotiques (IRCT) in 1946 and in 1949 the Compagnie Française pour le Développement de Fibres Textiles (CFDT), which were to supervise the improvement and production of colonial cotton production; the Institut des Fruits et Agrumes Coloniaux (IFAC) in 1946; the Institut de Recherches des Huiles et Oléagineux Tropicaux (IRHO) in 1942; the Centre Technique Forestier Colonial in 1949, and Bureau Minier de la France d'Outre-Mer (BUMIFOM) etc.[27] The role of these bodies in determining the future orientation of economic development can hardly be overemphasized. Since control over the purchase and sale of colonial export products remained, during the period of decolonization, in the hands of traditional colonial trading interests, the creation of specialized metropolitan 'semi-public' institutions such as those named above served to reinforce the existing organization of production and distribution and its domination by colonial interests, while the group responsible for a particular export crop or product continued to act independently of the others to maximize its own profits without regard for social costs or the future of the economy as a whole.

Although the European planters abandoned the cultivation of the major Ivorian export crops in the 1950s, they developed an increased interest in others. Four of these, palm oil, rubber, timber, and sugar, which could be grown, harvested, processed and marketed with very little peasant participation, increasingly became European crops. Others which were more labour intensive, notably cocoa, coffee, cotton, rice and bananas remained, as they have to the present, the responsibility of African producers. Even those export crops grown by African producers continued to be marketed by foreign companies. Moreover, where foreign interests were involved with agricultural production whether they produced or at least collected coffee, cocoa or palm oil, they were in most cases, the extension of metropolitan buyers of colonial primary products. Immediately after the war this monopolist organization of colonial trade was too blatantly exploitative to be wholly effective and in certain cases it even led to a fall in peasant output. One response to these difficulties was the creation in October 1946 of the *Caisse de soutien* or cotton fund to guarantee in theory a minimum return to peasant producers. But since it also guaranteed the margins of the private trading companies, the *Caisse de soutien* became, in practice, an alternative means of taxing the peasant producer and guaranteeing a 'super-profit' to the trading companies.

The role of the stabilization funds became still more transparent after the Korean war when prices collapsed and the funds were emptied. Returns to peasant producers were frozen while trading company profits were assured by convention and were maintained even though the reserves of the local budgets and stabilization funds were so exhausted as to require metropolitan subsidies. New *Caisses de stabilisation des prix* were created for this very purpose to replace the now exhausted funds. In 1955 a special metropolitan fund was created, the Fonds National de Régularisation des Produits Outre-Mer', to advance funds to the overseas *caisses*, establishing a pattern of subsidization not only of the peasant producers but especially of private trading interests and indirectly the local colonial administration. This pattern was to serve as an important precedent for the post-independence period. The latter role of the *caisses* was to become increasingly important.[28] The creation of semi-public metropolitan export promotion agencies together with the role played by the metropolitan backed stabilization funds reinforced the already integrated and often monopolist colonial economic agencies. To control production and marketing of the same export crop made it considerably easier to sell the product profitably abroad:

> If the firm which produces or at least collects the coffee, or cocoa, or palm oil, is at the same time a European sales agent, the problem of finding outlets is eased. Such a firm becomes, as it were, its own Produce Marketing Board. Moreover, in seeking investors the Ivory Coast will always see a special point in dealing with firms which already specialise in trading in local natural resources.[29]

These factors explain the extent to which local industry is dominated by French trading companies which expanded vertically into industrial activities as well as horizontally into different economic branches. Two examples illustrate this pattern. The overseas expansion of the French textile company, Boussac, through its subsidiary, the Compagnie de l'Industrie Textile Cotonnière (CITEC), led not only to the exporting of finished Boussac textile products to the Ivory Coast, but at the same time involved CITEC in the production and ginning of locally produced cotton, for the metropolitan industry and the Ivorian textile subsidiary, Ets. R. Gonfreville. A second typical example is that of the firm Blohorn. The company originally came to the Ivory Coast before the war to establish a soap factory, drawing much of its raw materials from local sources, as a hedge against competition and falling sales. It soon set up its own oil processing plants and later its own oil plantations.

The inheritance at political independence of a highly integrated structure of production and distribution had far-reaching implications. Among these was the almost total absence of industrial activities at the time of independence. When the colonies of French West Africa became independent, approximately 70 per cent of their imports continued to be purchased from France and about the same proportion of exports were sold there.[30] The dependence of the colonies on the metropolitan power for the supply of consumer goods and equipment was reinforced by the commercial and monetary policies of the franc zone. The privileged economic relations and high degree of protection assured French private interests by this centralized and authoritarian monetary framework remained of crucial importance. The persistence of the franc zone in an evolving yet unquestionably hierarchical manner, ensured the reinforcing of metropolitan links long after the granting of political independence. Commercial, monetary and industrial policies governing economic relations within this zone remained closely interrelated. The regulations concerning the flow of capital and merchandise did not merely control the flow of goods but placed severe restrictions on the monetary options of member states.

The persistence of this hierarchical framework explains why in the post-independence period, in order to maintain their position on the local market, the long-established export houses took the initiative and supplied much of the capital for the creation of local 'industrial' activities. Because of the manner in which local industry was initiated, the resulting activities were necessarily very often a function of, and integrated into, the existing metropolitan-dominated commercial circuit.

The colonial trading structure was dominated by such enterprises as the Compagnie Française de l'Afrique Occidentale (CFAO), the Société

Commerciale de l'Ouest Africain (SCOA), the Compagnie Optorg and the Compagnie du Niger Française. The multiplicity of areas into which these export–import houses have intervened, the effectiveness of co-operation among them, the flexibility of their organizational structures, the financial links with metropolitan banking interests and their long history of close relations with the colonial administration are well documented.[31] Some insight into the complexity of these relations can be obtained from considering the range of interests affiliated with a single colonial trading house, the SCOA in the Ivory Coast by the mid-1960s.[32]

Political independence has done little to modify foreign domination of local economic activity. Instead the previous orientation of colonial economic activity has been guaranteed by changes which have taken place both in metropolitan overseas policy and in the legislative and administrative policies implemented by the local group whose own economic and political power has depended on the continuation of the previous pattern of growth. Post-war metropolitan support for the creation of an infrastructure aimed directly to consolidate the export orientation of the Ivorian economy.[33] In addition, the improving quality of production, high world prices and preferential treatment for exports of coffee and cocoa on the metropolitan markets during the 1950s enabled the Ivory Coast to build up fiscal reserves from the price stabilization operations of the country's two principal crops.

Although metropolitan subsidies contributed only exceptionally and partially to the support operations of the Ivorian *caisses*, in which these reserves were held, the latter benefited the colonial trading companies at least as much as the peasant producers. Significantly the majority of the funds used for support operations in the Ivory Coast came from local resources:

> either from surpluses accumulated in favourable periods or, more frequently, and this was increasingly the case, from the taxes and duties paid on imported goods, or from subsidies from local budgets which in reality meant at the expense of African tax payers and consumers.[34]

Since independence the *caisse's* responsibilities broadened to include other agricultural products including cotton and in 1966, it assumed the name of Caisse de Stabilisation et de Soutien des Prix des Productions Agricoles. More importantly its status changed in 1964 from that of an *établissement public* to a *société d'État*, in recognition of its intimate relations with the private trading sector. Accordingly it differs in one fundamental way from the counterpart organization in the anglophone African countries. While in the latter case the marketing boards are responsible themselves for the purchase and sale of export products: 'The originality of the system which exists in the Ivory Coast stems from the fact that it permits the private sector to maintain its traditional role in the purchase, sale and distribution of products.'[35] In consequence it has served to preserve virtually intact the structures of production and distribution inherited from the colonial period. Its stabilization functions have, however, permitted the accumulation of important revenues for the use of the local state. In fact, in 1970 the *Caisse* was estimated to supply 34 per cent of public savings. In this regard the Ivorian *Caisse* appears to operate in a similar manner to the marketing boards of certain neighbouring anglophone countries. In Ghana, for example, in the early 1960s, the Cocoa Marketing Board continued to appropriate surplus from cocoa farmers to finance the state.[36]

In order to understand the negotiations by which political independence was granted, it is important to note that Ivorian fiscal reserves began to build up during the period of decolonization as a result of the privileged position which the Ivory Coast enjoyed on the metropolitan market. This pattern continued after the granting of political independence. Two of the principal Ivorian exports, coffee and bananas, continued during and after the period of decolonization to receive preferred treatment of the French market. In this regard, the coffee treaty concluded with France was of particular importance for by its clauses France agreed to purchase an annual amount of at least 100,000 tons (70 per cent of the country's production at the time) above current world prices. The treaty signed for the period of five years (1961–6) with the implementation of the Accord Général de Coopération Économique Franco-Ivoirien provided that France would import 100,000 tons of coffee until 1966 at 3.20 francs per kg (160 francs CFA), a guarantee revised in 1962–3 to 88,000 tons as a result of Algeria's independence, since Algeria's consumption of about 10,000 tons annually had been included in the 1961 agreement. These privileges remained important a decade after independence.[37]

The reserves built up during 'decolonization' from export crops in particular, explain why the Ivorian Caisse de Stabilisation, unlike those of certain other French colonial areas, did not require direct subsidies from the metropolitan budget. Its reserves were funded locally by the surplus collected when export prices were high and increasingly, from taxes, import duties and local budget subsidies. The reserves have thus played a key role in channelling the surplus from many small African producers into the hands of the local ruling group. The power of this group depended on ensuring rapid economic growth through a particular pattern of distribution of the accumulated surplus. The continuation of their dominant position thus depended on guaranteed export markets and the perpetuation of close metropolitan economic relations. But it also increasingly depended on the disposal of surplus accumulated locally and used to finance a pattern of rapid externally controlled economic growth.

Immediately before political independence the rate of accumulation had become extremely rapid, reaching 15 per cent to 16 per cent of gross internal product in the late 1950s and increasing to 17.5 per cent in 1964.[38] The dynamics of this growth rate reveal the preponderance of public investment up until 1960, and a balance between public and private over the next four years, with private investment taking a clear lead after 1964. Since just before political independence, France through FIDES and other metropolitan aid agencies was financing 50 per cent of public investment, and since according to the principles set down in the 'transitional programme of public investment' for 1962–3, internal sources were to cover less than 40 per cent of total expenses, the major part of Ivorian public investment immediately before and just after political independence plainly came from metropolitan sources. This pattern implied a corresponding continuity in patterns of public expenditure. Between 1960 and 1964, 50 per cent of total public investments in the Ivory Coast was placed in infrastructure. Of the remainder, 25 per cent was absorbed by social and administrative expenses and barely 20 per cent was devoted to investments:

> Such a structure of public outlays is a result of a purposeful governmental policy; the government tries to limit its own activity and merely create a set of favourable conditions for private initiative, believing that private enterprise should become the prime or even the exclusive motor of the growth of national economy.[39]

The local ruling group's early opposition to the emergence of an Ivorian *bourgeoisie d'affaires* thus implied the growth of foreign private capital and a continuation of the privileges accorded to metropolitan capital, techniques and personnel. These privileges are nowhere more clearly illustrated than in the Ivorian Code des Investissements, enacted *before* the granting of political independence on 7 August, 1960. The Code was drawn up by an expatriate, M. Raphael Saller, the Ivorian Minister of Economy and Finance. It extended far-reaching concessions in order to attract foreign capital into six branches of the national economy, in particular: real estate; industrial processing of local raw material; production and assembling of mass consumer goods; plantations; mining; and power supply (energy). Large foreign firms whose activities were considered of particular interest to the national economy were invited to conclude special agreements with the government. By these

81

agreements they became 'priority industries' and received favourable economic, fiscal and legal conditions for the establishment and operation of their activities. Such agreements guaranteed tax stability for twenty-five years and exempted the foreign firm from any higher tax rates or new taxes introduced after signature of the agreement. Since the income tax rate of the Ivory Coast at independence did not exceed 25 per cent (less than half the rate current in developed countries), it was and has remained (with long run guarantees) a major incentive to foreign investors. In addition, the Code included liberal provisions concerning the transfer of foreign company profits abroad. After 10 per cent of obtained profits – the sum to be reinvested locally – such transfers are unlimited.

It also exempted foreign investors on a long-term basis from paying import duties on raw materials and half-products used in the establishment and operation of their enterprises, a point which had a considerable impact upon the structure of industrial activity in the Ivory Coast. This exemption removed any stimulus to develop local raw materials and to increase the proportion of local half-products in the value of the final product. Besides its inhibiting effects on industrialization it also implied, along with the stabilization of tax rates on profits, a serious check on public accumulation by reducing the total tax levy. As significant as the extent of these concessions is their persistence without significant modification a full decade after the granting of political independence. This regime of economic liberalism is a fundamental point of departure for the analysis of the nature of state power in the Ivory Coast and of the objectives, scale and scope of state intervention in social and economic policy.

THE NATURE OF STATE POWER

The social and economic basis of the group who assumed political power at independence largely explains both the perpetuation of close relations with the former metropolitan power and the Ivorian ruling class's strict adherence to the philosophy of economic liberalism. As the president of the Ivory Coast declared a few months before the country's independence: 'The state has chosen a liberal economic option as its model for development and it will stick to this option regardless of the political orientation which it may adopt.'[40] It would be difficult to put things more clearly.

How has political power evolved in the face of the constraints implied by this option? More fundamentally, what has been the basis and scope of state power within its terms?

It is apparent that the philosophy of *laissez-faire*, *laissez-aller* presented as the dominant ideology in the Ivory Coast, does not accurately reflect the *policies* implemented locally in order to mobilize its resources and energies. On the contrary, the state apparatus has intervened during the decade and a half since political independence to maintain and reinforce a quite specific orientation to social, political and economic changes. The philosophy of economic liberalism has served ideologically to obfuscate and mask the privileges it confers on particularist interests.[41]

While the class character of the state specifies the class which is dominant in a given social formation, since this dominance must be enforced by the state, the class origins, class ties or class ambitions of the individuals who compose the apparatus of the state are not necessarily the same as those of the dominant class, and the state power need not reflect their own class interests except in a secondary way.[42] This is of crucial importance in the Ivory Coast case. The emergence in the post-colonial period of an important political and administrative group responsible for running an increasing number of state agencies and disposing, through the position which they occupy in the state apparatus, of considerable material wealth, does not necessarily imply, as some have suggested, that the basis of state power has shifted from rural to non-rural interests.[43] This growing politico-administrative group is unmistakably assuming a more and more important role in the administration and control of state power. But one must not confuse the origins, links and ambitions of this group, the functionaries of the state and the agents of its power, with the socio-economic basis of state power itself.

As long as a few agricultural products (cocoa, wood and coffee) represent 75 per cent of the value of exports, the basis and motor of the extraverted pattern of Ivorian growth,[44] the socio-economic basis of state power must be sought in the interests which continue to control the organization of production and commercialization of the economy's export sector. It is in this pattern of growth, with its dependence on foreign markets, foreign capital, foreign techniques and foreign personnel that the nature and basis of Ivorian political power lie.

As Colin Leys has emphasized: 'even if the state bureaucracy enjoy great "relative autonomy", and have a distinct class interest of their own, it doesn't follow that the class character of the state, or of state power, reflects this interest.'[45] While the Ivory Coast state bureaucracy has succeeded in appropriating the plums of office and has managed to do so rather greedily,[46] it has not significantly modified the external orientation and economic dependence on which Ivorian growth continues to be based. What the state has in fact done is to create the conditions for rapid economic growth to the benefit of foreign interest and a small local minority. The perpetuation of these conditions, moreover, precludes a more equitable distribution of the economic surplus created by growth. It is within this context that internal political activity must be understood.

Ivorian independence was above all political and was obtained at the price of a series of important 'co-operation agreements'. The strongly mercantilist regulations of the franc zone served to consolidate economic ties between the metropolis and former colonies to the benefit of French private interests in at least four ways. They secured guaranteed markets for a significant proportion of France's exports. They guaranteed supplies of essential raw materials without having to make the price of exports competitive or to use scarce foreign exchange. They facilitated unlimited transfers by French individuals and firms from overseas to France at a favourable exchange rate. They ensured that most French aid would be spent in France directly or indirectly even before most of the aid to be spent on imports was formally tied to procurement in France.[47] Within this framework more specific agreements such as the Protocole Franco-Ivoirien of 1961 were signed with each newly independent state. By this *accord*, France agreed to maintain preferential tariffs for the principle Ivorian exports – coffee, wood, cocoa, bananas and pineapples – as well as to continue to pay a guaranteed price for the coffee and bananas which it purchased. In exchange, the Ivory Coast accepted a maximum quota of 100,000 tons on the coffee to be exported to France which would continue to be subsidized. The Ivory Coast accepted as well certain limitations over its rights to import in order to ensure a privileged place for metropolitan products. This part of the arrangement included maintaining the 1960 level of imports (22·3 billion francs CFA) of French products even where these were not particularly competitive on world markets. More striking was the system of quotas by which the Ivory Coast agreed to buy all its imports of wheat and flour on the metropolitan market, along with 70 per cent of its wine and beverages and printed cotton cloth, 60 per cent of its milk, 50 per cent of its tractors and air conditioners, and 30 per cent of its radios and household electrical equipment.[48]

Despite the measures of trade liberalization which were to be implemented with the signing of the Yaoundé Conventions of 1964 and 1969, many similar trade restrictions remained a decade after political independence. In spite of the attempt in 1966 made by the Ivorian government to simplify and reform the quota system inherited from the colonial period, the categories of imports (four by source and one by use) remain essentially the same and their orientation unchanged. This can be seen clearly in a description of Ivorian trade practices circulated in 1972 within the Department of External Commerce:'Any product whose entry has not been the object of a specific liberating clause is restricted. In order to be imported, an importing license must be obtained. Only automobile parts may be imported regardless of origin. All products originating from the European Economic Community are liberated with the exception of a nominative list of sixteen import headings enumerated in Arrêté No. 7758.'[49]

Categories for which licenses are awarded remain fairly vague. Since greater precision would run too overtly against the obligations in favour of trade liberalization, the entry of specific products is effectively debarred and the privileged commercial circuit maintained by more supple measures.[50] A similar pattern may be discerned[51] in foreign investment aid to the Ivory Coast. Economic co-operation agreements over the period since independence have become more and more multi-nationalized in keeping with the increasing internationalization and con-centration of western capitalism. But in spite of the growing importance of such organizations as the FED (Fonds Européen de Développement) or the IBRD, the continuing predominance of historical links with France is clearly revealed by the continuing importance of loans advanced by the Caisse Centrale de Coopération Economique (CCCE) and by the French government.

A still more striking example of the perpetuation of dependence on the former metropolitan power is the updating of the agreements concerning military co-operation. The fundamental principle underlying these 'common defence agreements' was the option given to newly inde-pendent states of French West Africa which signed the *accords* of calling on the forces of the French army in order to guarantee both their internal and external defence. The Ivory Coast entered into this system of com-mon defence with France by means of the Entente Sahel-Bénin which was established in 1959 by Houphouët-Boigny and which was to serve as the framework for a four-way military agreement signed by France, the Ivory Coast, Niger and Dahomey on 24 April 1961. The Ivory Coast, like other members of the French Communauté which replaced the French Union in 1958, has also signed Accords d'Assistance Militaire Technique which confirm the priority, if not the exclusivity, of the former metropolitan power in the supply of military aid and equipment, and its sole respon-sibility for the training of national military forces. These agreements provided a framework for the perpetuation of a French military presence in the former colonial areas. More specifically in the years immediately after political independence, they permitted the intervention of the French forces in case of any threat of change or overthrow of the ruling group which had negotiated the independence and co-operation agree-ments.[52] Within this context the national forces and French forces stationed locally, as well as the *forces d'intervention* stationed in the metropole ready for rapid intervention, played complementary roles in both internal and external defence.

Although certain aspects were modified in keeping with other political and legal changes, French military presence in West African states persisted in different ways. The reduction of French troops on African soil after 1962 was matched by the establishment of national armies trained and equipped by French forces and incorporated into a common defence system. These national forces were backed by two levels of possible intervention: a reduced number of French forces who remained in Africa, based at strategic places amongst which was Port Bouet just outside Abidjan in the Ivory Coast,[53] and the *forces Inter-Armées* stationed in France itself. These two levels were seen as a deterrent to threats either from inside or outside the states of French West Africa.

These agreements were not simply a matter of military security but a vital part of the much broader framework of political and economic co-operation which still characterizes France's relations with her former colonies.[54] The existence of such military, diplomatic and political agreements has been crucial to the creation and to the perpetuation of a climate of stability and confidence favourable to the establishment of foreign economic interests. These conditions are naturally complemented by internal factors. The need to project a climate of confidence and internal stability for the eyes of external opinion, has been among the most important and constant factors conditioning the nature of political power and the articulation of public policies throughout the post-colonial period in the Ivory Coast. In essence, however, the need simply reflects the dependence of the dominant class within the Ivory Coast itself on another dominant class – a foreign bourgeoisie which resides abroad.

Within the Ivory Coast the need to maintain internal order and stability has had marked effects on the evolution of political institutions and on the nature of Ivorian political activity in general. Since independence those who control the state apparatus have made vigorous and not unsuccessful attempts to suppress or control all political activities, in municipalities or trade unions, in tenants associations and student organizations. Effective political monopoly was established by the local ruling group at independence and has been fully maintained since. The political role of the state has been increasingly dynamic and interventionist despite its vigorous advocacy of *laissez-faire* in the economic sphere. The apparent insubstantiality of civil society in the Ivory Coast is thus largely a product of governmental action designed to disarm or neutralize popular political activity and to marginalize and minimize such activity where it cannot be suppressed completely.

The absence of grass-roots political activity and control within the Ivorian single party, the PDCI, is of central importance in this regard. At its founding in 1946 the PDCI had developed initially along ethnic lines and its organizers did not try to rebuild the party on the neighbourhood principle.[55] Consequently, the organization of the PDCI after independence reflected this multi-ethnic membership with each individual *comité ethnique* linked to *sous-section* and thus represented in the *conseil national*, the *comité directeur* and *bureau politique*.[56] The repression of 1948–50 seriously weakened the party and its immediate structure tended to wither away. Many local and village committees of the PDCI which had emerged spontaneously after the war became deeply involved in ethnic conflicts which the ethnic basis of the local organization did little to reduce. Most formal links between the village committees and the territorial headquarters in Abidjan were broken off. As an integrated body the PDCI virtually ceased to exist at the district, canton or village level. Its surviving territorial leaders became preoccupied with the transfer of power and took on governmental duties in France, West Africa, the territorial government and the civil service. They failed to reconstruct the party structures or even to call a territorial congress until 1959. Even before the granting of independence, a pattern which was to reinforce itself after 1960 had become apparent. In theory the occasional conferences of *élus, sous-section* members and members of the *comités directeurs* chose candidates for elections and took important decisions. In practice power became progressively concentrated in the hands of President Houphouët-Boigny who showed no hesitation in grasping and retaining it.[57]

From its beginning, the PDCI has remained very hierarchical in structure:

> The PDCI, like the Syndicat Agricole Africain, 'grew from the top down'. The only grass-roots support it sought was that of the voters: and it used their support only at the territorial level, not in the grass-roots arenas . . . It is important to stress these points because the very success of Houphouët in releasing the peasants from forced labour can obscure how little he actually proposed to give them in the way of formal political participation . . .[58]

Since independence the party has become increasingly bureaucratized as an agency of the centre, 'the most important instrument of government control, and "auxiliaire d'autorité" '.[59] The hierarchical nature of the PDCI, however, simply reflects the nature of political power in the Ivory Coast. The role left for popular political participation by the dominance of foreign interests is well summarized by Philippe Yacé, secretary-general of the PDCI, as 'active acquiescence in the policies of government'.[60] Mass mobilization is now confined to party membership and since everyone has to join the party, membership is indistinguishable from citizenship. As a recent study states, with regard to the party's 1970 objectives:

> The stifling of opposition, the absence of debate concerning the country's most serious problems, the self-satisfaction of political leaders, are some of the factors which explain why the progress which has been made to date towards the realization of the two objectives defined by the Fourth Party Congress – national unity and economic independence – has been so very small.[61]

In this sense, the size and scale of the state apparatus does not merely reflect its past historical role as the instrument of the colonial administration to subordinate all indigenous classes. The post-colonial state certainly inherited a strong military–administrative apparatus and state bureaucracy, as well as a central role in the distribution and appropriation of economic surplus; but since independence its burgeoning growth has acquired a new dynamic of its own. Between 1958 and 1963, for example, the proportional contribution of public services to GNP doubled, from 13 per cent to 26 per cent.[62] It has required energy and political ingenuity to preserve this monopoly, even if one of the most important factors in sustaining it has been the sheer expansion of the size and scale of state apparatus. By 1976 the number of *sociétés d'État* in the Ivory Coast in which the state held more than 50 per cent of the capital had increased to twenty-nine. In all but one of these where public participation represented 82.35 per cent, the corporations were wholly controlled by state capital. These corporations exist in almost every area of the economy whether concerned with regional planning (AVB, Autorité pour l'Aménagement de la Vallée du BANDAMA; ARSO, Autorité pour l'Aménagement de la Région du Sud Ouest), foreign commerce (CICE, Centre Ivoirien du Commerce Extérieur), or agricultural production (SODEPALM, Société pour le Développement et l'Exploitation du Palmier à Huile; SODEFEL, Société pour le Développement de la Production des Fruits et des Légumes), etc.[63] To these must be added a list of eighteen additional *sociétés anonymes* in which the state also represents 50 per cent or more of capital. In addition there are a great many other companies where the Ivorian state is present but represents a minority participation.

By 1971 a World Bank mission had already reported that new state enterprises, which by that time numbered twenty-five, were springing up without careful planning and being operated with wholly inadequate financial scrutiny.[64] According to the Ivorian government: 'The public corporations have been created in the case of specific activities where administrative or private intervention alone would not have produced the necessary encouragement or permitted a sufficiently rapid development.'[65] Other factors, however, have plainly contributed to this expansion. The state-owned corporations are managed by leading members of the government, often deputies to the National Assembly. While they contribute to economic activity in a wide variety of sectors, they do so under the direction of the ministries of planning and economic affairs, a consideration crucial to the role played by foreign capital in very profitable sectors. Furthermore, as Cohen writes:

> The growth of state capitalism, through the many *sociétés d'état* and the departments of government, provided opportunities for economic activity to complement what had previously been only political and administrative roles. A study of the Ivoirien membership of the *conseils d'administration* of 88 enterprises and economic associations shows that 129 individuals hold the 287 seats involved.[66]

Cohen's significant finding is the fact that 62 per cent of the positions in eighty-eight Ivorian economic enterprises or associations are held by members of the government.[67] As he demonstrates, the role of public officials in economic enterprises is of the greatest importance and has developed largely since independence. He does appear to misrepresent the situation, however, by arguing that these trends imply the decline of the planter class in favour of a 'politico-administrative class' and that 'the planters have lost both their early political power and their ability to successfully request urban resources'.[68]

The nature of political power has certainly evolved with the development of the state apparatus. But the dominant class which assumed power at independence maintains control over the export-oriented pattern of growth and the particular pattern of surplus distribution which it implies. With the emergence, particularly after 1964, of an important politico-administrative group, the dominant class may have been broadened in its composition; but the interests of the planter bourgeoisie have remained firmly dominant. Within the *conseils d'administration* of the *sociétés d'état* the continuing importance of the members of the planter bourgeoisie is noted by Cohen:

> the SAA category, . . . has an extraordinarily high average [of seats on *conseils d'administration*], reflecting the many activities of Joseph Anoma, the grand chancellor and former SAA head, and late Alphonse Assamoi, a highly successful political and economic entrepreneur.'[69]

The control of the state apparatus has also tightened on the municipal governments. Municipal elections have not been held since 1956 and memberships in the councils of the three *communes de plein exercise* (municipalities with locally elected mayors) and six *communes de moyen exercise* (municipalities with centrally appointed mayors) have accordingly declined. Increasingly it is the Ministry of the Interior which has final authority over municipal affairs.

> Administrative centralization has weakened the communes in both procedure and substance: they are dependent on central ministries for approval of actions, and because they are perceived as weak, they are no longer able to collect taxes from local populations. The startling result for Abidjan is that while the city population has doubled every six years, municipal revenue has declined in absolute terms from 1966 to 1970.[70]

The communes are financially crippled and unable to provide their residents with social services. Even the possibility of the revival of local government has been officially discouraged, lest local involvement should promote autonomous political activity. The same effort to neutralize, or canalize political activity has emerged in relation to unemployment, land expropriation, student protests or labour disputes. The government-sponsored student organization the Union Nationale des Etudiants et des Elèves de Côte d'Ivoire (UNECI) and its successor, the Mouvement des Etudiants et des Elèves de Côte d'Ivoire (MEECI), which was placed directly under the control of the PDCI in 1969, are paralleled in the area of labour disputes by the Union Générale des Travailleurs de la Côte d'Ivoire, also directly under the PDCI and the sole legal representative of workers interests. Most unions in the Ivory Coast have submitted to labour policy because they do not have either sufficient membership or economic power to support their demands in the face of repression and harassment or the co-optation of their leaders. Their weakness is in fact merely a reflection of the capacity of the ruling class to extend and maintain its control over union activities.

It is important to consider the question of ethnicity in the context of this sustained governmental restriction of popular opportunities for political action. Just as rural ethnic responses to agricultural capitalism varied at independence, there have continued to be different ethnic responses to the socio-economic changes in the decade following independence. Baoulé, Agni, Sénoufo and Malinké migrants were, of the various groups, those best able, with political help, to establish themselves, obtain property and invest profitably. More important in relation to state power has been the continuing importance of ethnicity as an organizational principle of the single party. The persistence of the ethnic basis of the *sous-comités* of the PDCI in large urban centres such as Abidjan or Bouaké, in spite of

90

the divisive implications for national unity, requires consideration. Legislative elections are seen, for example, as the occasion to put forward a representative from one's own ethnic group and consequently elections contribute to the exacerbation of ethnic differences.[71] The exacerbation of these differences and the absence of horizontal communications among different ethnic committees not only obstruct national unity but also serve to reinforce the hierarchical nature of the party and so contribute to the centralization of political activity.

Cross-ethnic political activity, whether it occurs in tenants associations, among the unemployed or in the labour movement, where it exists outside accepted political structures, represents a serious threat to the Ivorian single party system and its ethnic principle of political organization. Under these circumstances it is important to examine the conditions surrounding the announcement as a result of the 1969 'Dialogue' of an end to the prohibition of non-ethnic associational activity. This modification was made public at the PDCI Congress of 1970 where P. Yacé announced the replacement of *comités ethniques* by *comités de quartier* as the basic unit of the party.

Although the change was not implemented immediately, public recognition of the need to end this obstacle to national unity appears to have coincided with more fundamental transformations in Ivorian society. Ten years of post-colonial rule had provoked new socio-economic cleavages and resulted in the emergence of new differences, new inequalities, new lines of opposition and contradictions. Although perhaps a little exaggerated, Cohen gives a forceful statement of the extent of this impact.

> Ethnic differences have proved to be of minor significance when contrasted to political activity resulting from public policy. Thus riots against foreign laborers, student protest at the university, unemployment demonstrations, conflicts over land expropriation, refusal to pay taxes, and many other demonstrations of opposition to public policy have become increasingly frequent in the urban environment as a result of public management of urban growth and not because some ethnic groups feel excluded from a particular kind of urban opportunity.[72]

Ethnicity, so long an instrument of control in the hands of the colonial power and those who assumed political control at independence, appears a decade later to be increasingly subordinate in importance to the emerging class struggle.

91

THE NATURE OF STATE INTERVENTION

In order to understand the nature of state intervention and to assess and to explain the different levels of success or failure which the Ivorian state apparatus has shown in the performance of its tasks, one must first attempt to analyse *how* these tasks are defined and *why* they are defined in this way. The contradiction between the particularist interests which state intervention may be shown to serve and the general interests which it is said to serve, clearly illustrates the class character of this intervention. The philosophy of 'economic liberalism' was proclaimed by the leaders of the Ivory Coast even before the declaration of independence in August 1960. Their continued adherence to this doctrine has been the guarantee for the perpetuation of close links with the former metropolitan power and the creation of conditions favouring foreign capital. This orientation has been summarized by the following four points:

1. co-operation with France in all fields;
2. the path of evolution, not revolution, and the rejection of the ideology of class struggle, on the grounds that classes 'do not exist in the Ivory Coast';
3. unrestricted reliance on foreign and local private initiative;
4. consolidation of national sovereignty in advance of any attempts to form larger African units, deemed illusory.[73]

The notoriously rapid rates of economic growth which have characterized the Ivorian economy during the decade after independence constitute the so-called *miracle ivoirien*. Over the period 1950–65 the rate increased, rising from 7–8 per cent during the decade 1950–60 to 11–12 per cent during the five year period 1960–5. After a brief slump, the rate between 1968 and 1970 increased to approximately 12 per cent which resulted in a yearly average increase of 11 per cent for the decade 1960–70. Since then the rate of increase has tended to decrease: 'Growth rates have been a little less rapid since 1970 when the rate was 8.4 per cent, to become 8.5 per cent in 1971, 5.8 per cent in 1973 and 6 per cent in 1974.'[74]

In purely quantitative indices, several factors explain the rapidity of the rates of growth up until 1970. One of these factors was the relatively late beginning of the *mise en valeur* and export crop production noted earlier in this article, with the result that the returns from this area came somewhat later than in Senegal or Ghana. Another factor was the important investment in infrastructure undertaken by the colonial administration just before political independence. Important public works such as the port of Abidjan and the Vidri canal created the conditions for rapid growth after independence. Moreover, post-independence economic growth in the Ivory Coast was based on a combination of quite specific circumstances: the use of extensive techniques of exploitation, a small number of agricultural export products sold at a guaranteed price on guaranteed markets, the relative abundance of arable land at that moment and the considerable use of foreign migrant workers drawn from neighbouring poorer Sahelian countries.[75] Last but not least, the rates of growth were based increasingly on the first easy phase of import-substitution industries, of an assembling or finishing nature. The counterpart to these growth rates was a model of extraverted development, dependent for its continuation on increasing supplies of foreign capital, foreign techniques and foreign labour.

In conformity with its economic liberalism, state intervention and economic planning in the Ivory Coast has not aimed to co-ordinate socio-economic changes and attain well-defined social objectives. Instead it has intervened to create a climate of confidence and stability favourable to foreign economic interests, in the past for the most part private interests, but increasingly multilateral and public. More specifically, the government's role in economic planning and growth has been to create the infrastructure and guarantees necessary to growth – roads, ports, buildings, telecommunications, etc. The initiative, the responsibility and especially the control over the creation and management of productive economic activities is left to private interests. It is possible to explain this orientation at several levels. Officially, the leaders of the Ivory Coast have always claimed that this option is best able to enrich the population as a whole. It is important to grasp the political and ideological implications of this claim.[76] In the guise of economic planning for rapid growth and national development, the state masks growing internal inequalities and contradictions and projects a climate of stability and confidence, playing a highly political role in the perpetuation of a specific type of growth. Preoccupation with creating the conditions for quick short-term returns to capital to attract the necessary supplies of foreign capital is a central factor in many Ivorian state policies. In consequence, as the first decade after political independence progressed, more emphasis was placed on attracting foreign capital and foreign personnel to promote import-substitution-type industry, instead of diversifying agricultural exports or for that matter, training Ivorian managers.

Since the agricultural sector is the basis of the livelihood of the vast majority of the population it is important to consider the nature of state intervention within it. The vulnerability of the Ivorian economy at independence, with coffee and cocoa providing 90 per cent of the value of exports in the 1950s, led in the post-independence period to attempts at

93

agricultural diversification. The Five-Year Ivorian Economic Plan (1971–5) proposed to reduce the joint contribution of coffee and cocoa to total agricultural production for export or industrial use by 1980 to 66.5 per cent by contrast with their 77.4 per cent of 1960 or 77.7 per cent of 1965.[77] The programme of agricultural diversification was directed not towards creating a more equitable distribution of the agricultural surplus among the local population, but to the reproduction of existing distributive inequalities on the basis of a slightly larger number of export products.

Although no formal barriers prevent Ivorian peasant producers from growing oil palms, rubber, sugar, pineapples or anything else in addition to or in place of the crops with which they are familiar – although they are free to dispose of their produce through the same marketing channels, and on the same terms as European producers of the same crops; although African producers can also, for a minimal fee, receive technical help from a variety of French technical service companies operating as agents of the Ministry of Agriculture, such opportunities remain essentially formal. Few African small-holding peasants are in a position either to meet the cost or to face the psychological challenge involved in utilizing such facilities. Indeed French private enterprise in agriculture has apparently increased since independence mainly by expanding already existing non-agricultural business. Of the eight principal products of diversification, oil palms, rubber, cocoa, pineapples, timber, cotton, rice and sugar, five (all except rice, cocoa and cotton) are grown, harvested, processed and marketed essentially by Europeans without – at the extreme – the need of any peasant participation at all. Bulk production is undertaken on large or medium plantations run by European concessionnaires and worked by paid African labourers.[78] The case is different with cocoa, cotton, rice, and two important crops, coffee and bananas. By long custom, these five products are all peasant crops and their cultivation is still carried out largely by Africans on a family basis, on holdings of one to three hectares without hired labour. Before independence there were no European-owned cocoa plantations and 97 per cent of the coffee output came from African plantations.

Government diversification policies in the first decade and a half since independence have had an important impact on this situation. The government policy to discourage the expansion of coffee-growing was to be offset by increased yields per acre, and by conversion to oil palm, coconut palm or rubber. The socio-economic basis of agriculture production was, however, to be transformed simultaneously:

What is more, agriculture which is the basis of the economy of the

Ivory Coast, is less and less characterized by small-holding property. This trend had not been anticipated. At the beginning, 'village plantations' were expected to benefit from the external economies which resulted from the large plantations. The reduction of small-holding coffee production was to be compensated by an increase in small-holding cocoa production. But nothing of the sort happened. And in spite of the government's intervention concerning the producer prices of coffee and cocoa which were raised in 1966 to their 1962 level, *there is no doubt that the relative weight of the small peasant producer is declining.*[79] (Our italics)

The reproduction of a hierarchical socio-economic pattern which is explicit in the nature of Ivorian state intervention in agriculture is also the implicit consequence of the government's liberal approach to agricultural change.

Although the sum to be invested in agricultural diversification projects, 88 billion francs CFA over the period 1971–80 may appear impressive, the manner in which it is to be invested is far less so. Of this sum, 56 billion francs CFA is to be invested in industrial plantations: 'palm oil trees, coconut trees, rubber plants, bananas, pineapples, but also coffee and cocoa plantations, the production of cotton, kenaf, and sugar cane.'[80] Most of the funds involved, however, are to be invested on large or medium sized plantations (oil palms, rubber, pineapples, sugar cane, wood), managed by European concessionaires and worked by salaried African labourers. The reforestation programme for 1971–80 will receive a further 8 billion francs CFA, in addition. However, it is the 'Plan palmier', the oil palm development plan, which will absorb far the largest share – 40 per cent of the public funds for agricultural investment between 1970 and 1980. This project is particularly revealing in terms of the income distribution pattern it implies.

The state corporation in charge of the programme, (SODEPALM), has had to decide between the expansion by means of *blocs industriels*, (i.e. large plantations run by European concessionnaires), and by means of *plantations villageoises* entrusted directly to peasant farmers. Without ruling out the latter, the SODEPALM has opted heavily for the conversion of smaller coffee plantations, cultivated on an individual or family basis on plots between one and five hectares, into large industrial block allotments of oil palms. This choice is explained pellucidly by a long-time defender of French colonial interests, M. René Charbonneau:

> This distinction results from the fact that the material difficulties which accompany the creation of industrial block plantations are considered as more easily overcome than the psychological dif-

ficulties which accompany the establishment of village plantations. In the first instance it is a question of means and finance and in the second, of time and patience.[81]

Ivory Coast expansion is plainly 'to continue to be confined to the 15 per cent of the population who understand about means and financing. The 85 per cent whose pressing need is education can safely, even preferably, wait while the regime builds up a buffer stock of time and patience.'[82] This overall strategy is epitomized by the sectoral growth rates projected by the Five-Year Development Plan. Agricultural production for export or industry is expected to grow by an annual rate of 5 per cent between 1970 and 1975 and 6.8 per cent between 1975 and 1980; foodstuff production and cattle raising are expected to increase at a rate of 3.7 per cent and 3.9 per cent for the same two periods respectively.[83] In consequence as the Plan notes, 'the relative importance of foodstuff, agriculture and cattle raising will be reduced by half over the period 1965–80 and will decline from having represented 17 per cent of gross domestic product in 1965, to 9.1 per cent in 1980.'[84] The intervention of the Ivorian state in favour of agricultural sectors ensuring the highest short-term returns, and directed towards export markets or local industry, perpetuates a particularly uneven distribution of surplus in favour of foreign interests and a small local minority.[85] Ivorian industrial policy shows a remarkably similar pattern. The importance of state intervention in creating and determining the nature of industrial activities can hardly be overestimated. The importance of this intervention to the detriment of agricultural diversification became increasingly clear as the first decade of political independence progressed.[86] Since this pattern requires the continuous creation of new possibilities for rapid short-term returns, it was implicit in the development strategy from the outset, though the planners plainly did not care to assert it too clearly. Since 1970 the priority of the industrial and service sectors has become still more marked.[87]

The protectionist policy and industrial concessions granted to foreign interests at independence in the Ivory Coast stemmed from changes in both metropolis and colony. Post-independence Ivorian legislation legitimized this new orientation and the form of capital accumulation in which established interests now became involved. The concessions set out in the 1959 Code des Investissements suited the monopolistic distributive position of the large trading companies which increasingly participated in the creation of local finishing and assembling industries. The concessions determined decisively which goods were imported, which were produced locally, and even how they were produced. Among the Code's concessions, extensive import privileges fostered the creation of consumer goods 'industries' concentrating on minimal finishing operations to manufactured inputs imported duty-free.[88] Complete tariff exemptions on imported industrial inputs of firms granted priority status have encouraged the implantation of processes which minimized the degree of local value added. The greater the component of duty-free inputs imported from the cheapest source, the lower the costs of production, the more substantial the profits of the foreign investors.

In order to accommodate industrial interests in finding the cheapest source of inputs, certain modifications have been made to the rigidly protectionist commercial policy – for example, through the granting of licences to import industrial inputs. In this way, Ivorian fiscal and monetary policies have reinforced the bias of the Code des Investissements in determining not only which goods were produced but also the techniques of local production. The import-substitution orientation of Ivorian industrial policies has encouraged local production of previously imported European goods which reflect and incorporate the advanced technology of the industrialized metropolitan power. This structural bias in favour of capital intensive techniques, inherent in the demand patterns which have resulted from colonial trade, has been reinforced by other areas of economic policy. The availability of metropolitan credit for overseas projects which favour the use of metropolitan capital equipment, serves as a further impediment to the introduction of 'middle-range' techniques of production adapted to the resource availability of the local environment. Adherence to the franc zone has also meant the maintenance of low interest rates, artificially lowering the cost of imported capital goods and hence favouring capital intensive techniques at the expense of Ivorian labour. These concessions have not only influenced the structure of local industry but impaired the financial viability of the economy and distorted the distribution of resources within it.

Tax and tariff exemptions of up to twenty-five years have mortgaged the economic future of the country even if they have not demanded immediate sacrifices. But since they are not linked to criteria of economic performance, it is impossible to determine their net impact on the economy. Returns to investment were guaranteed to 'priority' enterprises through a system of uniform price fixing, but there was little guarantee that the profits were reinvested locally. Ivorian industrial policy allowed for unlimited transfer of company profits and savings, subject after an initial 10 per cent reserved for the purchase of bonds or certificates from the Fonds National d'Investissement.[89] The size of yearly outflows of private capital and the relative rates at which public as opposed to private investment have grown over the last decade show the inadequacy of this provision. Public investment rose much faster than public saving, since the public sector drew its funds increasingly from existing productive activities; but private investment has grown less rapidly, although net outflows of private savings, interests, dividends, income remittances, debt repayments and capital transfers have all increased.

Annual private transfers from the Ivory Coast between 1950 and 1965, in constant 1965 value, increased three and a half times, from 7 billion to 25.2 billion FCFA.[90] During the same period the relative size of private transfers remained fairly constant at about 11 per cent of the country's GNP, a constancy explained by the stability over the same period of national urban income distribution as a whole, half of which continued to accrue to private firms, individual entrepreneur and non-African salaries.

By 1969 foreign transfers had increased to almost 29 billion FCFA.[91] The consequences of these transfers are apparent in the balance of payment position in recent years.[92] The overall deficit since 1971 is largely due to unilateral private transfers, a net drain which has risen from 11.8 billion francs CFA in 1970 to 25.2 billion in 1973.

A key factor in this transfer has been the extent of foreign control of local industry. Unlike other West African states like Nigeria, the Ivory Coast made no initial attempt to introduce measures to promote the control or management of local industry by nationals or to oblige foreign firms to include Ivorians among their directors. In consequence the private sector and more particularly French firms dominated the formation of industrial capital. Half total investment came from wholly foreign sources and a good two thirds were devoted to industry.[93] The state has nevertheless participated importantly in this process. Its stake in the capital of private firms (12–25 per cent) is too small to guarantee control but plainly helps to legitimize the scale of foreign economic activity in local eyes, to say nothing of reassuring foreign interests. It has also spent heavily on creating necessary conditions for capital accumulation through, for example, the Bandama hydroelectric project (92 million dollars) and the Port of San Pedro (146 million dollars). Quite apart from their sheer size, such projects committed the economy more heavily to the growth of the foreign sector.[94]

In a similar fashion the perpetuation of colonial monetary ties has entailed keeping interest rates at externally-set low levels. These in turn have favoured the keeping of large balances abroad, encouraging the transfer of funds and discouraging accumulation and reinvestment of domestic savings. They have also favoured capital intensive projects by under-rating effective 'foreign' capital costs and consequently restricting the employment of local labour. National private savings in the Ivory Coast have been much smaller than domestic savings because of transfers by immigrant workers from neighbouring countries, by employees from

France who transfer part of their salaries, and by foreign enterprises which transfer profits. This tendency has produced in recent years a net inflow of private capital lower than the outflow of corporate profits (investment income payments) alone. The obvious consequent burden on balance of payments will require increasing external borrowing.

The absence of institutions capable of effectively tapping Ivorian domestic savings and ensuring their reinvestment contrasts strikingly with other non-franc zone West African nations – notably Nigeria, where institutions were established for the 'Nigerianization' of the economy before 1967. Easy access to the French capital market through the Caisse Autonome d'Amortissement (which handles the central government's debt) has permitted the Ivory Coast to sell bonds guaranteed by the French government. Privileged access to metropolitan funds has thus inevitably stifled local initiatives:

> The countries of the West African Monetary Union are headed by an oligarchy of functionaries who are concerned above all with the evolution of the state budget and who for a long time have favoured foreign capital. As a result they have developed almost no local *bourgeoisie d'affaires*.[95]

The lateness of the creation of institutions in favour of local participation is in itelf an indication of the Ivorian leadership's attitude to the emergence of a local entrepreneurial group. The performance and mediocre results of the institutions created after 1968 for this purpose are even more revealing.

The decision to establish these institutions in the late 1960s was prompted by several factors. The early phase of easy import-substitution activities was beginning to run out. The need to redefine industrial strategy was recognized in a report of the Banque Ivoirienne de Développement Industriel in 1967, which recommended:

> that it was necessary to create the conditions for a second generation of industries based on the transformation of local raw materials and on the production of intermediary goods; that the Ivorian Development Bank should orientate its activities in favour of private Ivorian enterprise; that industrialization would only become permanent if the new industries were more solidly implanted in the country than were the already existing enterprises; in other words, that what was needed was the creation of Ivorian entrepreneurs and the mobilization of Ivorian capital.[96]

One may presume that a further motive for the creation of such institutions was the simple wish to placate opposition discontent in the early

1960s over the foreign dominance of the economy. The institutions created were in any case in little danger of realizing the stated aims of the BIDI. In July 1968, the Office for the Promotion of Ivorian Enterprise, OPEI, was created to develop and improve the efficiency of Ivorian commercial, industrial and agricultural enterprises. Its activities were to include studies, technical assistance and training in finance and admini-stration. After three years of operation, OPEI statistics revealed that out of 7,363 enterprises in the Ivory Coast, less than 20 per cent were Ivorian. Of the 332 principal industrial enterprises included in this total, (busi-nesses with a minimum annual turnover of 12 million CFA), only twenty-five or 8 per cent proved to be Ivorian controlled. The proportion declined to 3 per cent if state and para-state enterprises were excluded. The actual activities of the OPEI and similar organizations and finally the formation of the Ministry of Training in January 1970, strongly suggest that they were created more to mitigate pressures for greater Ivorian participation in the productive sectors of the economy, than as serious efforts to transform the structure of production. In an economy as exter-nally controlled as the Ivory Coast, the creation of local 'promoting' institutions, and even the allocation of sizeable quantities of funds to such institutions, can on its own represent no more than symbolic action.

Fifteen years after independence it is apparent that the Ivorian lead-ership will not contemplate redefining metropolitan economic relations sufficiently to permit Ivorian participation the least element of real control. If a reorientation had been envisaged, government policy would necessarily have included the progressive transfer of control. Ivorian policies have been directed, however, at updating rather than modifying in any significant manner the extraverted and dependent economic and political relations on which Ivorian state power is based.

THE IMPLICATION OF STATE INTERVENTION

How far has the Ivorian state succeeded in the performance of its task? And, more urgently, how adequate analytically is it to assess this per-formance (necessarily favourably) by the sole criterion of the rapidity of economic growth?

The conditions which permitted rapid growth in the first decade were based on factors which had relatively little to do with the intervention of the Ivorian state. Rapid growth in the short term has been based on heavy borrowing and may thus have mortgaged possibilities of such growth in the future. Moreover, to the extent that the continuation of the foreign investment necessary for growth is dependent on a climate of stability and confidence, the portrayal of the Ivory Coast as a 'miracle of development' becomes in itself an important factor in the perpetuation of the past orientation of growth.

THE RURAL SECTOR

In the rural sector, as elsewhere, the state has sought actively to foster growth in those agricultural sectors with the highest assured short-term returns. This has led it to favour *blocs industriels* rather than *plantations villageoises* in the oil palm programme, and to support ever since independence a variety of un-integrated projects for the intensive production of agricultural products for export and industry, at the expense of foodstuffs for local consumption. In consequence techniques in the production of local foodstuffs have stagnated and their producers remain poor and isolated, while it has also been necessary to import food in bulk.[97]

Because no measures were introduced between 1950 and 1965 to allay the increasing disparities between the northern savannah region of subsistence agriculture and the southern coastal forest area, these disparities have intensified:

> the social and economic changes have not as yet transformed all the Ivorian countryside in spite of the fact that the traditionally isolated and stagnant regions only represent one third of the rural population as against 60 per cent in 1950. These economic and social changes have been less extensive in the northern cereal-producing areas which represent 8 to 9 per cent of the rural population and where the monetary income per capita has increased from 1,400 francs CFA in 1950 to 5,200 in 1965 (in 1965 prices) than they have been in the southern plantation region which has expanded considerably. The zone characterized by ordinary plantations which represented 23 per cent of the rural population in 1950 (with a per capita income of 11,700 francs in 1965 prices) represented 49 per cent in 1965 (with an income of 15,300 francs per capita). The privileged areas which represent 8 to 10 per cent of the rural population have benefited from an increase in per capita income from 19,400 francs in 1965 prices to 26,000 francs.[98]

As Gilbert Compte notes, these disparities are clearly shown in the 1971 IBRD report:

> Up to now an annual effective average income per person in the north and in the rural areas of thirty dollars as opposed to a hundred dollars in the cities and in the coastal region of Abidjan conferred

101

sufficient privileges on the urban dwellers to make them accept a considerable number of sacrifices. However, a decrease in the number of jobs available together with inflationary tendencies and a new increase in prices could make them turn their discontent against their employers, the majority of whom are French.[99]

What has been the impact of government employment and wage policies upon the agricultural sector? According to planners' estimates for the period 1970–80, the number of wage workers in agriculture will grow by only 3.3 per cent a year compared with the growth rate of the rural working age population which is expected to increase by at least 4 or 4.5 per cent annually. The increase in the number of self-employed farmers is likely to be even smaller than the increase in the number of wage workers in agriculture. Rural areas are therefore likely to have increasing numbers of surplus labour and the tendency will be for increasingly larger flows of workers to the cities. It is the question of labour which will reveal the shortcomings of the Ivorian pattern of agricultural development. The bottleneck created by labour could only be broken by a change in the entire growth pattern to permit the intensification of techniques in all areas of agricultural production and put an end to rural unemployment and enforced migration. More recent programmes of agricultural diversification represent no change in orientation. It is now clear that changes have been to the detriment of the small peasant producer, and that they have created an increasing number of landless wage labourers who either work for larger landowners or for the industrial plantations.

The Ivorian government's wage policy has contributed directly to worsening the position of agricultural wage workers and to the inflow of thousands of migrant workers from neighbouring Sahelian countries, Upper Volta, Mali and Niger. Because the government has exempted owners of coffee and cocoa plantations from paying the labour which they recruit the minimum agricultural wage and since to this day these are not tied by the minimum wage regulations which apply to other agricultural sectors, Ivorian workers have avoided the plantation sector.[100] Consequently, it is in the plantation zone that the proportion of foreign migrant labour has increased fastest. According to the Ministry of the Plan, by 1965 the population of the Ivory Coast included 670,000 non-Ivorian African 'residents' as well as over 300,000 African seasonal plantation workers. By 1970, well over half of agricultural wage labour was non-Ivorian. The social tensions created by the presence of such an important non-Ivorian component of the African labour force both in the plantations and in urban areas have led to serious outbreaks of violence

102

against non-Ivorian Africans such as those which took place in Treichville in October 1969. Ivorian resentment of African foreigners (accused of taking jobs away from them) exists also among petty traders and even trained *fonctionnaires*. The presence of so many African foreigners as a target for Ivorian frustrations may serve temporarily to shelter expatriate interests; but it cannot be expected to do so indefinitely. While African foreign workers supply vitally needed labour, the presence of such a large non-integrated social group is a source of considerable political instability.

Even President Houphouët-Boigny suffered a major rebuff on this issue in 1966. The refusal of the Ivorian population to accept the President's resolution favouring the creation of double nationality – an almost unprecedented occasion, as the President's initiatives were practically never refused – indicates the depth and seriousness of the problem created by the presence of so many non-Ivorian Africans in the Ivory Coast. Their number has been estimated at about one quarter of the country's population in 1966–7.[101] The absence of recent official statistics for numbers of foreign Africans suggests that this group may be more strongly resented than is the European community for whom figures are available. The number of Europeans, 90 per cent of whom are French, has increased since independence from 10,000 in 1956 to 20,000 in 1963 and 40,000 in 1970 and was officially given as between 40,000 and 50,000 for 1975. The problem of unemployment has rendered the position of non-Ivorian Africans increasingly critical. Rightly or wrongly, they are seen as occupying jobs which could have been occupied by Ivorians more easily than the management positions held by the Europeans.

By 1970 probably half the agricultural wage labour in the Ivory Coast was non-Ivorian.[102] The problem created by the presence of so many foreign workers cannot be analysed apart from the broader framework of the overall employment and salary policies of the Ivorian government. The stagnation of traditional agriculture, because of government emphasis on agriculture for export and for industry, has encouraged important migratory movements of labour towards the southern plantation zones. Furthermore, the use of public funds to promote products with the highest returns (palm oil, rubber, cocoa, etc.) particularly in *blocs industriels* has created a situation in which productivity is encouraged at the expense of employment. In consequence a pattern of resource distribution has persisted very similar to the pre-independence balance between the modern European-dominated and the peasant producing sectors of agricultural production. Social disparities have scarcely altered and improvements in the productivity of Ivorian agriculture introduced

103

through the programmes of diversification have come almost exclusively in the export crop sector. Changes in control over production and changes in income distribution reflect this bias and extend the patterns of social differentiation discernible in the mid-1960s.

By 1965 a wealthy planter class of about 20,000 had emerged and employed approximately two-thirds of agricultural wage labour. Any attempt to analyse the evolution of the Ivorian planter class since this time is made particularly difficult by the conspicuous absence of official statistics concerning the distribution of land within each agricultural sector. We need urgently to know the distribution of land ownership, the employment of wage labour and the control over production in the 280,000 coffee plantations which in 1976 covered 700,000 hectares and the 200,000 cocoa plantations which the same year represented 900,000 hectares. In the absence of such figures, one must resort to the few existing studies which examine the rural impact of state intervention.

Lawson suggests that agricultural diversification schemes designed to reduce the number of small coffee producers have not been offset by an increase in small cocoa producers. The relative decline of peasant production is unmistakable.[103] The same pattern is revealed in a study which analysed the socio-economic impact of agricultural improvement schemes such as those for the mechanized production of cotton.[104]

The criterion of short-term profitability has not only accentuated differences within particular sectors, it has also reinforced disparities in favour of the southern plantation zone and in particular of the country's capital.

> If, as some economists argue, it is true that the concentration of infrastructure and productive enterprises in Abidjan has served as an important stimulus for economic growth, it is also clear that the public resources devoted to Abidjan, if distributed upcountry, could have transformed the lives of many more people.[105]

Official figures may indicate that the annual consumption of the African population is expected to increase more rapidly during the present decade (1970–80) than that of the European population; but this comparison has little practical meaning in the absence of figures indicating the amount of income on which the comparison is based. Furthermore, if the actual income spread between various groups is taken into account, it becomes clear that in 1980 the non-African urban population, the Europeans, are expected to consume an annual market value of 947,000 francs CFA per person more than the market value consumed by the rural African population (in contrast to the 1970 difference of 701,000 francs

CFA), suggesting that disparities will have increased in real terms by the end of the decade rather than decreased. Moreover, in 1980 the urban non-African population, the Europeans, will continue to consume a market value forty-four times larger per person than the rural African population.[106]

THE URBAN SECTOR

The loss of economic freedom that the Ivory Coast government has been willing to forego through its dependence on foreign private capital is considered the 'economic cost' of the country's rapid growth. Governmental efforts to foster rapid rates of return in the short-term in the quest for foreign capital, have resulted in a particularly distorted import-substitutive industrial structure characterized by a lack of inter-industry flows, a lack of local value-added, small sized industrial units and important transfers abroad with increasingly serious balance of payments effects.[107]

A further direct consequence of the government's reliance on foreign capital has been the restricted place allotted to Ivorians within the industrial sector. Most West African states have recently made sustained efforts to Africanize the more lucrative employment opportunities in the modern sector, along with equity capital in privately-owned local firms in commercial or industrial sectors and entrepreneurial access where this does not require very large initial supplies of capital or technical expertise. In this respect the Ivory Coast is a striking exception. The reasons for this distinctive posture throw considerable light on the class character of the Ivorian state. Ivorians have played a decidedly marginal role in the creation, management and control of local industry as the suppliers of capital, as entrepreneurs, or as qualified labour and in the share of the industrial wage bill which they receive.

The Ivorian share in a total industrial investment of 42 billion CFA up to 1968 consisted of some 1 billion CFA in the form of state participations in the capital of the various enterprises (excluding the 850 million capital stake in the Ivory Coast Electric Power Enterprise, EECI); 120 million CFA in the form of direct investment and 4.7 billion CFA in the form of loans to the Ivory Coast Development Bank (BIDI), which was formed with the participation of a large number of foreign private and public banking institutions; 2.3 billion in the form of loans from the banking system rediscounted by the Central Bank; and lastly, about 300 million CFA in the form of Ivorian private capital principally invested in four large-scale industrial enterprises whose corporate capital ranges from 40 million to 200 million CFA. By 1968 only two Ivorians were in entrepreneurial control of large scale industrial enterprises, two of the four previously mentioned. By 1968 the government had, it is true, created two agencies to promote small and medium scale enterprises. But institutions created to encourage enterprises of an artisanal nature (bakeries, joiners' shops, and service trades – plumbing, and tailoring) can scarcely provide the material for top industrial management positions – a prerequisite for the Ivorization of local industrial activity. Recent studies have made it clear, too, that expatriate control over the industrial sector remains virtually unmodified and continues to restrict Ivorian access to managerial and more highly skilled posts in industry. The absence of local industrial activities explains the continued dependence of urban salaried labour for employment on foreign firms. Although the number of non-agricultural wage workers has increased from 115,400 in 1963 to 142,000 in 1965, to 192,000 in 1971 – an annual rate of 12 per cent – this dependence has been fully maintained.[108]

In the Abidjan area the widespread use of foreign Africans in less skilled jobs and non-Africans in more skilled jobs means that an estimated 50 per cent of jobs are held by foreigners.[109] In 1965 almost half of urban labour was employed directly by foreign enterprises, with the colonial trading companies still preponderating.[110] During the same period over four-fifths (83 per cent) of value added in urban economic activities resulted from the foreign sector. The overriding importance of foreign interests in urban economic activities was beyond dispute: 'apart from the foreign sector, the national productive economy consists of very little indeed.'[111] By 1970 this situation remained unchanged. A 1971 enquiry estimated the non-agricultural wage labour force at approximately 192,000 workers, including 8,000 household help; 41,485 civil servants and 142,299 workers employed by 2,454 private firms. The overriding importance of the employment provided by the foreign sector was matched by the continuing absence of local entrepreneurs on the one hand, and the decline in importance of artisan activities on the other, the latter often displaced by the establishment of foreign industrial activities.[112] Indeed, the country's planners overtly anticipate that the contribution of artisan production to GNP will fall from 3.4 per cent in 1965 to 2 per cent in 1980.[113]

The dominant role which foreign enterprise has played in creating urban labour has largely determined the employment structure and income distribution of the Ivorian urban population. As has been pointed out concerning urban wages, these consist almost exclusively of 'dependent wages'.[114]

The disproportionately small wage bill accruing to Ivorian workers reflects the continued expatriate monopoly over management positions.[115] Africans, on the other hand, have had to accept the role of unskilled labour for foreign firms at disproportionately low wages:

> They consist moreover of subordinate labourers who, when considered as a group, only receive 60 per cent of the wages which these firms distribute (a sum of 18.1 billion out of a total of 30 billion in 1965).[116]

Their situation leaves Africans little chance to accede to positions of greater responsibility or management which are effectively circumscribed.[117]

In 1968 a Manpower Bureau study of 44,000 wage earners in industrial activities, including electric power and trade, showed that only 6 per cent of managerial and professional–technical staff of enterprises were Ivorian or non-Ivorian Africans. (Subsequently, the term 'African' will be used to designate non-Ivorian Africans.) The corresponding figures for supervisory technical personnel (foremen) was 35 per cent. One quarter of these were non-citizen Africans. Thirty-four per cent of the employees at higher levels (book-keeper, personal secretary, etc.) were still Europeans; and whereas 35 per cent of the skilled workers were non-citizen Africans, in the case of unskilled workers the proportions rose to as much as 60 per cent. The higher levels of industry have remained firmly in the hands of non-Africans (see table 2).

TABLE 2

	Total	Ivorian	African	European
Managerial personnel	503	20	4	479
Professional–technical personnel	792	31	13	748
Supervisory technical personnel (foreman)	1,659	435	157	1,067
Supervisory personnel	1,233	581	230	422
Subordinate personnel	2,818	1,759	1,018	41
Skilled workers	5,668	3,769	1,831	68
Semi-skilled workers	15,638	9,989	5,647	2
Unskilled workers	15,751	6,230	9,515	6
TOTAL	44,062	22,814	18,415	2,833

An estimated 15.9 billion CFA or 30 per cent of the total wage bill – 40 per cent if the non-artisanal urban economy is considered – accrued to Europeans in 1965.[118] An inquiry into Ivorian wage labour employment patterns and wage distribution, conducted in 1971 by the Ivorian Ministère de l'Enseignement Technique et de la Formation Professionnelle, reached similar conclusions (see table 3, page 108).

The portion of the wage bill accruing to Europeans has thus in fact increased slightly, while in the private sector over half the jobs and nearly two-thirds of the wage bill accrues to non-Ivorians.

These disparities have become increasingly difficult to ignore. As Cohen's study on the distribution of urban resources (housing, land, secondary school education or social services) amply documents, the issue of Ivorization is as much concerned with living standards within the Ivorian population as with employment and management of economic and public affairs. Frustrations felt by Ivorians have already on several occasions led to anti-foreign riots. Ivorian agricultural and urban workers resent the competition of non-citizen Africans for scarce jobs. Another less publicized consequence of Ivorian reliance on foreign capital and the free market is the domination of upcountry commerce by foreign Africans.[119] Even more highly trained Ivorians are coming to share these resentments as employment within the administration closes up and careers in private enterprise remain largely pre-empted by established foreign interests, or by the existence of fiscal, monetary and credit institutions which favour these interests. A changed pattern of growth, creating basic rather than light industries, could alter this bleak employment position; but such a growth pattern could hardly be financed in the manner which has characterized Ivorian growth over the last decade. For the availability of savings up until now has been very much a function of the manner in which they have been used.

TABLE 3

Wage Labourers by national origin	Percentage of urban wage labour force	Percentage distribution of global wage bill
Ivorians	48	36.4
Africans (non-Ivorians)	45.2	31.4
Europeans	6.8	32.2
TOTAL	100.0%	100.0%

THE POLITICAL IMPLICATIONS OF STATE INTERVENTION

Ivorians, as Cohen notes,[120] are perfectly well aware that the employment of foreigners is a consequence of official decisions, even if their government rationalizes these decisions in terms of investment climate, labour costs, or skills and relations with France. What they can as yet perhaps see less clearly is the extent to which the policies of economic liberalism and openness to foreign interests are in fact the very basis of the power of those responsible for taking official decisions. Central to the successful perpetuation of this pattern inherited from the colonial past has been the role played by the dominant ideology. Formulated in quantitative terms and resolutely discreet on the matter of distribution, the ideology of 'economic growth' put forward by the Ivorian ruling class has been an important tool of obfuscation and an effective instrument of class struggle. Important externally in the attraction of foreign investment, its internal implications are no less crucial. In the face of specific demands such as those made by unions for higher wages or by tenants for proper lodging, the ostensibly impartial and universal ideology of economic growth has served to mask the successful defence of minority interests under the benign and mystificatory guise of a wholly spurious 'public' interest.

But political control in the Ivory Coast has not been confined to the reiteration of ideology. Not only was an effective monopoly established at a fairly early stage; it has been very actively sustained and reproduced ever since independence. Particularly important in this regard are the government's policies over the emergence of a local entrepreneurial group and its policies concerning Ivorization. Government initiatives in the late 1960s and since in this area show the strains resulting from the limited role played by Ivorians in the control of production, without altering the hierarchical and extraverted economic relations on which past growth has depended.

In delaying the emergence of a group of local entrepreneurs, moreover, governmental policies have ensured a specific orientation within local activities. Emergent Ivorian interests have been directed into speculative, administrative and managerial functions rather than into production. Since productive activities are largely pre-empted by the foreign sector, since the mid-1960s new opportunities for Ivorians who can no longer be integrated into the civil service have been created by the government's participation in certain sectors of the economy. The large palm oil projects are an important example of the creation of such openings. The posts created are those of administrators and managers in semi-public, or public companies. To the extent that through intervention in the economy, the Ivorian state can channel the participation of Ivorians in economic activities, local initiatives may be prevented from competing with foreign interests for whom the most productive sectors will be reserved. This pattern serves to perpetuate the colonial orientation of relations on which Ivorian economic growth and local political authority have been based. The dependence of accelerated growth on close relations with the former colonial power requires that the emergence of a local

109

group, which would imply altering the structure of the economy, must be blocked. The use of local economic policy to this end ensures that the capital which accrues in the hands of Ivorians is put to work in the tertiary sector, in real estate, in very small enterprises or exported to foreign banks. The 'non-productive' or expansionist orientation of local capital is assured by a policy of local promotion which reinforces the speculative outlets for local Ivorian private savings and impedes the emergence of a group of local entrepreneurs whose activities would rival already existing interests.[121] Domestically, the activities of a local entrepreneurial group would threaten the economic authority of the Ivorian ruling group and more fundamentally the foreign interests sanctioned by and backing this group.

Consequently, where credit and opportunities for local investment have been made available, it has been above all to those already holding political authority, and for certain kinds of activities. 'The political leaders, who have close ties with foreign capial, monopolize by far the largest part of the meagre funds advanced on credit by the banks to local African businessmen.'[122] Since the emergence of an alternate source of economic authority might well threaten established interests, the local state has become an important instrument of self-preservation:

> It organizes methods of aggression and extortion against local merchants and industrialists who do not have connections and protection within the state apparatus. One does not succeed in business in Africa if one belongs to the opposition or if one opposes the existing order or even if one is simply outside the control of those in power.[123]

Local credit and investment opportunities are consequently made available to the Ivorian *haut fonctionnariats* who possess both an immediate interest in increasing Ivorian participation in the circulation of capital, and an interest in seeing that Ivorian participation is of a kind and in areas which will not alter the existing political and economic structures. The relation between political authority and involvement in local productive activities could hardly be clearer: 'In the Ivory Coast, the local business bureaucracy receives gifts of shares, in their capacity of honorary cadres of the party or the government. By this practice, the attempt is being made to create a *néo-bourgeoisie économique*.'[124] The orientation of such local groups is particularly evident in the nature of the economic activities which they undertake:

> One need only glance at those groups who, in the Ivory Coast . . . constitute what are known today as African businessmen, men set

110

forward as window-dressing among the executives of the Chambers of Commerce. The vast majority of them come from governmental and political circles where, thanks to the widespread system of prebends, they have accumulated the small amount of capital for which they are responsible. For the most part, they are mere façades (*prête-noms*), and generally are active only in the service sector, (transport, handling, consultancy, import, export, processing of export products, management of public corporations, etc.). All their activities amount to little more than a series of compromises and concessions which foreign and metropolitan capital has been ready to allow them.'[125]

The most decisive manner of control over the emergence and activities of a local industrial group is the restrictions on access to and use of local funds. Since the funds which supply the newly created organizations for the promotion of indigenous enterprise depend more or less indirectly on external sources of financing, it is most unlikely that the local activities encouraged would run contrary to external interests. While the funds of the Fonds National d'Investissement are specifically allocated for local reinvestment, its own source of financing, a 10 per cent business tax and 16 per cent real estate tax, depend on the continued presence of foreign investors. The same holds good for the SONAFI and the Fonds de Garantie des Crédits aux Entreprises Ivoiriennes, founded in 1968 to provide guarantees for commercial bank credit to local enterprises whose activities are found compatible with existing interests.[126]

Ivorian monetary, credit and industrial policy has served to prevent the emergence of a local entrepreneurial group. The belated and cramped Ivorian *bourgeoisie d'affaires* which has begun to emerge has been shaped to the requirements of this extraverted pattern of growth. The ruling class in the Ivory Coast has been able to control the timing and manner of the process of Ivorization because of the more general and far-reaching control which it exercises over the organization of any activity which might serve as an alternative base for political opposition. The control exercised by the Ivorian state over trade unions and student organizations has restricted associational freedom.

> Although no formal prohibitions on associational life existed during the 1960s, it was in fact well understood that associational activity outside of ethnic organizations was frowned upon. The absence of the right of assembly in the Ivory Coast adds to the government's ability to make its presence felt whenever it so decides.[127]

Immediately after political independence the PDCI controlled the

111

youth through the Jeunesse RDA de la Côte d'Ivoire (JRDACI) and the trade union movement through the Union Générale des Travailleurs de Côte d'Ivoire.[128] As the decade after independence progressed, several new developments began to be discernible. The regime responded to the reported *coups* of 1962–4 both by a series of short-term repressive measures, and by initiating longer-term projects designed primarily to anticipate difficulties by institutionalizing more adequate structures of political control, communication and participation.[129] The experience of the crisis years revealed that existing party structures were faction-ridden, inadequate to control administration or populace and in no sense an effective network of political communication.

Party reconstruction began immediately; but in the latter half of the decade (1964–9) the regime came to rely increasingly on the development of an effective territorial state bureaucracy for the performance of critical tasks.[130] This reinforcement of the state bureaucracy appears to have reduced certain aspects of the single party's autonomy in relation to the state, redefining for example the spheres of responsibility of the Secretary-General of the party's *sous-sections* and the *sous-préfets*. As the party's Secretary-General carefully affirmed in 1970, the notion of *primauté politique*, 'n'a jamais signifié le droit pour le parti de se substituer à l'Exécutif'.[131] The increasing importance of the state in controlling the distribution of public resources, opportunities and constraints represents less a 'decline of the single party'[132] than a growing fusion of party and government and an increasingly firm subordination of the former to the latter.

On the other hand, unmistakable signs of popular discontent have begun to appear. The president's 'Dialogue' with his people between September and December 1969 is particularly revealing in this context. His meetings with the representatives of the various groups, cadres, unions, employers, the Lebanese, the tenants, the students, the army, clearly illustrate the absence of alternative structures of effective political participation and communication. While it may in the short term have alleviated the mounting pressures which had precipitated it, Dialogue as an instrument of political control could only seek to accommodate political discontent within a system incapable of remedying its roots.

Although it produced a number of changes in the form of political activity, proclaiming the eventual replacement of the *comités ethniques* as the basic unit of the party by *comités de quartiers*, ending the prohibition on non-ethnic associational activity, advancing a number of younger members of the party, the Dialogue produced no major socio-economic or political change. Symbolic participation in mass meetings may serve to reduce political tension; it can scarcely resolve serious socio-economic problems. Given the existing orientation of growth there is no possibility of resolving the serious problems which made the Dialogue necessary. Its occurrence was not, however, without significance. Not only did it plainly reinforce the role and position of the President himself; it also served to consolidate the dominance of the existing ideology by reiterating its premises. Once again it proclaimed that specific demands of the oppressed sectors of the population must be subordinated to what those in power defined as the interests of the many. As the Minister of Labour and Social Affairs stated, Dialogue 'teaches man to accept less because he knows more'.[133] The very occurrence of the Dialogue constituted a recognition that serious socio-economic problems exist in the Ivory Coast; but its significance was more or less exhausted by this recognition. The policies, programmes and modifications announced since go no distance towards resolving the contradictions which made the holding of the Dialogue necessary.[134] Nothing essential has changed. As the report of the Commission on Economic and Financial Policy reiterated at the Sixth Party Congress in 1975 five years after the Dialogue:

> The Commission on Economic and Financial Policy has concluded in this regard, that since that date (1970) the freedom to establish enterprises had been preserved, the country's policy of openness towards the exterior had been broadened, private enterprise had remained the basis of activity in the economy's modern sector, the freedom of transfer had not been impaired in any way, and as a result, *the continuation of the option in favour of economic liberalism* had been guaranteed in a consistent manner by the government throughout the last five years.[135]

The question of Ivorization reveals both the character and the contradictions of the Ivorian post-colonial state with particular clarity. The emergence of a local group which might have acted as a potential basis of opposition to the traditionally-based planter ruling class was delayed until its emergence was compatible with the interests of the dominant class. The number of expatriates continues to increase; and at the same time, as the Commission Report of the Sixth Party Congress expresses it, the results of past efforts to promote Ivorian entrepreneurs have been *très inégaux*.[136]

The planter–politician group who have become the country's ruling class have thus met with considerable success in perpetuating the past pattern of accumulation and distribution of surplus between their foreign partners and themselves. They have succeeded at the same time in transmitting their past scale of privileges and their effective hold on national income. Especially striking is the sheer effectiveness with which political monopoly was established and has been perpetuated since the granting of political independence. For an explanation of the 'durability' of the basis of political power, one must look to the conditions surrounding the emergence of the local ruling group and to the factors which have contributed to their reinforcement. In this regard one may identify several internal factors including the circumstances which led to the creation of an African planter group before independence, the relative homogeneity of this group, their rapid enrichment due in part to the relatively late development of export crops in the Ivory Coast and in part to abundant sources of migrant labour, arable land and colonial investments in infrastructure. These internal factors were reinforced by a series of external conditions. Among the most important of these, metropolitan treaties and institutions, whether related to the commercial, monetary, stabilization or military spheres provided a framework favourable to the perpetuation of a particular orientation to economic growth and consequently the reinforcement of a certain group of local interests.

Because of the conditions surrounding the negotiation of political independence, it soon became apparent that it was the interests of the *bourgeoisie de planteurs* which were to determine the class character of the Ivorian state. Moreover, as the analysis of the post independence period suggests, this ruling group has succeeded in maintaining the class character of the Ivorian state for quite specific reasons. But their success has imposed heavy costs on the rest of the Ivorian population. Economically, it has meant a steady outward flow of profits on foreign investments and of surplus exported through the highly unequal terms of market exchange. Politically, it has meant sharp restrictions on political freedom and on popular participation in public affairs.

Although the Ivorian state has evolved in some respects since independence, these changes have modified the form and not the orientation of its intervention. There has been increasing centralization, an important increase in the size of the state bureaucracy and the formation of numerous public or semi-public corporations. At the same time, the single party has become more clearly the subordinate instrument of state power. Through its intervention, the Ivorian ruling class has successfully reproduced the control over the organization of production and distribution of national wealth on which its power depends. This clearly implies the preservation and transmission of the current hierarchical pattern of surplus distribution although the precise details of this pattern of distribution between the local ruling class and their foreign partners and between different groups within the local population require further research before class analysis can be applied with any rigour.[137]

The external constraints implied by the present pattern of growth and the internal inequalities which it will necessarily continue to imply will compel the state to become increasingly centralized and authoritarian. New strategies of political participation compatible with these trends will have to be evolved, including perhaps the eventual creation of new, centrally controlled arenas of activity in which political opposition is permitted if channelled through a legalized party system with clear ground rules. Under these circumstances, a 'multi-party system' with the material rewards which each party hopes to win, rather than different ideological programmes as the prize of victory would represent 'an ideological mechanism (*appareil idéologique*) which operates to the advantage of the ruling class and the status quo.'[138] The continuation of this pattern of extraverted growth will depend on at least two categories of factors which are themselves dialectically related. The first is the continuation of international market conditions, sources of capital and credit for foreign investment and the capacity of the Ivorian ruling class to organize accumulation and redistribution of surplus value in such a way as to meet the flow of payments to international capitalism. The second is the increasingly important and delicate question of internal political control and legitimacy. In this regard it will be increasingly necessary for the state to intervene to mask, control, marginalize or suppress the opposition which is certain to arise. The increasingly 'political' nature of this intervention may be suggested by the kinds of questions which are likely to assume increasing importance:

(1) Until the present, hostility towards strangers has been largely, although by no means exclusively, directed toward non-Ivorian Africans rather than the more fundamental and deeper cause of inequality, the European community. Under what circumstances may this be expected to change and the small more strategic European minority become the object of hostility?

(2) To what extent and under what conditions might one expect the Ivorian *néo-bourgeoisie d'affaires*, whose emergence is so clearly linked to state intervention in the economic sector, to become more nationalist and challenge the past policies of 'openness'?

(3) To what extent can the state bureaucracy use its position to gain access to private property or to other means of production through government contracts, land speculation, and governmental loans or credit etc.?

(4) To what extent is the increasingly important 'parasitic' capital which the state bureaucracy amasses being transformed through private investment into productive capital thus creating a new identity of interests compatible or in conflict with those which existed previously?

(5) With the worsening of the unemployment situation and the increas-

ing social inequalities, under what circumstances might one expect a growing number of artisans and members of the petty bourgeoisie to be brought into opposition to the ruling class and hence allied more closely with the growing number of unemployed and unhoused?

(6) Will external economic conditions permit the Ivorian ruling class to continue to use the state apparatus to channel, neutralize and control eventual opposition and so preclude the creation of political opposition seeking to alter past patterns of growth and consequently, the basis of power of the present ruling class?

The continuing 'success' of the Ivorian ruling class will depend on its capacity to meet and to overcome the internal problems raised by questions such as these – questions whose emergence is intimately related to and in fact conditioned by the evolution of factors external to the Ivory Coast.

5

Liberia

CHRISTOPHER CLAPHAM

The Republic of Liberia is almost the smallest of West African states, its population of a million and a half in 1973 being exceeded by every state in the region save only The Gambia.[1] Its insignificant size, coupled with its peculiar heritage as the region's only non-colonial state, sometimes give it the appearance of being insulated from its neighbours in an uneventful stability of its own. Certainly, the more dramatic events of recent West African history have passed it by. Yet the Republic of Liberia has been subject to many of the same pressures as its fellows, both externally and domestically, and the way in which it has managed them has more than a merely idiosyncratic interest.

The most salient features of the Liberian experience over the last twenty or thirty years have been political stability and economic growth. The first of these is sometimes exaggerated by a mistaken impression of instability in the ex-colonial states: of the eight states of the West African littoral from Mauretania to the Ivory Coast, only one – Sierra Leone – has had a government overthrown by violence since independence. Even so, the Liberian record is impressive. The same party, the True Whig Party, has held office continuously since 1877, its tenure unbroken by any coup or extra-constitutional succession, a record equalled by no other political party anywhere in the world. Its capacity to manage succession to high office was most recently exemplified by Vice-President Tolbert's orderly takeover on President Tubman's death in 1971. Of course, political stability may be only a negative virtue – some would claim, not a virtue at all – but if we are looking at the role of the state, then the capacity of those who control the instruments of state power to maintain themselves in office does provide some indication of the effectiveness in its setting of the state itself.

Economic growth has been fairly continuous. Gross domestic per capita income, at $288 in 1973, was the second highest in West Africa, a little higher than Ghana but appreciably lower than the Ivory Coast, and has risen steadily over the previous twenty years.[2] This figure tells one nothing about the distribution of income, which is unlikely to be any more equal in Liberia than in other West African states, nor does it show the means by which the economy has grown or the extent to which this growth can be maintained. But it does indicate the level of resources on which the state can draw, and hence its capacity to meet the demands made on it.

To account for the Liberian state's performance, it is necessary to look a bit more closely at the state structure itself. This was formed at much the same time, in much the same way, and for much the same purposes as the equivalent colonial structures in, say, Senegal, Sierra Leone or Ghana. In each case, the impetus for state formation was entirely external. Settlements were founded at some coastal anchorage, in Liberia from 1822, which for most of the nineteenth century were content to maintain themselves as trading posts with occasional pacificatory forays into the interior. Only in the late nineteenth and early twentieth centuries did these settlements make good their vaguely articulated claims to the hinterland by imposing their rule on the peoples of the interior and establishing some kind of permanent administrative apparatus. The means by which the Liberians did this, the resistance which they encountered, and the centralized hierarchies which they set up, were not essentially different from their British or French equivalents, even though there were variations in the honesty or efficiency of the administrators and the legitimizing myths on which they called; Manifest Destiny replaced indirect rule or the civilizing mission. The state structure was then used, in Liberia as elsewhere, to pacify the interior and extend the trade in primary products which was channelled through the coastal capital. As elsewhere, foreign companies were introduced to intensify this process, and in so doing to create a source of government income. In Liberia the major, and until after the Second World War almost the only, such company was the Firestone Rubber Company which from 1926 established rubber plantations to meet the American demand for car tyres. Since the war, rubber has been overtaken by iron ore as the major source of foreign investment and government income, and Firestone has been supplemented by a host of other corporations. The state has extended its functions in fields such as education and local administration, but in this too it has paralleled its ex-colonial neighbours.

Where the Liberian state differs from its fellows is not so much in what it does, as in who does it. Even though its origins were no less external than those of the colonial territories, since it was set up and for a while maintained by American money and influence, it was established for repatriated black settlers from the Americas and, after independence in 1847, governed by them as well. These settlers came to form a ruling elite

– the term is not so vacuous in Liberia's case as in most of the contexts in which it is used – which achieved a high degree of institutionalization, and in at least certain respects a comparatively high degree of effectiveness. Whereas the inescapable alienness of the colonial regimes provoked in time an inevitable nationalist reaction, the Liberian state was able, partially at least, to legitimize itself through a formula of common African identity between rulers and ruled which allowed some assimilation of indigenous Africans into the governing community. As a settler regime, moreover, it was less inhibited than the colonial governments in restraining, as repressively as the occasion required, any systematic politicization of anti-government sentiments.

Looked at in this light, the Liberian state may be seen to have established, from the start, a brokerage role between indigenous and external pressures not altogether different from that which many ex-colonial regimes have come to occupy as the legacy of the nationalist movements has died away. The state is maintained on the one hand by its capacity to tax and regulate the flow of goods to and from the international economy, on the other by its ability to retain the obedience of its subjects. The principal difference from its ex-colonial neighbours is that the political formula underlying the regime continues to be that of association with an immigrant core, rather than that of a coalition (on varying terms) between the indigenous peoples inhabiting the territory left within the colonial boundaries. This formula, incorporating established identities, institutions, and rules of political action, provides in the short term a surer recipe for political stability than the combination of inter-group bargaining and personal management which has to serve in states without an established core, but is subject to obvious dangers should association with the centre become unacceptable for any substantial section of the political community. The questions of how and why the Liberian state has performed over the last twenty years or so, and of how it may be expected to perform in the future, then resolve themselves into three further questions. How has the central elite maintained itself and regulated political competition? How, and with what success, has it involved the remaining people of Liberia in the political process, and coped with the problems arising from social and economic change? And how have the economic resources been produced and distributed to maintain the political structure? The remainder of this chapter will discuss each in turn.

THE CORE

No discussion of the Liberian state can get very far without assessing the position of the Americo-Liberian community: the descendants of the settlers from the United States and elsewhere who landed on the coast from 1822 onwards, established an independent state in 1847, and have controlled it ever since. Despite attempts to play down the name and the extent of Americo-Liberian dominance in recent years, and despite a certain blurring of the distinction between immigrant and indigenous communities due to intermarriage and cultural assimilation, the fact remains that the majority of the most important politicians in Liberia are of immigrant descent, and, equally important, that the government as a whole operates through institutions created and constraints set by the immigrant community. The two presidents who have held office over the last thirty years, William V. S. Tubman and William R. Tolbert, have had no trace of indigenous blood; nor have their vice-presidents. In the Tubman cabinets of 1967 and 1968, 75 per cent of ministers belonged to the immigrant group, though one or two of these were of mixed descent; by 1973, when Tolbert was president, the proportion had dropped to 58 per cent.[3]

They are an astonishingly small group. In the 1962 census, only 6,452 Liberian citizens out of just under a million did not claim any tribal affiliation, and can thus be reckoned as Americo-Liberian, well under one per cent of the total population.[4] It is not surprising, therefore, that they are closely linked. A high proportion of senior politicians can be brought together in a single genealogical chart, through a complex network of family relationships and intermarriages;[5] and in addition to their family and political contacts, members of the immigrant core are also constantly associated with one another through churches, business associations, and clubs and societies, the most famous and important of which is undoubtedly the Grand Lodge of Freemasons. Politics is a highly important part of the group's activities. It is the major source of wealth, employment and status, and the source also therefore of numerous factional divisions within the immigrant core. But the group's size and coherence, and the fact that it shares values and activities outside the political sphere, enable it to contain political rivalries within reasonable bounds. Only once during the last thirty years has any faction within the core resorted to violence in order to try to achieve political goals, when an attempt was made to assassinate Tubman in 1955.[6]

Much of the recruitment process within the core can be described simply as jobbery, an eighteenth-century English term entirely appropriate to the Liberian political scene. Members of leading families easily acquire the educational skills which are a prerequisite for high office, and possess the contacts through which to work their way up inside the governing community. All the usual mechanisms for advancement within a well-institutionalized political community – reasonable diligence, a

120

decent respect for social norms, a prudent attachment to leading men already well-placed in the system – apply also in Liberia. So, President Tubman's son Shad Tubman Jr becomes senator for Maryland County. President Tolbert's brother Stephen becomes Minister of Finance. Stephen Tolbert's legal adviser Cecil Dennis becomes Minister of Foreign Affairs. Cecil Dennis' cousin William Dennis becomes Minister of Commerce. When Stephen Tolbert is killed in an air crash, his place is taken by Deputy Minister of Finance Edwin Williams, son of the Defence Minister, Allen Williams. It is all quite an intimate affair.

Nonetheless, the immigrant community has succeeded in maintaining sources of initiative and political skill which have prevented it from degenerating simply into a conservative and inward-looking oligarchy. The major source of initiative is the presidency, which in the hands both of Tubman and of Tolbert has proved a very effective instrument for adaptive changes which have helped to maintain the system while leaving its fundamentals unaltered. Tubman was to some extent an outsider, in that he came from Harper, capital of Maryland County on the Ivory Coast border, rather than from the main political dynasties established in Monrovia. He constantly remained aware of the need to retain sources of support outside the central elite, and in particular did a great deal to extend political linkages beyond the Americo-Liberian community. Tolbert was selected by Tubman as his understudy largely, it used to be said before Tubman's death, because he was too venal and unpopular ever to present any challenge to his principal. Even so, he blossomed out once he became president himself, and without doing anything to jeopardize the structure which he inherited, reformed some of its less popular features and extended participation in the hinterland.

Even in the Tubman years, though – and he was by far the most dominant president Liberia has ever had – political leadership was to some extent dispersed. Other figures within the established hierarchy possessed authority which could be used to sustain and adapt the system after Tubman's death. The representative system is one such source of authority. Each of the nine counties into which Liberia is divided provides two senators and a varying number of representatives, who are effectively co-opted through the TWP machine, but who are at the same time generally expected to have some standing within their local community. Senior senators such as Charles B. Sherman in Grand Cape Mount County or James E. Greene, later vice-president, in Sinoe County, become local bosses with established positions from which the president cannot easily remove them. Something of the same standing in national politics is enjoyed by men who, though their posts are formally at the president's disposal, are so well entrenched in the governing community

121

that they too have to be accepted. The classic example is McKinley DeShield, Minister of Posts and National Chairman of the TWP, who played a critical role in the brief hiatus between Tubman's sudden death and Tolbert's accession. The system also maintains itself through the recruitment of young politicians into senior posts: the ministers of Finance, Information and Commerce are all in their early thirties, those of Foreign Affairs, Public Works, Health, and Mines in their early forties. The establishment has not hardened into a gerontocracy.

THE PERIPHERY

The Liberian state's capacity to maintain its hold over the minuscule Americo-Liberian community is not particularly surprising. It would have had to have been very badly managed to do otherwise. What is more important, and more surprising, is its capacity so far to maintain a hold over that 99 per cent of the population which does not enjoy privileged access to political power, and is not involved to any great extent in the web of social institutions which give coherence to the core community. Perhaps the first point to emphasize is that this is made possible to a large extent by simple geographical conditions which do not obtain in most other coastal West African states. The indigenous population of Liberia is small and scattered over the territory at an average density estimated in 1973 at fifteen per km. sq. This compares with figures of thirty-seven for Sierra Leone, forty-four for Ghana, sixty-five for Nigeria.[7] It is also composed of many different peoples, for the most part formed into very small political units, who were forced into the forest by their inability to compete with stronger groups in the western Sahel. There is no equivalent, therefore, to the powerful indigenous polities of, say, Nigeria, Ghana or Senegal. Had there been, then not only would the task of the Liberian state have been much more difficult, but it might well have proved impossible to establish such a state in the first place, in the absence of the powerful military support available to the direct colonial regimes.

Like its colonial equivalents, the Liberian state imposed itself on the hinterland by force, and to some extent maintains itself in the same way. But it is important to recognize that continued effective control would be impossible without the existence of a political formula which treats all Liberians as formally equal, and which allows the development of political mechanisms which help to integrate the periphery into the state structure and reduce the need for any overt use of force to very small proportions. Liberia is not a sort of black Rhodesia.

These mechanisms take several forms. Assimilation of outsiders into Americo-Liberian society is one of them, though its importance is easily exaggerated. There is a certain amount of intermarriage – Americo-Liberians selecting wives or concubines from the indigenous population, ambitious hinterlanders marrying up into the elite – and a well established tradition of adopting country boys into coastal families, but the process as a whole is too leisurely and on too small a scale to bridge the gap. However, some assimilation is implicit in the much more widespread mechanism of simply recruiting hinterlanders to government posts, since this involves some acceptance of coastal standards of social and political behaviour, incorporation into the patronage-dominated bureaucracy, and deference to the leaders of the political community, especially the president. Tubman started the practice of appointing a few hinterlanders to ministerial positions and Tolbert has extended it, even though few of the appointees are men of substantial political weight.

More generally, bureaucratic expansion serves largely as a mechanism for involving the indigenous peoples in government, since they account for the great majority of those seeking employment, including most of the two or three hundred who graduate annually from Liberia's three university-level institutions.[8] I can find no consistent series of figures for the government payroll, but Lowenkopf suggests an annual 10 per cent growth during the 1960s, and quotes government figures of 14,000 employees in 1967 (or 20,000 with the police and armed services), and 18,000 in 1969.[9] Other government figures give a total of nearly 24,000 in June 1971, followed by a pronounced cut to 17,000 after Tolbert's accession, rising to nearly 19,000 by the end of 1972.[10] Personnel and other services accounted for $47.7m in 1974 and a projected $60.8m in 1975, 50 per cent and 52 per cent of government spending respectively.[11] This proportion has been fairly constant over the last ten years, during which time government revenues have trebled.[12]

A particularly intriguing outlet for patronage purposes is the provincial administration. The coastal Liberian counties, controlled by Americo-Liberian settlers, have traditionally enjoyed a fair amount of autonomy in that by far the greatest number of local government officials, including the local representatives of central government agencies, have been selected from local residents. The convention of senatorial courtesy, taken over from American practice, has strengthened this tradition. In 1963–4, the county system of administration was extended to the hinterland provinces, hitherto governed by provincial and district commissioners of coastal origin directly responsible to the department of the interior in Monrovia. The result was a rapid increase in the degree of local self-government, and correspondingly in the amount of administrative patronage, available in the hinterland. The superintendents, heads of the county administrations, have almost all been natives of their counties and have enjoyed considerable local initiative, though always subject to instant replacement if they lost the president's support. Lower down, the proportion of local men depends on how many qualified individuals are available. In Lofa County, in north-east Liberia on the Sierra Leone and Guinean borders, all but one of the forty local officials whom I was able to identify in October 1973 were natives of the county. In Bong County in central Liberia, with a much shorter history of local secondary education, the proportion of natives was only 40 per cent, the deficit being mostly made up by educated tribal men from the coastal counties.[13] The chiefs, who are government officials at the lowest administrative level, have small salaries but are also well placed to acquire land and services from the local population.[14] Hence the disadvantaged position of tribal Liberians in central government has to some extent been compensated by giving them protected posts in local administration.

Another important channel for indirect political participation is the extension into the hinterland of the patronage networks of coastal politicians. To some extent, this is an offshoot of the common practice of acquiring hinterland 'farms' or estates, which combine the functions of commercial plantations and leisured weekend retreats. Tubman had such a farm at Totota in Bong County and Tolbert has one at Bellefanai on the Guinea border. Each of these has served as a centre for hearing petitions, distributing benefits, and building up a useful network of protégés and hangers-on. Other politicians – county superintendents, senators, representatives – are expected to maintain similar networks in their regional centres of influence. Superintendents are likely to be dismissed should 'troubles' arise in their counties which they are unable to control, and legislators need to have local sources of support which are kept up by providing services for local petitioners. Both Tubman and Tolbert have maintained local linkages by constantly travelling round the country to receive petitions and discipline officials. The system is certainly elitist and also rather haphazardly organized, but it is not closed. For most Liberians, and particularly for those who through status in local society, wealth or education have acquired interests which the government needs to take into account, some channel exists through which these interests can be expressed, and these channels as a whole have so far proved capable of meeting the demands made on them. The political structure of the core has thus extended its scope to form an alliance of interest with those hinterland elements which would otherwise be best placed to oppose it.

What these channels do not do – and what in fact they are specifically prevented from doing – is mobilize the interests and identities of local communities. Where Liberia most strikingly differs from other West

African states is in the complete absence of that period of rapid politi-cization – 'the time when politics came' as it has been called in Ghana – during which nationalist or regionalist politicians activated local interests and identities in order to provide themselves with a support base to use in a contest for central government power, against one another or the colonial regime. There has been no 'Green Uprising'.[15] This political mobilization is so much a part of the common experience of the region that a political society which has not undergone it is instantly anomalous. One area where its absence makes itself felt, for example, is the politics of tribe. Liberians – 99.4 per cent of them anyhow – belong to 'tribes', and few of them have any difficulty in identifying to which particular tribe they or their associates belong. But this has not been a source of political identity, because there has been practically nothing, politically speaking, that one could do with it. Whether this is to be seen as a benefit or a loss depends partly on a straightforward value judgement on the respective merits of order and representation, rather more on whether Liberian state has simply postponed the inevitable moment, or whether it has devised enduring mechanisms which will render the politics of tribe unnecessary. That question is still unanswered.

The non-mobilization of hinterland identities is clearly a condition for the maintenance of the regime. Were Liberian politics to be polarized into a confrontation between the indigenous and immigrant com-munities, then a hinterland based government would inevitably take over in one way or another, displacing as it did so the existing core-centred institutions. The regime therefore has a strong and obvious interest in preventing any such mobilization. But the use of force to do this, beyond a localized and limited level, is bound to be self-defeating, partly because it would increase the consciousness of differentiation, and thus intensify a numerically unequal confrontation, and partly because the coercive resources at the government's disposal would in such circumstances be unreliable. The Liberian armed forces, even up to the highest ranks, are heavily composed of tribal men. In 1973, two of the three generals on the active list were Lomas from Lofa County, and several of the colonels were Kru, a tribal group with some history of opposition to the central govern-ment. Americo-Liberians are also well represented in the officer corps, but scarcely, if at all, in the ranks. The government has therefore had to keep an eye open for any sign of hinterland mobilization, and then nip it in the bud before it got out of hand. From time to time some alleged plot breaks the surface, usually involving hinterland army officers, which shows this process at work. In 1963, an army colonel of tribal origin was reported to have said that 'if 250 Togolese soldiers could kill President Olympio and overthrow his government, an army of 5,000 in Liberia can do wonders'.[16] He swiftly found himself in jail. Ten years later, an assistant minister of defence and two lieutenant-colonels were imprisoned for plotting to assassinate the president. Civilian politicians are prevented from building up sources of hinterland support which appear to threaten the government; the clearest case is that of Henry Fahnbulleh, an ostensibly assimilated Vai arrested in 1968 for attempting to mobilize tribal opinion against the government, allegedly with communist aid solicited when he was Liberian ambassador in Nairobi. He spent four years in jail, but was released by Tolbert, and in 1976 was appointed superintendent of his home county, Grand Cape Mount: a striking case of the way in which the regime attempts to incorporate potential opponents.[17] Others, including several of the hinterland superintendents who occupy an especially sensitive linkage role between government and indigenous population, have been abruptly dismissed. But these are little more than sporadic incidents. Most political actors understand the limitations imposed by the regime, and work within them. There is little sign of organized challenge to it.

PRODUCTION AND REWARDS

One critical element in the Liberian state's performance has been its capacity to generate and distribute enough wealth to meet the expectations made on it. Here, as in the state's dealings with the indigenous peoples, happy geographical accident has come to its aid. Since resource stocks are high in relation to population, there is a comparatively large amount available to be handed out. Liberia lies entirely within the forest belt, and since it is sparsely inhabited, large stands of timber exist to be exploited wherever roads can be built to take them out. The forest land can be used to grow a large variety of cash crops, the chief one being rubber. In addition, there are considerable deposits of iron ore, some of them, especially those on the Guinea border, of exceptionally high purity.

However, it is equally important that since the economy has grown under the guidance of an established indigenous regime, it has been used to support that regime in a far more closely-knit fashion than in territories where economic growth took place under the aegis of the colonial power. In the ex-colonial states, certainly, the new governments have not been slow to seize control of economic resources and use them in support of the existing political structure, the use of oil revenues in Nigeria being perhaps the classic example; but none of them have had the time, and few of them the domestic political stability, to do it as systematically as the Liberians.

Most of the wealth is actually produced by international corporations. Firestone's rubber plantations are the best known in the outside world, but their contribution to exports and national income has long been overtaken by the iron ore companies, notably Lamco, a Swedish–American group, and Bong Mining Company, a West German consortium. In addition, there are a host of minor concessions attracted to Liberia by the Open Door Policy for foreign investment, which is effectively underwritten by the use of the US dollar as the national currency. The iron ore companies have 50/50 profit-sharing agreements with the government, which produced 21 per cent of the total government revenues in 1967, falling to 14 per cent by 1974. The growth of the concessions sector as a whole has produced an astonishing increase in government revenues, from $3.9m in 1950 to $32.4m in 1960, $46.7m in 1966, $66.5m in 1970, and $97.6m in 1974.[18]

These revenues, of course, finance the expansion in government employment through which the new hinterland county administrations have been created. In a marginally less direct way, they also finance the private business enterprises which are run by members of the elite. Liberia is exceptional in the extent to which government employees openly and legitimately supplement their salaries through private commercial ventures. A great many of them, perhaps the majority, have some alternative source of income. For local government officials, this is usually something fairly modest, such as a rice farm or a small rubber plantation. For ministers in the central government, it is usually something much more ambitious, which combines a modicum of productive activity with the ability to use one's government position to extract profits from the government itself, foreign traders or companies, or the public. There are any number of ways of going about it: the former Secretary of Defence who ran a tailoring business supplying uniforms to the army; the police chief who owns a fleet of taxis; the ministerial law firms which accept retainers from foreign companies to smooth their relations with the government; the private landowners who lease out buildings for government offices, including for instance Presidents Tubman and Tolbert. This all comes under the heading of legitimate trade, and is openly conducted. To some extent, opportunities are thus gathered into Liberian hands which elsewhere would be enjoyed by foreign entrepreneurs; agencies for imported goods handled by the Mesurado Group (owned by President Tolbert's late brother and Minister of Finance) would in Sierra Leone or the Ivory Coast be dealt with by UAC or CFAO. To some extent also productive opportunities are created which would otherwise be lost, especially in agriculture. For the most part, however, the economic activities of the elite are parasitic on government.

The impact of the state structure on the economic opportunities open to other Liberians is much more difficult to assess. Only about 45,000 Liberians, some 12 per cent of the adult male population, were in wage employment in 1971, about half of them in plantation agriculture.[19] The remainder of the population consists of a sizeable proportion of urban non-wage earners (about a third of the adult male population was classed as urban in 1971) and of subsistence or cash crop farmers. Numerous publications refer to the exploitation of peasants by government agents, through land alienation, involuntary labour, or simple confiscation of crops, but the extent of these practices on the ground is hard to pin down. To some degree, the opportunities to be gained from trade, government or the big companies lessen the need for members of the elite to supplement their incomes by direct exploitation of the peasantry, and complaints in this line are mostly directed against chiefs, local government officials and soldiers who miss out on the big chances. And in one area where quantitative comparison is possible, the prices paid to peasants for cash crops such as coffee and palm kernels by the government buying monopoly are on the whole higher than in Sierra Leone, and much higher than in Guinea.[20] I find it impossible to say, therefore, whether Liberian peasants are better or worse off than their equivalents in neighbouring states.

The state itself takes very little part in directly running economic enterprises, and even the Produce Marketing Corporation is managed not by the government itself but by a Danish company which shares its profits with the government. There is therefore little of the inefficient and corrupt state business sector found in many West African states, its functions in converting political influence into private wealth being performed by the doubtless equally corrupt, but very possibly less inefficient, concerns of individual politicians. In other respects, however, the Liberians have been quick enough to adopt indigenization measures pioneered by more radical African states. Concession agreements with iron ore producers have been revised to give the Liberian government a larger return – though its returns per ton of ore were in any case better than the Sierra Leone government received from the inefficient and now defunct Delco mine at Marampa.[21] Legislation for the Liberianization of trading opportunities has been seized on by members of the elite as a chance to establish themselves as sleeping partners in Lebanese-run businesses. President Tolbert has warned foreign companies to make more jobs available to Liberians, and has directed criticisms against some of them, the most popular target being Firestone. But the essential productive operations which foreign traders and companies carry on have not been disturbed, and the openness of

128

the economy is ensured by retaining the US dollar as Liberian currency.

CONCLUSION

Compared with most West African states, Liberia has quite a simple political system, which has operated in quite a consistent way. It has not been complicated by the rise and fall of political parties, overt ethnic rivalries, military coups, rapidly changing governing groups, or switches in economic policy. The main features of its performance can be summarized and accounted for fairly simply and briefly.

Over the last thirty years, Liberia has undergone a vast expansion in most of the indices customarily associated with 'modernization': in literacy and education, communications networks, monetarization of the economy, the proportion of the population in wage employment, government services, even political participation. The rate of growth in GDP, which was the highest in the world during the 1950s, slowed but was still maintained during the 1960s and the first half of the 1970s. These changes were not accompanied by any radical change in the political structure, which maintained itself subject only to a few alleged plots, none of which appeared on the face of it to present any substantial danger.

The first reason for this stability can be seen in the nature of the political institutions themselves, and their relationship with the social structure. These institutions, whatever their formal imitation of United States models, developed from the existing structure of Americo-Liberian society and were well adapted to the closely-knit patronage system through which it operated, as well as to the existence within the community of diverse centres of influence. They were not simply introduced from outside in pursuit of ends, and subject to distributions of effective influence, which ceased to be relevant the moment the colonial powers withdrew.

Secondly, those who managed the system showed considerable wisdom and skill in adapting it to the changed conditions created by social and economic modernization during the 1950s and 1960s. They were able to identify and incorporate within the state structure potentially rival sources of power, and especially those created by the economic development of the hinterland, the accession of hinterlanders to western education, and the desire for political rewards of those who enjoyed positions of local authority. These were given access to the political system by establishing their own centres of influence in the new hinterland county administrations, recruiting a number of individuals to high central government office, extending central patronage networks to the periphery,

129

and providing opportunities for the acquisition of personal wealth. At the same time, they were inhibited from challenging the regime by the maintenance of strict boundaries of permissible political action, beyond which it was hazardous to step. Thus, the Liberian government weathered the period of rapidly expanding political participation among its neighbours, and survived to an era in which authoritarian central government was once more the norm, and comparisons with conditions beyond the frontiers provided no very alluring alternative to the *status quo*. This process was aided but by no means ensured by fragmentation of Liberia's indigenous population into numerous small groups lacking powerful traditional institutions.

Thirdly, the system has been able to generate, in close association with foreign extractive industries, the very rapid expansion in revenues which this strategy required. These revenues have made it possible to increase the wealth of the elite while at the same time extending government employment. Again, circumstances were favourable, especially in the discovery and exploitation of iron ore deposits which made it possible to reduce the degree of direct elite extraction from the agricultural sector; but again, these circumstances were aided by comparatively skilful management. An explicitly capitalist ideology encouraged a display of uninhibited venality among those in a position to make money, but it is not clear that the process is qualitatively different, except perhaps in its efficiency, from the mechanisms used more furtively and under other ideological guises elsewhere.

So much for the past. What of the promise? The underlying weakness of the Liberian state structure is that, for long into the future, it must continue to depend on a political formula which may well become unacceptable, and on a distribution of rewards which it may well be unable to maintain. The political formula by which the Americo-Liberians presented themselves as Africans enabled them to head off a hinterland nationalist movement by encouraging the incorporation into the governing structure of potential leaders of the tribal people who might otherwise have opposed them. At the same time, it enabled the regime to perform its brokerage role vis-à-vis the international economy more effectively than those governments which have felt obliged to make gestures to their domestic supporters in the form of nationalist rhetoric and restrictions on foreign businesses. If, as is sometimes claimed, this formula had led to the replacement of an essentially ethnic-based Americo-Liberian government by an essentially class-based bourgeois one, then the Liberian state would probably be safe in something close to its present form for many years to come. In fact what has happened is that elements outside the historic core have been associated with the regime and allowed to acquire both rewards and critical positions in it, without at the same time being fully merged in the governing structure. The potential leadership for an opposition movement thus continues to be available in the existence of hinterlanders who have attained positions essential to the state, but who feel their promotion, especially to the topmost posts in government, to be blocked by the presence of the existing elite. These could rationalize and gain support for their challenge to the system either on ethnic (immigrant/indigene) or on ideological (capitalist/socialist) grounds, and in either case might reckon on initial backing from any section of the society which felt itself to be comparatively disadvantaged by the present distribution of power. The most obvious location for such a challenge is in the armed forces, which are quite large enough to launch a coup, and heavily composed of hinterlanders; but analogous though less strategically placed centres of potential opposition exist in the provincial administration and the educational system. These are the classic dangers to a modernizing oligarchy. In order for them to be overcome, much will depend not only on the skills of the elite but also on the economy, since a crisis could most easily be provoked by a failure to keep rewards more or less in line with expectations. The Liberian economy does not face such immediate failures in its mineral reserves as, say, that of Sierra Leone, and forest land remains in plentiful supply. But it would be optimistic to assume that the economy can continue to expand indefinitely at the rate required, particularly since the heavy external dependence on which Liberian prosperity has been built leaves it vulnerable to changes in the outside world. Whereas 'failure and promise' is the title of this volume, 'success and danger' might be a more appropriate verdict on the recent Liberian experience.

6

Nigeria

GAVIN WILLIAMS and TERISA TURNER

POLITICS AND POLITICAL ECONOMY

'Politics is a dirty business', as the *Concise Oxford Dictionary*[1] reminds us. It is also 'the science and art of government'. In its first aspect, politics is a particular, and discreditable activity, whose virtue is to be 'scheming, crafty', and which turns on the private advantage of its practitioners. In its second aspect, politics is concerned with the administration of the common affairs of the public, a matter of universal rather than particular concern, whose virtue is to be 'judicious, expedient' in both defining and promoting the common good. The contradiction between private interests and the public interest gives rise to, but is not resolved by, the state.[2] The state is required both to mediate among competing interests, and to reconcile or subordinate them to the wider requirements of the public interest.

Politics thus has two related dimensions, the competitive pursuit of private interests, and the determination of public policy. But the nature of both private and public interests is defined by class relations. Classes are groups which arise out the division of labour in society. They are defined by their place in the process of production, their access to markets for commodities, including labour power, and their relation to the state. Where producers have access to their own means of production, surplus expropriation takes place through control of market and state relations. Class relations link together different groups within societies, and between societies.

Classes may be stabilized into accepted relations of domination and subordination, or organized into relations of patronage and clientage. Class relations may be contested, both in their particular forms, and in general. Both stabilization and contestation require references to values to justify claims and inspire actions. Thus politics comes to be a contest over values, and not simply over interests.

132

Thus any study of politics must examine:
(a) the allocation of scarce resources;
(b) the determination of public policy; and
(c) the relations and conflict among classes.
These require an examination of production, market and state relations, and the ideologies through which these are defined, defended and challenged. Politics cannot be studied separately from political economy.[3]

POLITICS AS THE ALLOCATION OF SCARCE RESOURCES

In Nigeria today resources are neither socially allocated among alternative common ends nor distributed through an unfettered market mechanism. They are allocated both to private and to public ends. This process of allocation takes place through the state and its several agencies, by the profit-seeking activities of corporations and businessmen, and in paying for the commodities produced by peasants and craftsmen, and for the labour-power of workers. As Weber[4] points out, profit-making does not only take the form of organizing productive enterprises or the purchase and sale of goods in competitive markets. Profits may be acquired by speculating in money, in commodities and in the financing of enterprises and political activities, by acquiring booty, by the imposition of compulsory labour, by trade monopolies and taxes, and by what Weber delicately calls 'opportunities for profit opened up by unusual transactions with political bodies'. Even the production or the marketing of commodities requires the favour and co-operation of agencies of the state, and monopolistic firms, whose substantive powers and purposes undermine the formal rationality of market competition and impersonal bureaucratic rules. Access to resources, including opportunities for profit-making, thus requires the favour of those who control the resources, or who control the private and public institutions which allocate them. Consequently, politics turns, as the drafters of the current Nigerian constitutional proposals remind us,[5] on gaining the 'opportunity to acquire wealth and prestige, to be able to distribute benefits in the form of jobs, contracts, scholarships, and gifts of money and so on to one's relatives and political allies'.

Politics thus comes to be the process of gaining control of public resources for the pursuit of private ends. This sort of politics can only take place within an appropriate framework. In Nigeria since the Second World War, several items constituted this framework. Nigeria continued to depend on foreign markets for the export of primary products, and on foreign imports of manufactured, intermediate and capital goods. The state gained control and influence over a significant share of strategic

133

resources. A category of politicians and state functionaries, later joined by military commanders, was established, with the exclusive claim to allocate state resources. Specific constituencies were delineated, through which the resources were allocated, and to which politicians looked for loyalty and support in return for such rewards.

The competition for access to resources in Nigeria has taken place predominantly between ethnically-defined constituencies. These constituencies were not simply given, but are defined in the process of political competition itself. Ethnic identities do not present themselves ready-made, determining in advance the lines of political conflict. They are socially constructed in relation to the exigencies of specific historical situations. Differences and similarities of language, custom, religion and historical experience are used selectively to define and legitimate particular claims to solidarity and exclusion. These constructed identities may use the language of kinship. But they are founded not on the primordial ties of close kin, but on solidarities based variously on communities under a common political authority and with corporate claims to land, or on a common language or a common religion. These criteria are themselves ambiguous and may cut across one another. The definition of appropriate solidarities and the choice of political alliances is made according to calculations of relative advantage and political judgement. The conquest of Nigerian peoples led to the definition of provincial and divisional boundaries, based in part on pre-colonial polities, as modified and amalgamated to meet colonial administrative requirements. These boundaries defined the areas for which a distinctive status and administration would later be claimed, and claims for fair treatment in the allocation of funds and opportunities would in due course be made.

To maintain the system of allocation, the following conditions must be met. Formal and informal rules must be defined, which govern competition among politicians and other claimants to resources and opportunities. Political alliances must be formed which incorporate powerful contending interests, and sustain an adequate share of rewards to these, while enforcing the exclusion of other interests. Popular tolerance of the system of appropriating and allocating rewards must be secured, by coercion and by the spread of opportunities and rewards among constituents.

POLITICS AS THE DETERMINATION OF PUBLIC POLICY

The regulation of conflicts among contending private interests requires a state which is capable of enforcing decisions and legitimating its authority over various interests. State power which is seen consistently to favour

134

particular interests at the expense of others not only forfeits the support of the excluded interests but also undermines the legitimacy of its own claims to authority. The state comes to depend only on force and on those who control the instruments of coercion.

The state itself organizes and engages in economic activity. It is responsible, directly or indirectly, for the allocation of strategic opportunities and resources. Therefore, the state itself becomes an arena for political conflict, rather than an institution capable of standing above and mediating such conflict. State authority is constrained, in principle, by impersonal rules which do not discriminate formally among competing interests. But state institutions themselves have particular interests which conflict with those of other public and private bodies. And different state agencies form links with private interests with which they are involved in their day-to-day business activities. Thus conflicts among private interests come to be repeated in, or even to penetrate and engulf, state institutions.

There is a basic contradiction within the state. On the one hand, the state and its agencies are required to regulate conflict among contending interests. On the other hand, the state serves as the instrument of these contending interests. As the introduction to the Nigerian draft constitution declares[6]: 'Such is the pre-occupation with power and its material benefits that political ideals as to how society can be organized and ruled to the best advantage of all hardly enter into the calculation.'

There is a need for political ideals, embodying public goals and values, which are above politics and define the framework within which political conflict is to take place. The drafting committee sought to embody such ideals in the Nigerian draft constitution.[7] They are all the more necessary in Nigeria 'because of the heterogeneity of the society, the increasing gap between the rich and poor, the growing cleavage between the social groupings, all of which combine to confuse the nation and bedevil the march to orderly progress'.

This reconciliation of the interests of 'rich and poor' requires a common 'collective conscience',[8] embodied in a universal value transcending particular interests. The draft constitution recognizes the need to define such a universal goal:[9] 'What do we really want for the generality of Nigerians in the foreseeable future? The answer must surely be that we seek to enhance the welfare of the individual through providing better educational facilities, housing, health facilities, more jobs and a rising standard of living for the people as a whole'.

This is to take place within the framework of Nigeria's established 'ideology, namely, Mixed Economy'.[10] By assuming that growth precedes distribution,[11] they justify inequality as a means to the universal goal of

135

'development'. The common value of welfare, as the guiding value of public policy, has the virtue of overriding claims of sectional interests, and the 'confusion' these cause the nation. It offers an ideology under which all can contribute instead to 'the concerted march to orderly progress', and in which public objectives are taken out of political contention. As Marx and Engels[12] point out, each class which aspires to rule must present its particular interest as a universal interest. Further, the universal interest of the bourgeoisie in creating and maintaining the most favourable conditions for capitalism conflicts with the competing interests in making their own profits of particular capitalists.

POLITICS AS THE RELATIONS AND CONFLICTS AMONG CLASSES

The constitutional draft itself, true to the impersonal principles of constitutional liberalism, makes no reference to conflict between classes, either in its explicit provisions, or in devising its array of checks and balances between the powers of the institutions of state. But the very nature of both private interests, and of the public interest embodied, in principle, in the state and its national ideology, are defined by the relations among classes. The determination of class relations in practice cannot be derived by *a priori* deduction from the functional requirements of the reproduction of capitalist social relations.[13] This not only grants the state, defined as that institution which reproduces the social relations of production, an omniscience and an omnipotence which should properly be confined to theological discourse. It also fails to recognize the contradictory requirements of social relations within civil society, and between civil society and the state, and within the state itself. These contradictions are the basis for the social action of contending groups and are resolved and reproduced through a political process of conflict and contention.

'Class' relations, defined to include production, market and moral relations, do not only, or necessarily, take the form of the organization of 'parties', or political groups for collective action, on the basis of class affiliation and solidarity. Groups, defining themselves around criteria other than class, such as status or ethnic affiliation, will organize themselves to gain privileged access to means of production, and to appropriate market opportunities and state resources.[14]

Political conflicts may be based either around communal solidarities, or on solidarities based on identity of, or more often, an alliance of class interests. More commonly, politics draws severally from both communal and class identities. A person's political identity is not unambiguously given, but is adopted in relation to particular contexts of action. In such contexts, salient identities will be acted on, in accordance with criteria of practical rationality. In turn, the salience of alternative identities will be governed by the social relations which constitute the changing contexts of political action. Thus, John Peel[15] has pointed out that where the most strategic and lucrative sources of opportunity are controlled by the state, and distributed among communities, politics may be expected to continue to turn around competing communal loyalties. This does not, of course, mean that class considerations are eliminated from politics. Class relations develop round the appropriation of resources by and from the state, and take the form of relations of patronage and clientage. Where patrons compete for clients, and clients seek opportunities to become patrons, such relations themselves become a focus for both resentment and contention.

Oil, Sheik Yamani reminds us, comes from God. Even when oil does provide a manna from heaven, or perhaps Hades, so that contention focuses on its distribution, rather than production, its revenues are invested in, and may provide a market for productive activities. These market and production relations remain a focus of class opposition. Conflict over the command of state power escalates because of the increasing concentration of resources in state hands.

Class conflicts may be regulated and reconciled by reference to considerations of mutual advantage and to shared values. But they may also raise questions as to the interpretation and implementation of particular values, or lead to the counterposition of different sets of values. Thus, the demand for 'fairness', 'justice' and the 'rights' of the common people may be, and has been, counterposed to the values and pursuit of personal advantage, and those of progress and development.

THE POLITICAL ECONOMY OF NEOCOLONIALISM, 1939–66

Capitalism in Nigeria has always taken a primarily commercial form. Control of the terms of exchange of commodities has been the major source of profit. The state has regulated access to commercial opportunities. The import–export trade has held a strategic position in the hinterland of European commercial activities. The staple exports have changed from slaves to export crops to mineral oil. Imports of cheap cloth, liquor and guns have been replaced by more expensive versions, by cars and cement, by machines and semi-manufactures. But the trade has always required both foreign commercial firms on the one hand, and on the other, local compradores[16] who organize foreign access to local supplies and markets. The terms of these relations between imperialists and compradores have always been the source of

137

competition among parties within each side, and of antagonism between the two sides.

The foundations of the neocolonial political economy were established in five ways. In 1939 the British government set up state monopoly marketing boards. The state bought crops at well below world prices, so that it withheld income from producers, and transferred it to the state and its beneficiaries. Initially these funds were used by the colonial government to finance Britain's sterling and trade balances. Nigerian politicians sought to gain control of these revenues to finance their political and commercial activities, the expansion of the state administration, and the development projects with which they would reward themselves and their constituents. The marketing boards established the fiscal basis for post-war Nigerian politics, and financed the creation and expansion of a commercial and a bureaucratic bourgeoisie.

In 1947, the British government initiated a strategy of planned decolonization in West Africa. Colonial government was to be replaced by government of politicians. Administrative and political office, state revenue, and state authority were ceded to Nigerian politicians and bureaucrats between 1947 and 1960. In this way, the British sought to create a new stratum of intermediaries through whom they could protect British strategic and commercial interests. Constitutional reforms created a stratum of professional politicians. Politics turned on the competition for the spoils of political office.

Between 1947 and 1966 foreign firms carried out a strategic shift in the nature of their operations in response to the opening of international competition for access to the Nigerian market, local commercial aspirations and protectionist legislation. They left the local trade in produce and the wholesaling of cheap, staple lines to Nigerian and Levantine traders, and imported more expensive and capital-intensive products, the market for which was expanded by the state's transfer of income from export crop farmers to wealthier consumers. They substituted the import of semi-manufactures, machines and raw materials for their factories, for the import of cheap manufactured goods, following the lead of the United Africa Company. Another Anglo-Dutch corporation, Shell, established its claims to, and began production in, the Nigerian oilfields. The dominant position of foreign firms was consolidated, and Nigerian businessmen increased the opportunities open to them as compradores.

Between 1954 and 1966 state institutions such as the Central Bank were created for regulating the national economy and the terms of its relations to the international economy. The state extended its regulation of access to commercial opportunities, for both foreign and local businessmen, in the form of marketing board licences, tax reliefs, loans and

138

contracts, and later import tariffs and exchange controls. Increasing state activity and Nigerianization dramatically expanded the opportunities for bureaucratic employment. Political and economic competition thus extended to the control of bureaucratic, as well as judicial, offices despite the institutions designed to insulate them from 'political' influence.

Nigerian governments, politicians and businessmen competed amongst themselves for the rents and profits to be derived from foreign business activities and foreign state capital ('aid'). They acted as agents for foreign firms and foreign governments, wishing to establish themselves commercially and politically in Nigeria. This facilitated the diversification of foreign trade and investments.

THE POLITICS OF RESOURCE ALLOCATION, 1939–66

'Politics' was the competition among, and the alliances between, politicians and their clients and associates. Its object was to control the resources of the state, and the rents and profits from foreign and local business activities. It was not limited to competition for electoral office. Academic, bureaucratic and judicial positions, and commercial opportunities were all equally 'politicized'. Politics was the means of class formation, financing the accumulation of money by the Nigerian bourgeoisie. It was the means of class competition, through which resources and opportunities were distributed.

Conflicts firstly concerned the allocation of particular resources, such as jobs, public funds, foreign aid, and via the population census, voters and constituencies. Secondly, parties disputed more general questions regarding the constitutional framework within which competition takes place, such as revenue allocation, the creation of new states, and the proper relations between regional and federal governments. Although such issues were often argued in terms of general principles, disputes turned on the consequences which their application would have for particular groups, defined in regional or ethnic terms.

During the nineteen-fifties, the British government remained the arbiter in the constitutional conflict and electoral competition. It directed developments by playing Nigerian politicians off against one another, and by protecting the institutional base of northern conservatism in the Northern Region government and the Native Authorities. Politicians accepted compromise as the price of access to state office, and thus to the revenues of state.

Between 1948 and 1951 politicians sought office as spokesmen for their communities, within their regions. The AG (Action Group) and NPC (Northern People's Congress) were formed as regional parties in the

139

West and the North in response to the nationalist challenge of the NCNC (National Council of Nigeria and the Cameroons) and NEPU (Northern Elements Progressive Union), and to the threat of Igbo and southern competition. In 1951, each party claimed the allegiance of a majority in one of the three regional assemblies, though in the 1954 federal election the NCNC would win a majority of western as well as eastern seats.

Regional government control of patronage was consolidated in 1954. The Macpherson Constitution of 1950 had not granted self-government, and thus Nigerian control of state funds. In 1953, both the AG and NCNC demanded self-government by 1956. The NPC rejected this. They retired to the North and produced a plan for confederal government, which would give them autonomy from southern competition and protect their authoritarian social and political institutions. The promise of regional security won some AG sympathy for confederation. However, insults to northerners in Lagos were answered by attacks on Igbos in Kano, provoked by a southern (AG) political meeting. The ensuing constitutional conferences compromised by agreeing to self-government for those regions which desired it by 1956. The fiscal base for the three regional governments was established by regionalizing the commodity marketing boards, and allocating revenue to the regions on the basis of 'derivation'. Lagos was made a separate federal territory, and the North was allocated half the seats in the federal legislature.

These decisions met the immediate demands of all three ruling parties. The AG's immediate concern was to gain for the Western Region government control of the lucrative marketing board and tax revenues derived from the export of cocoa. The NPC was primarily concerned to defend the 'unity' and 'traditions' of the North. This meant defending the authority of the Native Administrations, and excluding southern competitors from jobs and commercial opportunities controlled by local and regional governments and marketing boards. It required the incorporation of non-Muslim peoples into the 'northern system',[17] in which the NPC claimed a monopoly of political representation, with which they could protect northern interests at the federal level. Neither the NCNC's policies of new states and a stronger federal government, nor the East's interest in a different allocation of revenues were realized. Yet the NCNC agreed to the new constitution because it gave them access to state funds with which the party leaders could pursue their political and commercial ends.[18]

The first priority of Nigerian politicians was to establish control over their regional fiefs and eliminate opposition within them. Between 1956 and 1961 the party in power in each region consolidated its control of local government and its legislative majority. Parties combined appeals to ethnic and regional interests with the manipulation of patronage to individuals and communities, administrative coercion against opposition councils and simple repression of opponents. In each region, political minorities demanded new states which they would be able to dominate. In 1957, in the Yoruba West, the NCNC proposed a separate state for the colonial Oyo province in which they expected to win an electoral majority. In all three regions, ethnic minorities claimed new states, and allied with parties in power in other regions, the NCNC in the case of the Mid-West, and the AG in the case of certain northern and eastern minorities. But the established interests of regional governments and the colonial administration took precedence over the claims of minorities to separate status.

At the 1957 constitutional conference the colonial secretary, Alex Lennox-Boyd[19] exposed the conflicts among the Nigerian delegations. The North adamantly opposed new states in the North, which would end its majority of seats in the central legislature. The AG and NCNC proposals for new states varied according to their respective calculations of the political benefits. The colonial secretary insisted that the creation of new states would delay self-government and eventual independence. The issue was passed on to the Willink Commission which duly recommended against change. The conference agreed to self-government for the West and East in 1957. The question of independence was postponed to conferences in 1958 and 1960 at which agreement to the Anglo-Nigerian Defence Pact was secured. In 1953–4 and 1957–8, constitutional issues were determined by the interests of each party vested in their control of regional governments.

However, the 1957–8 constitutional and fiscal provisions increased the economic and police powers of the federal government. Control of the federal government became a means of controlling, or protecting, regional governments. Between 1960 and 1964, two attempts were made to challenge the federal domination of the NPC and its dependent allies. But these were followed by compromises in which the politicians sought the protection and patronage of the established federal and regional governments.

In 1959 the NPC and NCNC formed a federal coalition based on the numerical preponderance of the North and their shared antipathy to their regional rivals, the AG. The NPC resented AG 'interference' in the North in the form of support for a Middle-Belt State. The violent resistance of the Tiv to NPC rule in 1960 and 1964 failed to secure their new state, but angered the NPC. The NCNC hoped to use federal power to end AG control in the West, and to establish a separate Mid-West Region. The AG sought to develop a national opposition, adding an

141

ideology of 'democratic socialism'[20] to its base in the West and its support for new states. The Western Region premier, Chief Akintola, and several of the party leaders saw no reason for the west to finance the national political ambitions of the party leader, Chief Awolowo. They sought access to federal patronage through a rapprochement with the NPC, and made no secret of their hostility to socialism, democratic or otherwise. In 1962, the AG persuaded the governor of the West to replace Chief Akintola before parliament met, to prevent him dissolving it before they could recoup their election expenses. His supporters and members of the NCNC provoked a fracas in the House of Assembly when it met to reinstate his successor. The federal government used the occasion to declare a state of emergency. By 1963 they had been able to reconstruct a new majority of AG defectors and the NCNC in support of Chief Akintola, and to charge Chief Awolowo and his close associates with treason for which they were duly convicted. In 1963 the Mid-West Region was duly established.

Shared antipathy to the AG was insufficient to sustain the NCNC's alliance with the NPC. The eastern NCNC resented the NPC control of federal government policy, and its allocations of expenditures in favour of the North. This was sharpened by the rising share of 'eastern' oil in federal revenues. The mid-western NCNC was, by contrast, aware of the economic dependence of the new region, where oil production had yet to begin, on federal favour. The Eastern Region returns for the 1962 census clearly inflated the count. Together with a sharp increase in the West, this would have ended the North's numerical majority of the 'population', and thus of parliamentary constituencies. The North replied by 'verifying' their figures by adding $8\frac{1}{2}$ million to the original $22\frac{1}{2}$ million. A new census was arranged in 1963 in which all regions inflated the figures to retain the political status quo.

In 1964, Chief Akintola formed a new party, the NNDP (Nigerian National Democratic Party), taking most western NCNC parliamentarians with him. He tried to win Yoruba support by taking to a shrill extreme the old AG theme of Igbo favouritism, focusing on appointments to the federal universities and bureaucracies. This did not win the allegiance of his western opponents. It did focus attention on the real rivalries between Yoruba and Igbo academics and administrators for preferment. Ethnic conflicts was exacerbated in 1965 when Dr Njoku, Igbo vice-chancellor of the federal University of Lagos was summarily replaced by Dr Biobaku, a Yoruba. The politics of ethnic competition was far from a monopoly of politicians.

In 1964, the NCNC formed the UPGA (United Progressive Grand Alliance) with the rump of the AG and NEPU, though without abandoning their federal ministries. The NPC united with the NNDP and their minor allies in the NNA (Nigerian National Alliance) built on their common determination to control state power, and their common hostility to the Igbo. The decisive features of the campaign were administrative coercion and licensed thuggery, backed in the North by refusals to accept nominations. Clearly, no challenge to the ruling parties would be tolerated. UPGA declared an electoral boycott which was completely successful only in the east. UPGA candidates were elected throughout the mid-west and in twenty western seats, but elsewhere the boycott only let in NNDP nominees. The president refused to recognize the results and reappoint the premier, but the military refused to accept his authority on judicial advice. A compromise was reached, under which the NPC–NCNC coalition was continued. New elections were held in areas where no polling had taken place, enabling the NCNC to recover its seats in the East, but abandoning the AG to NNDP predominance in the West. In April, federal ministerial offices were expanded to seventy-six, to accommodate eleven NNDP ministers. Yet again, politicians had demonstrated their solidarity with the holders of power and patronage.

This willingness to join the winning side under pressure was celebrated as the Nigerian ability to compromise. But the conditions for compromise no longer existed. British arbitration had been removed. Federal control of the rules of political competition was itself the object of conflict. The accumulation of wealth and the conspicuous consumption by politicians and their clients, and the cost of state administration could only be financed by exactions on export crop farmers, and control of urban wages. At the same time the prices of export crops were falling and the cost of living rising. In the October 1965 Western Region election, the NNDP could only retain power by blatant rigging. Victimization, intimidation and the distribution of largesse to NNDP supporters were insufficient. Fraudulent electoral victory was followed by a drastic cut in the price paid to the producer for cocoa. Arson and riots were directed against the NNDP and their local supporters, and in some places against local Hausa. The NNDP retaliated with thuggery and repression, creating opportunities for robbery and mayhem. As with the Tiv resistance to the NPC in 1964, the army was needed to impose order. Government by politicians could not sustain the conditions necessary for its existence.

The conflicts of the era of politicians were not resolved when the military assumed power in January 1966. Instead the army itself became the focus and source of such conflicts. The overthrow of politicians was popularly welcomed in the south and tolerated in the north. But the majors who initiated the coup failed to seize power, except briefly in Kaduna. The rump cabinet was forced to cede power to Major General

Ironsi.The coup-makers, who were mainly Igbo, did succeed in killing the federal, northern and western premiers, and several senior army officers, mainly northerners. They failed to kill the two Igbo premiers and most Igbo officers, notably Ironsi himself. The killings undermined authority within the army and the solidarity of the soldiers. General Ironsi detained the coup-makers but failed to decide what to do with them. Northerners saw them as assassins of brother officers. Southern radicals saw them as deliverers of the people from the oppression of politicians in general and the NPC in particular.

The new military rulers shared with the majors a contempt for politicians and a belief in the military virtues of discipline, hierarchy and central command. The country's ills would be corrected by applying these virtues to civil administration. Ironsi relied for advice on a small circle of civil servants and officers, mainly Igbo, even on matters affecting the North. Like the British he preferred to deal with traditional rulers, and rebuffed the advances of northern opponents of the NPC. Chief Awolowo remained in prison. The sins of the era of politicians were blamed on regionalism, a view widely shared among radicals in the south. Northern fears of unitary government were ignored or treated as reactionary. The terms of reference of the Constitutional Review Group emphasized the evils of regionalism and party politics. In April, the Northern Region government announced that local courts, prisons and police would be taken from the control of the Native Authorities, the organizational base of the NPC. In May, the Ironsi government announced that the 'former regions are abolished', the public services would be unified, and all political associations banned. Then, and again in June, they emphasized that this was an administrative measure, taken by a 'corrective' regime, without prejudice to the constitutional review. They refused to recognize the dire political consequences of their administrative measures. These measures threatened the power base of the NPC. But they also threatened the ability of all northern groups, including the 'minorities', to protect themselves from competition in education, employment and commerce. Some Igbo in the north blatantly proclaimed 'their' victory over the NPC. Army promotions appeared to create an Igbo hegemony. The killings of northern officers and political leaders in January remained unavenged. In May, northern students demonstrated against the unification decrees, proclaining '*Araba*' ('let us secede'). More sinister forces, apparently organized by local merchants, contractors and other former NPC clients attacked and killed Igbo in the major commercial cities of the North.

On 29 July, northern officers carried out a counter-coup. They killed General Ironsi and his host, Brigadier Fajuyi, military governor of the

144

West, and Igbo commanders. Northern troops, both Hausa and 'minorities' like the Tiv, murdered Igbo soldiers and some civilians. Initially, northern officers and troops appear to have favoured secession and withdrawal to the North. They refused to accept the authority of the chief of staff, who resigned, but negotiated with Lt.-Col. Gowon, a northerner. Gowon, advised by senior civil servants and judges, as well as the British high commissioner and US ambassador, persuaded them against secession and took power as Supreme Commander and Head of the Military Government, announcing that the 'basis for trust and confidence in our unitary system of government has not been able to stand the test of time', and that 'the base for unity is not there'.[21]

Northern secession had been checked, but national political authority no longer existed. For the coup had failed in the East, and the military governor, Lt-Col. Ojukwu, was unwilling to recognize the authority of Gowon and his government. From then on the East consistently demanded regional autonomy, both in the control of security forces and in constitutional matters. They would not concede to any proposals for new states in the minority areas of the East, where their major source of revenues, the oilfields, were largely situated. On 27 August, Ojukwu declared a day of mourning, and proclaimed that 'there is in fact no genuine basis for true unity'.[22]

Gowon sought a political solution to the problem. He released Chief Awolowo and other Action Group supporters. Regional meetings with 'leaders of thought' were convened, preparatory to a constitutional conference. The conference was formally constituted by representatives of the four regions and Lagos, each primarily concerned with its own security and interests. The East and the North both proposed a confederal arrangement, and accepted the right to secession. Only the Mid-West opposed it, though the West and Lagos preferred a federation with more states. Between 16 and 20 September 1966 the conference was adjourned and the northern delegation changed its position. They now accepted a strong central government, repudiated the right to secession and supported the creation of new states. This change was brought about by two influences. The first was the northern minorities, and northern minority troops in particular. The second was those northern army officers, bureaucrats and academics who saw the economic disadvantages of secession, and who recognized that only by creating new states could an effective central government and a united army be retained. On 30 September, the government reported agreement that Nigeria should continue as a political entity, and 'substantial, but as yet not unanimous, agreement that more states should be created'.[23]

While the conference deliberated, a series of attacks began on Igbos

145

leaving the North. The governments denied the killings until the tragic broadcasts of 28 and 29 September, when Radio Kaduna relayed unsubstantiated reports of killings of northerners in the East. This seems to have sparked off the appalling massacres of 28 September to 2 October. They were more widespread and better organized than they had been in May. Soldiers as well as Native Authority officials both instigated and participated in the slaughter. The pogrom appears to have resulted from the evident vulnerability of the Igbo refugees, and the political uncertainties of the period. It was encouraged by those northerners who feared the loss of regional security, and the protection and patronage of the regional government. On 3 October, the constitutional conference was adjourned. The East never returned to it. Non-easterners, other than Mid-West Igbos, were expelled from the East. Constitutional arrangements could no longer guarantee to the military government of Eastern Nigeria the protection of Igbo lives and property. The conditions for conciliation no longer existed. The politics of compromise and crisis had reached a bloody impasse.

THE DETERMINATION OF PUBLIC POLICY, 1939–66

Competition for sectional advantage defined the politics of the era of politicians. Issues of public policy only came to be political when they were brought into the struggle for party and sectional advantage. As Dudley says, 'politics in Nigeria . . . is not about *alternative policies* but about the *control over men and resources*.'[24] The politicization of policy issues, and of public administration, was seen as a threat to sound policy and to good government.

Politicians, bureaucrats and the public at large shared a commitment to a common conception of development. They all welcomed the provision of more jobs, roads, schools and health services without questioning the character of the jobs, roads, schools and health services provided. Development would be promoted by increasing government spending and encouraging private investment, both local and foreign. The task of the state was to establish the conditions for the development of capitalism. The 1954 World Bank mission outlined a strategy of industrialization by invitation.[25] Government should finance infrastructure and encourage 'the free development of private initiative and private capital formation'.[26] Since the advantages of attracting foreign capital are self-evident, they must be secured by liberal incentives and 'assurance of free transferability of profits and repatriation of capital',[27] which all four governments duly gave in 1956. After independence, ministers in all four governments attacked any discussion of nationalization as irresponsible.

146

The World Bank report does not mention protective tariffs. Individual firms secured from the government appropriate import duties, and exemption from import duties, to ensure their profits. What appeared to be a strategy of encouraging market competition in fact required the state to protect the accumulation of money capital.[28]

Nigerian businessmen depended on the favour of the state and of foreign firms for their operations and profits.[29] Yet they also wished to expand the arena within which they had access to profitable opportunities. They expected the state to finance, subsidize and patronize them. Government contracts and produce licences backed by public credit created an area of politically-protected profit-making. Businessmen demanded that foreign firms act with local partners and through local agents who could thus interpose themselves between foreign importers and manufacturers and retailers and consumers to reap monopolistic profits and control the allocation of petty trading opportunities. They even asked to be relieved of taxes to free them to meet family responsibilities and accumulate savings. Only where Nigerian private business was unable to invest should the state set up firms whose shares could later be transferred to private owners.[30] An ethic of private entrepreneurship, assisted by the state, could be legitimated in the contending party slogans of 'pragmatic' or 'democratic' socialism, summed up as: socialism 'is the right of everyone to own his own business'.[31]

After 1957 the federal government acquired the fiscal and constitutional powers to regulate the national economy. It increased its share of tax revenues, and acquired powers over foreign loans and investment, banking and the money supply. Regions retained certain taxes, as well as the marketing board surpluses and half the royalties and rents on mining, but had to finance expanding expenditures, particularly on education. The 1962–8 development plan was based on wishful thinking.[32] It relied on a level of foreign public and private investment which was simply not forthcoming. The growth of manufacturing and state employment increased the demand for imports. The consumption of the newly enriched accentuated this. Outflows of profits and interest had to be financed. The prices of export crops continued to fall. Only the expansion of oil production promised some relief. Strategic investment decisions were decided, or left undecided, according to considerations of sectional political advantage and the interests of specific foreign firms. The Kainji Dam hydro-electric project in the North was preferred to the development of natural gas in the East. The planned iron and steel complex was never built because of disagreements as to whether it should be sited in the North, or the East, or both. Regional governments directed industries to inappropriate locations to share out patronage and reward particular constituencies.

Colonial labour policy had been mainly concerned to keep wages down. Between 1938 and 1946 the government set up institutions for regulating industrial relations. Both the colonial government and its successors, wished to 'isolate industrial disputes from political agitation',[33] by encouraging 'responsible' trade unionism and voluntary collective bargaining. They failed to carry out the measures required to establish either.

Most Nigerian unions have been organized by professional trade union secretaries. They competed to accumulate unions in different firms and government departments, and to establish their rival claims to speak and negotiate for workers at a national level. Rivalries for members were exacerbated by their dependence on financial sponsorship from competing international trade union centres, in return for their protégés' allegiance to their ideological and diplomatic postures. Successive government commissions repeated the same recommendations for strengthening and rationalizing trade union organization, without effect. Trade unionism continued to be an entrepreneurial activity, financially dependent on foreign patronage.

Periodic wage increases have been the result of government awards, usually following commissions of enquiry. Commissions have been set up, awards conceded, and then extended to the major private employers, in response to general and specific strikes, or to the threat of these, and to the electoral calculations of regional governments. NECA, the Nigerian Employers Consultative Association, advocates collective bargaining to free the private sector from being tied to government awards. But the combination of permissive legislation and occasionally repressive practice has understandably failed to institutionalize collective bargaining or to prevent periodic confrontations of workers against government and employers.

Colonial and mission schools educated people for subordinate clerical positions. The transfer of authority required the expansion of higher education to create the administrators and managers who would take over the offices, assumptions and indeed the privileges of colonial officers and managers. Regional governments competed to expand schools and to found universities which provided the qualifications which governed access to employment and salary levels. Political controversy did not centre on the content and purposes of education, but on the uneven geographical distribution of schools and universities, and the ethnic distribution of academic appointments.

Nigeria's economic dependence on capitalist countries was matched by

148

the government's commitment to the assumptions and objectives of western foreign policy. Issues of foreign policy provided a focus for popular nationalist and pan-African sentiments. Demonstrations against the Anglo-Nigerian Defence Pact and over the news of the murder of Lumumba both led to riots in Lagos. The All-Nigeria People's Congress, initiated by NCNC ministers, and the Nigerian Youth Congress attacked the policies of the government. The AG reversed Chief Awolowo's pro-western stance to win nationalist sympathies for its programme of 'democratic socialism' to the alarm of AG conservatives. The 1964 UPGA manifesto took up the AG support for the principle of nationalizing foreign firms, for non-alignment and for pan-Africanism. But politics was not realigned around ideological issues. It continued to turn on the mundane issues of office and patronage.

The basic lines of federal economic and foreign policy remained unchanged. Certain symbolic changes were made. The Anglo-Nigerian Defence Pact was formally rescinded. Nigeria broke off diplomatic relations with France over atomic tests in the Sahara. But Nigeria remained a pillar of African conservatism. It maintained a military contingent with the UN in the Congo. It supported a two-Chinas and one-Germany policy at the UN. It adopted a moderate approach to Southern African problems, and a supportive stance towards Britain's Rhodesian dilemma. Calls for national independence in both economic and foreign policy were brushed aside.

Failed by the politicans, radicals and nationalists looked to the military to use state power 'to establish a strong, united and prosperous nation, free from corruption and internal strife', as Major Nzeogwu, the January coup leader declared in his broadcast to the nation.[34] A strong centralized state was required to override sectional interests, to establish national control over the economy, to determine and execute a rational development strategy, and to create a pride in national achievements. Immediately after the July 1966 coup, the tendencies to regional security and secession seemed to predominate. But they were countered by bureaucrats and officers who recognized the economic advantages of unity and saw a need for centralized direction of development policy, while conceding to the states the satisfaction of sectional aspirations. Oil revenue would not only win regional support for national unity, but would finance the predominance of the federal government. Both Britain and America recognized the need of international capital for a strong central government, to which the Soviet Union was to give unqualified support. The development of capitalist production required a centralized authority and rational administration. There was a clear contradiction between the politics of commercial capitalism in

Nigeria and the policies required for the development of capitalist production.

RELATIONS AND CONFLICTS AMONG CLASSES, 1939–66

Colonialism transformed the class relations and political institutions of Nigerian societies. Specific class groups challenged on occasion the terms of their relations to the capitalist market system and the colonial state. Merchants, professionals and clerks opposed the monopolistic and racist practices of government and foreign firms which excluded them from access to opportunities. Their methods were constitutional. They formed associations, wrote editorials, sent petitions and delegations, and sought legislative office. Farmers, petty traders and workers focused on other issues: harassment and extortion by government officials, increased taxes, high import prices, low export prices and stagnant wages. They also sought to present their grievances constitutionally, but were forced back onto direct resistance: strikes, refusing taxes and attacking buildings and officials of the government, and sometimes of foreign companies.[35] Certain politicians and journalists presented or explained popular grievances, but they gave no lead to popular action. They identified with the explicit values of their colonial rulers, and shared the colonial disdain and distrust for the masses. Even in protest against colonial abuses, they acted as intermediaries.

The Second World War accentuated the grievances of each group, and post-war controls exacerbated resentments. The marketing boards and import controls lowered export prices, raised consumer prices, and limited commercial opportunities. Nigerian businessmen joined American and British commercial interests in defence of 'free trade' and the 'open door'. Merchants opposed the marketing boards. Petty traders opposed 'conditional sales' of controlled commodities by foreign firms. Farmers' unions opposed low crop prices, new taxes and agricultural regulations. Ibadan farmers' *Maiyegun* League resisted the cutting out of cocoa trees infected with swollen shoot.

The expansion of wage-employment increased the number and bargaining power of workers. Rising living costs and stagnant wages provoked demonstrations, and increased union membership. In 1942 a government commission conceded an increased cost of living allowance. In June 1945 government workers, defying the caution of their union leaders, sustained a forty-four day general strike. A further commission then awarded a 50 per cent wage increase. In 1949, the shooting of striking miners at Enugu led to attacks on foreign firms in the East. UNAMAG, representing United Africa Company workers, tried to sustain the offensive in 1950 with two strikes, the first successful, the second a disaster.

The grievances of different classes provided a popular basis for national politics. Nationalists rejected the limited reforms of the 1945 Richards Constitution. They used popular grievances to establish their own claims to state power with the authorities. Radical nationalists and labour leaders, united in the Zikist movement, sought to force politicians into a confrontation with the authorities. In 1948, and again in 1950, the colonial government acted firmly to repress the Zikists, at the same time as they opened commercial and administrative opportunities to Nigerians, and steered nationalist politics into responsible electoral competition. Dr Azikiwe and other party leaders carefully distanced themselves from nationalist and labour radicalism.

Decolonization devolved power to regional governments, controlled by a bourgeois *stand* (status group) of politicians, businessmen and professionals, whose social and commercial ties extended across the region. Petty traders and contractors, and artisans, who had previously been able to influence customary authorities at the local level, could not take advantage of the new opportunities for political participation, except as clients to merchants and politicians. In several commercial centres, they supported populist opposition parties, such as NEPU in the North, and NCNC in the Yoruba West. They often organized locally, in defence of the prerogatives and honour of their communities, as with the Ibadan *Mabolaje* and the Kano People's Party. Adelabu[36] built the *Mabolaje* around the political, occupational and convivial societies of the Ibadan commoners and the farmers' *Maiyegun* League, over the concrete issues of jobs, contracts, taxes and the imposition of officialdom, and not, as Sklar[37] suggests, around the defence of communal sentiments by the heads of chieftaincy lineages. His supporters looked to Adelabu to work the system for their benefit. Class conflict was thus incorporated into local politics, which was subordinated to the regional government's control of the instruments of patronage and coercion. Farmers' unions depended on the patronage and purposes of politicians and bureaucrats, to the point of formally agreeing to reductions in the cocoa price. Unions and co-operatives were concerned with credit and commercial marketing rather than farmers' grievances.

By 1960 it was clear that hopes for 'life more abundant' were only to be realized for the few. The ethics of entrepreneurial initiative and of patronage, shared among all Nigerians, are double-edged. They legitimate the unequal gains of the rich, but demand that the rich provide opportunities and assistance to the poor.[38] Nigerians found that colonial rule had been replaced by politicians' rule. Politics itself became the focus of

151

resentment. It was identified with the corrupt and blatant enrichment of the few at the expense of the many, and the nepotism, tribalism and repression with which the politicians kept themselves in power.

The 1964 general strike articulated the class resistance of workers and the popular resentment against politicians. Workers' restiveness led the rival unions to form a Joint Action Committee in 1963, and sustain it through the strike. A brief general strike in September 1963 led the government to establish the Morgan Commission. The unions threatened and then called a general strike to force publication of the Morgan report, and implementation of its awards, which the government arrogantly rejected after the start of the strike. Some 750,000 workers, by no means all of them unionized, went on strike for thirteen days, in defiance of arrests of leaders and threats of dismissal, and gained partial implementation of the Morgan awards. As in 1945, the strike was actively supported by market traders and the urban poor. Despite the declared support for the strike of AG and NCNC leaders, a demonstration of 30,000 people at Ibadan race course chanted, 'No AG, no NCNC'. Workers' defence of their 'rights' focused popular grievances against all politicians and their practices.

Trade union unity did not survive the 1964 elections. Labour parties made little impact, and a strike called against the election results failed. People gave their support to the political parties they had renounced, acting according to the rules of electoral politics, of competition to control the allocation of state resources. The strike was not about 'politics', but about justice. It was in effect a strike *against* parliamentary politics.

In Tivland in 1960 and 1964, in Ibadan districts after Adelabu's death in 1958, and in Yorubaland in 1965, supporters of opposition parties resisted the forcible imposition of regional government power upon their communities. They attacked government buildings, tax clerks and police. They vented their wrath particularly against local supporters of the ruling party. Post[39] suggests that the violence took the specific form of punishing offences against their communities. The violence did not simply involve people in the politics of resource allocation. It was also a popular rejection of the rule of politicians.

THE POLITICAL ECONOMY OF CRISIS AND RECONSTRUCTION, 1966–75

The coup of 29 July 1966 created a crisis of state authority. It was finally resolved by the consolidation of the power of the federal government and military victory over Biafran secession. Between 1969 and 1974 the production and price of oil both increased dramatically. These led to significant changes in the forms of state authority, of state intervention in the economy, and of Nigeria's relations with foreign countries.

In 1966 and 1967 federal permanent secretaries acted decisively to maintain federal authority. The creation of states ended the power of the regions. The federal government appropriated an increasing share of the rising oil revenues, and controlled the allocation of the remainder to the states. Military rulers depended on bureaucrats, and particularly the federal permanent secretaries, to define policies. The war and increasing oil revenues expanded state economic activities. The federal government extended its control over imports, banking, foreign exchange and the relations between foreign and indigenous capital. This accelerated the substitution of imports of machinery for imports of consumer goods, and expanded factory production, thus extending state control over access to private commercial opportunities. Military, and federal and state government spending increased rapidly with decreasing budgetary controls. Federal and state governments formed numerous parastatal corporations to spend government money and promote development activities. The federal government took shares in foreign oil companies and joined the Organization of Petroleum Exporting Countries (OPEC).

After the war, oil production and oil prices both increased dramatically. In 1971/2 oil revenues of ₦640 million provided half of government revenue. By 1975/6 they had risen to ₦4,600 million, out of a total revenue of ₦5,300 million. Oil then provided 93 per cent of export earnings. Yet the industry employed only some 6,000 people. The vertically integrated activities of oil companies generate backward and forward linkages, which stimulate production abroad rather than in Nigeria. Oil income arrives as manna from foreign firms. Political competition centres on the distribution of oil rents, rather than on the appropriation and distribution of surplus value produced by export crop farmers. Foreign corporations compete for access to Nigeria's oil supplies and lucrative markets. A secure market position requires not simply sales and purchases, but investment in and the provision of technology for manufacture and mining. 'The export of capital thus becomes a means for encouraging the export of commodities.'[40] In Nigeria, as elsewhere, oligopolistic, transnational firms are reluctant to engage in price competition, and pay 'considerations' to gain access to market opportunities; '. . . monopolies introduce everywhere monopolist principles; the utilization of "connections" for profitable transactions takes the place of competition on the open market'.[41] The expansion of state expenditure and state regulation of economic activities increases the scope for bribes. State officials increasingly take over the comprador role of organizing foreign access to local supplies and markets.

153

Production by foreign firms also requires an efficient administration and provision of services and the development of government and other institutions that mirror their corporate values and organization. Thus the shift of foreign capital from trading to production creates the need for local technocrats. They increase local productive capacities, which may alter the terms of the state's relations with foreign capital, enabling foreign firms to withdraw from direct investment to the international marketing of services and commodities, 'developing new lines of business in the provision of technical advice and support'.[42] Foreign firms have often trained technocrats, as in the case of the staff of NNOC (Nigerian National Oil Corporation). They 'produce' technocrats in another sense. Just as comprador middlemen are the historical creation and local counterparts of foreign commerce, so technocrats are the historical creation and local counterparts of transnational capitalist production.

THE POLITICS OF RESOURCE ALLOCATION, 1966–75

The initial consequence of the coup was a retreat to regional security. Constitutional negotiations took place among civilian and military representatives of each region. Regional military governors defined their stances in terms of the interests and security of their respective regions. However, the East was unwilling to accept guarantees of regional security within a framework of federal sovereignty. Its military government consistently demanded maintenance of its military and constitutional autonomy, and territorial integrity. Central authority could only be conferred by the regions.

Both federal institutions and interests based in the regions wanted a strong federal government and the division of the regions into states. Federal civil servants had vested interests in and attached value to an effective central government. Army officers, outside the East, wished to maintain its unity. Political and ethnic minorities in each region, and Lagosians, sought states of their own. Key permanent secretaries came from minority areas, and the Mid-West. After September 1966, northern political leaders consistently supported new states. However, the West remained ambivalent. With the Mid-West, they repudiated the use of force against the East, and also demanded that northern troops be withdrawn from the region. On 1 May 1967, Chief Awolowo agreed to the regionalization of revenue, security forces and the public debt, and declared that if the East were allowed to secede, then so must the West and Lagos.

Federal policy shifted back and forth from support for new states to conceding Eastern demands for regional autonomy. Senior military offic-

154

ers appeared to agree at Aburi, Ghana, in January 1967, but only by leaving the exact relations between federal and regional governments ambiguous. The ambiguities were rapidly exposed by federal permanent secretaries, who adamantly opposed the cession of political, military and administrative powers to the regions, on which the East insisted. New states were finally promulgated on 27 May to pre-empt the declaration of Biafran secession on 30 May 1967. Civilian commissioners, notably Chief Awolowo, were appointed to the Federal Executive Council, after over one year of government by permanent secretaries and senior military officers.

In July, Nigerian forces advanced from the North and landed at Bonny on the coast. In reply, Biafran forces, assisted by Mid-West Igbo officers, seized the Mid-West. Their Yoruba leader Col. Banjo appealed to 'progressive' southerners to unite against 'reactionary' 'Fulani-Hausa' domination. This simple dichotomy did not rally the support of the West and Mid-West. Instead the invasion committed them to the federal cause. Col. Muhammed checked Banjo at Ore, and the Biafrans retreated rapidly across the Niger, with both sides committing atrocities in their wake. Banjo's vision of a 'progressive' Nigeria had no appeal to Ojuwku either. Banjo was executed with three others, including Ifeajuna, a leader of the January 1966 coup, for planning to overthrow Ojukwu. For thirty months, the Biafrans combined stubborn resistance from their shrinking enclave, with an international propaganda offensive and an adamant refusal to concede their claim to sovereignty over the whole of the former Eastern Nigeria, most of which they no longer controlled.

Nigeria's war was fought with foreign arms purchases, and became a focus for international concern and intervention. Rival powers sought to establish their diplomatic and commercial standing in Nigeria, or to challenge the predominance of their rivals by supporting Biafra. France and its allies in particular provided the means to sustain Biafran resistance from August 1968 by which time Nigerian victory was clearly inevitable. A motley group of supporters provided financial, military and diplomatic support to Biafra: Ivory Coast, Gabon and France; mercenaries and international charities; Rhodesia and South Africa; Zambia and Tanzania. Established firms and the British government supported the federal cause, though not without apparent equivocation. The United States followed Britain's lead in what Dean Rusk brazenly called 'Britain's sphere of influence'.[43] The Soviet Union provided aircraft and heavy artillery, and established stronger commercial links with Nigeria Egypt and mercenaries supplied pilots. Eventually, Nigeria's massive superiority in supplies, arms and troops ended the war in January, 1970. Federal authority had triumphed. Igbo were welcomed back into Nigeria,

155

except for Port Harcourt in the Rivers State. Biafrans were again Nigerians.

The assumption of state power by military commanders and top civil servants did not eliminate the politics of resource allocation. It simply changed its form. Access to opportunities was now controlled, not by elected politicians with constituents to reward, but by military governors, permanent secretaries, army officers and civilian and military commissioners. At both federal and state levels, resources were allocated by a clique of insiders. Far more resources passed through fewer hands, and were allocated to a narrower clientele.

The state controls access to oil supplies and lucrative contracts. The state itself, and its civil servants thus becomes the focus of a mass of distributive conflicts. Bureaucrats act as 'gatekeepers', monitoring the outflow of oil and agricultural exports and the inflow of imported goods and services. As they open and close the gate, they can exact a toll on the exchange. Foreign buyers and sellers secure supplies and contracts by gaining the favour of state officials. 'Commercial triangles' are formed of private Nigerian middlemen, state 'gatekeepers' or compradores, and representatives of foreign firms. Foreign businessmen come to Nigeria to sell their firms' products. They hire Nigerians to act as go-betweens with state officials. If the official who has jurisdiction over the particular matter awards a contract, the Nigerian middleman may reward him appropriately. The 'triangle' manifests itself in many forms, since the state issues a variety of dispensations, oil sales, import and foreign exchange permits, and contracts. Alternatively the private Nigerian middleman is simply cut out and the 'triangle' is replaced by a bilateral relationship between the state comprador and foreign firm.

Commercial triangles are exemplified by the billion naira cement racket, which clogged Lagos roadsteads with ships, without solving the cement shortage. Increased government and private spending created a massive shortage of cement. Under the authority of the permanent secretary in the Ministry of Defence, and the Defence Commissioner, General Gowon himself, contracts were freely awarded to overseas suppliers operating through the small ring of local middlemen. Sixteen million tons of cement, far in excess of Nigeria's import capacity was contracted and paid for by the Ministry of Defence alone. Much of the world's surplus shipping was then loaded with cement and anchored off Lagos at the expense of the Nigerian government.[44] Military arms purchasers established bilateral relations with suppliers: 'To be an army officer means to be the granter of licences for deliveries to the armed forces.'[45] Bilateral relations were formed between the Ministry of Mines and Power and the largest oil producer in Nigeria, Shell-B.P., which was assured access to supplies of oil on favourable terms. Rival US and European oil companies sought allies within the state opposed to the special relationship between the oil ministry and Shell-B.P.

The expansion of the direct economic activities of the state increased the scope for senior officials to deal directly with foreign firms, at the expense of private middlemen, and their bureaucratic collaborators. Businessmen resented state officials who had privileged access to information about, and to the patronage of, foreign companies selling shares to comply with the Indigenization Decree. They similarly opposed the purchase of firms or shares by state governments at the expense of out-of-state businessmen. State involvement in commerce and manufacturing threatens to pre-empt the intermediary position which Nigerian businessmen occupy between foreign capital and the local state or consumer market. The full rhetoric of unfettered private enterprise was marshalled by the Chamber of Commerce against state capitalist usurpation of their middlemen's activities.

The major issues in contention in the era of politicians were perpetuated under the Gowon regime. They included the relations between federal and state governments, revenue allocation, the creation and boundaries of states and a new federal capital, appointments to administrative, political and academic office, the population census, and the return to and constitutional arrangements for civilian rule. Each of these concerned the terms on which oil revenues would be allocated. Non-existent political parties, banned since the Ironsi regime, pursued their rivalries and alliances to gain office, sectional advantage and public following. For example, in the West, the ex-NNDP sought to use farmers' grievances to pay off old scores and to demand their own Oyo state. Northern politicians maintained their links through the Barewa College Old Boys Association, and the Ali Akilu Memorial Fund. Party and sectional interests were promoted by newspapers and by informal but effective patronage networks, like the 'Mid-West Line'. Some politicians used public office to build up a following and an election fund. Others distanced themselves from, and even opposed, military government. Awolowo and Aminu Kano did so while holding public office, riding two horses in opposite directions, with varying degrees of agility.

The new states created protected areas of jobs and opportunities. They could not eliminate rivalries within each state. In the Yoruba West, and Igbo East-Central state for example, numerous petitions asserted the historical and ethnic distinctiveness of particular combinations of Yoruba and Igbo groups and listed their specific deprivation of jobs and amenities. The 1973 census sought to adjust state population figures to changing political, fiscal and constitutional circumstances. Western and

157

south-eastern figures were below the imaginary 1963 returns. But the four predominantly Hausa-Fulani-Kanuri states, which dominated the old North, and through it the Federation, now increased their total by 78 per cent to claim the controlling majority previously held by the six states making up the old North. Gowon recognized the need to deal with such contentious issues before the promised return to civilian rule in 1976. But he failed to act decisively on them because of the Pandora's Box of sectional conflicts which they opened up. Thus under Gowon the issue of new states remained open, and the census figures 'provisional'.

The dynamics of resource allocation generated divisive conflicts. Military and bureaucratic officials competed to control the allocation of revenue, jobs and contracts. Middlemen competed for access to state officials. Foreign corporations competed by proxy through their local agents. The operations of commercial 'triangles' perpetuated nepotism, tribalism and statism. The clique of 'insiders' swells. The form of commercial relations leads towards closed government. The more triangles formed around a particular contract, the more competition; the fewer triangles involved, the easier the settlement. The shift towards bilateral deals further increased the premium on secrecy and the concentration of decision-making.

The public resented the increasing corruption and incompetence of government. Politicians, businessmen and academics resented the appropriation of opportunities by small cliques of military rulers and 'super' permanent secretaries. They saw themselves as qualified and competent to share in the government of Nigeria. Army officers, including those who had brought the regime to power, resented their exclusion from decision-making and opportunities. In 1974, civilian rule was postponed indefinitely. Gowon promised to replace the military governors and civilian commissioners, but this only encouraged them to spend the oil money while the going was good. Evidence of corruption was met by actions against those who laid allegations 'against highly placed officials with a view to discrediting the military regime'.[46] The rejection of civilian rule would perpetuate the domination of, and appropriation of resources by, a small clique of military and bureaucratic rulers and their local and foreign associates. Army officers decided to remove their seniors.

THE DETERMINATION OF PUBLIC POLICY, 1966–75

Capitalism makes contradictory requirements of the state. Profit-making requires the appropriation of commercial opportunities by colluding cliques of businessmen and bureaucrats. At the same time, the development of capitalist production requires that disinterested civil

158

servants determine policy in the public interest. State officials would like to increase national control of economic opportunities. Nigerian businessmen would like to expand their activities at the expense of foreign firms. Yet both depend on foreign capital for their activities. The contradictory requirements of capitalism generate conflicts both within civil society, and in the state itself.

In 1973, Allison Ayida, secretary to the federal military government between 1975 and 1977, proclaimed an 'institutional revolution'.[47] He identifies it with increasing national control and technocratic direction of the allocation of resources. Its proxy vanguard has been the 'super permsecs' like himself, who came to determine public policy under military licence.

The federal government appropriated an increasing share of the oil revenues, and controlled the allocation of the remainder to the states. In 1969 the government rejected the proposal of the Dina Commission that only 10 instead of 50 per cent of royalties and rents from on-shore production should go to the state of derivation, but in 1975 itself reduced the share to 20 per cent. The remainder go into the distributable pool, from which half is divided according to population, and half shared equally among the states.

The war required the state to increase its capacity to intervene in and to direct economic activities. It imposed import controls on specific items, and on imports from particular countries. It increased excise duties and import tariffs, except for certain commodities which factories in Nigeria would process. The Central Bank increased its powers over banks, financial houses and the money supply. Exchange controls were applied to the sterling area and payments abroad restricted or deferred. The federal government created an apparatus for economic planning, and published two plans for National Development, which prove to be non-binding guidelines for spending money. Industries of strategic national importance, such as oil and iron and steel, have been reserved to the state.

Administrators and technocrats disagreed over their relative salaries and standing, and as to whether authority over state corporations should rest with officials of the ministries or with officials of the corporations. These disagreements concerned the relations of the Nigerian state to foreign capital. They were not simply the result of rivalries generated within the state itself. Senior administrators wished to keep central control over relations with foreign firms, and thus of the payments made by foreign firms for access to supplies and markets. This brought them into conflict with both Nigerian private businessmen and their collaborators in the bureaucracy, and with Nigerian technocrats. Technocrats apply professional skills and impersonal calculations, in co-operation with one

159

another, to produce tangible results, measured in terms of outputs and profits. Technocrats employed by the state define their objectives in terms of increasing Nigerian control of productive activities, and ensuring the maximum benefit to the 'nation' from the operations of international firms. This brings them into conflict with comprador administrators.

In 1971, Nigeria joined OPEC. By 1974 it had acquired 55 per cent undivided interests in major oil producing companies. If it was to increase its control over the oil industry and reap the maximum financial benefits from participation, Nigeria needed to engage in production, marketing and refining of oil, and to establish petrochemical industries. In 1971, NNOC was established ' . . . to engage in prospecting for, mining and marketing oil and in all other activities with the petroleum oil industry'.[48] In 1974, all remaining and relinquished concessions were vested in NNOC. NNOC's capacity to carry out these tasks was systematically limited. Philip Asiodu, permanent secretary in the Ministry of Mines and Power, was chairman of the NNOC board. Expenditures over ₦100,000 required the approval of the Federal Executive Council, on the recommendation of the NNOC board and the Commissioner for Mines and Power. The post of general manager of NNOC was left vacant for four years, leaving the corporation under control of the permanent secretary, rather than a manager responsible to the Federal Executive Council. General Gowon's eventual appointment of Asiodu's nominee as NNOC general manager, over the explicit opposition of the Federal Executive Council, may have precipitated his downfall.[49]

In 1973, the government failed to complete an auction of crude oil, despite very high price offers which followed the Arab–Israeli War and the embargo by AOPEC (Arab Organization of Petroleum Exporting Countries). The ministry subsequently revised NNOC price calculations downwards. Price negotiations with Shell-BP and the smaller producers were delayed during 1974 and 1975, while oil prices were falling, Shell-BP, the major producer and purchaser of oil in Nigeria was assured supplies on favourable terms. The ministry also resisted state operational involvement in foreign oil companies. In mid-1977, operational agreements between the state and foreign oil companies remained unsigned. Regional rivalries delayed, and determined, decisions on the siting of the iron and steel complex, liquefied gas plants and two new oil refineries so that, in 1975, Nigeria suffered persistent shortages of petrol, gas and kerosene.[50]

During the nineteen-sixties salaries of senior public servants fell behind salaries of managers and professionals in foreign firms. The 1971 Adebo and 1974 Udoji Commissions[51] were invited to compare and harmonize the two. Both commissions recommended greater managerial autonomy over the staffing, pay and operations of public industrial and commercial corporations. For the civil service itself, the Udoji Report proposed a result-oriented executive model of management. The Government White Papers, drafted by the permanent secretaries, rejected these recommendations, suggesting that 'the Review Commission seems to have overplayed the so-called "tension" between the administrators and professionals in the public service'.[52] The unified grading scheme which Udoji proposed for the civil service, oddly including NNOC, was extended to the entire public sector, thus maintaining the superior salaries and status, as well as the authority, of administrators over technocrats.

The 1972 Indigenization Degree redefined the relations of foreign to Nigerian capital. Foreigners were excluded altogether from some businesses, and required to have a minimum size and 40 per cent Nigerian shareholding in others. They were encouraged to move towards more complex productive activities, and to associate Nigerians with their activities as shareholders or distributors. The government took 40 per cent of the shares of commercial banks and required them to allocate 40 per cent of loans to Nigerian businessmen. In this way, and through state banks, the government financed private acquisition of shares and firms from foreign companies by managers, bureaucrats and businessmen.[53]

The decline in the production of export crops, and the rebellion of farmers against the government of the Western State in 1968–9 led the federal government to take over responsibility for fixing produce prices. It can set prices in the light of world prices, local production costs and rural unrest, instead of in terms of the immediate revenue needs of state governments and their clients. The Third Plan commits vast sums of money to rural development. Productivity is to be increased by directing peasant farmers to use state-provided inputs according to state-directed methods to meet state-defined targets. On past experience, money will be wasted or diverted to commercial activities. The burden of state marketing will be extended from export to food crops, thus opening a new avenue for monopolistic profits to colluding bureaucrats and businessmen. Rural development increases bureaucratic employment and commercial opportunities at the expense of peasant farmers.[54]

Since 1968, labour legislation has been increasingly directive and restrictive. Decree 53 of 1969 banned strikes, permitted the police to detain anyone who had been, was, or was likely to be, engaged in acts prejudicial to industrial peace, and created a standing Arbitration Tribunal. Decree 31 of 1973 finally took up some of the proposals made by the Tudor Davies Commission[55] in 1945. The registrar could refuse to register a union where an existing union covered the same category of

161

workers. Registered unions can apply to the Commissioner of Labour for a compulsory recognition order. Formal industrial relations institutions are limited to the state and to large, mainly foreign, companies. Elsewhere, a personal style of entrepreneurial authority prevails.[56] Strike bans and detentions of union leaders did not stop workers from taking industrial action and going on strike. Delays on the part of the Industrial Arbitration Tribunal and the Commissioner of Labour have provoked strikes, rather than stopped them. Central labour organizations formed alliances to campaign for government wage reviews. Rivalries for position, and for foreign funds prevented labour unity, despite the wishes of both workers and government. Wage determination has not broken from the old patterns. Periodic government commissions reviewed wages and were then followed by waves of strikes to demand implementation of their awards, and the extension of these awards to the private sector.

The federal government established a National Universities Commission, and assumed shared jurisdiction over primary and secondary education. It committed itself to universal primary education, and increased facilities at all levels. This expansion will not remove the geographical imbalance among different states: at best it will enable disadvantaged states to run fast in order to stand still. The rich continue to use private primary schools to perpetuate class privilege through the educational system.[57]

Nigeria's civil war experience led her to define foreign policy objectives in terms of Nigerian and African interests, rather than her traditional, that is, colonial ties with Britain. The civil war brought Nigeria into diplomatic and military conflict with the commercial and political ambitions of France, and her African associates, and with Portugal, South Africa and Rhodesia. If Nigerian industrialization is to extend beyond import substitution, Nigeria needs free access to export markets in Africa. Foreign capital might then use Nigeria, rather than the Ivory Coast, as a base for penetrating West African markets. Thus, Nigeria wished to renegotiate the relations between the European metropoles and their former African colonies, and to resist South African diplomatic and commercial penetration in Africa. Nigeria took the lead in forming the Economic Community of West Africa (ECOWAS), and the negotiation of the Lomé Agreement of association between the European Economic Community, and African and other underdeveloped countries. Nigeria joined the radical African governments in rejecting detente with South Africa in 1971. Though her commercial links with capitalist interests were strengthened, Nigeria's diplomatic posture shifted towards pan-Africanism and non-alignment.

In 1969, Allison Ayida[58] declared:

162

Those who would like to involve the representatives of the people and members of the political class who are not in office, in the planning process, should recognize the limitations of representative institutions in the formulation and maintenance of plan objectives. It is the executive, made up of Ministers, planners, administrators and other public officials, who are in a position to determine and maintain the objectives and targets of development policy. . . .

Politics is seen as the conflict of sectional interests. Development issues should not be touched by considerations of sectional politics or the challenges of the exploited classes. Bureaucrats failed to direct public policy according to technocratic criteria. Regional rivalries have delayed decisions, such as the building of new oil refineries. Comprador administrators have turned the government into a racket, as in the case of the cement scandal, and maintained the dominant position of foreign companies, as in the case of the oil industry. They had the authority within the state, and the allies among local and foreign capitalists outside it, to override technocrats' state capitalist policy initiatives. But they failed to create the conditions under which capitalist production, local or foreign, could flourish. Government corruption, mismanagement and lack of policy produced port and road congestion, lack of water, fuel and electricity, increased food, labour and import costs, incompetent administration and social unrest. Bureaucratic rule both discredited and overreached itself. Two weeks after the coup, permanent secretaries were barred from meetings of the Federal Executive Council.

RELATIONS AND CONFLICTS AMONG CLASSES, 1966–75

The class relations of Nigerian society generated ethnic conflicts. The Nigerian section of the international bourgeoisie lacked the capacity to finance and organize production. It depended on foreign patrons and the state for money and markets. Politics took the form of communal competition for control of public resources. Even after the civil war, the state proved incapable of regulating this competition. Instead the state and its officials became an integral part of it. The war itself showed the predominance of communal over class loyalties. Easterners made up a significant proportion of the wage-earners in the North. They were killed or expelled in the massacres with the rest of their communities. As secession and civil war approached, most central trade union leaders played down the demands of eastern refugees for payment of wages and compensation. During the war the union centres vocally supported the federal cause, while their eastern affiliates formed a Biafran TUC.

The war also exacerbated conflicts between classes. Workers, farmers, artisans and petty traders had to meet the costs of inflation, higher taxation and import restrictions, while the price of export crops and level of wages were held down, just as at the time of the Second World War. War-time austerity meant suffering for the poor. For the rich it meant inconvenience at worst, and new opportunities for income and profits at best. As the Adebo Commission commented,[59] *'the suffering* [of the lowest income group] *is made even more intolerable by manifestations of affluence and wasteful expenditure which cannot be explained on the basis of visible and legitimate means of income'.* The spread of oil money has not alleviated the problem. Comprador bureaucrats and businessmen have appropriated the largest share of income and opportunities. Again, workers, farmers, artisans and petty traders have borne the costs of the consequent inflation, without being able to exploit the opportunities it creates. As demonstrating workers in Ecuador expressed it,[60] 'More petroleum, more poverty, more hunger, more joblessness'.

In 1968, increased taxes were resisted by western state farmers in the areas of declining cocoa production. Farmers attacked council officials, police, and local rulers who harassed and extorted from them, and supported the government against the farmers. In July 1969, mobile army-police units were sent to the farms to arrest tax defaulters. Farmers, armed with 'dane guns, matchets and dangerous charms' maintained their resistance, invaded Ibadan prison, and forced the authorities to accept their demands for the reduction of taxes and removal of officials. Two demands were not granted. The demand for an immediate increase in the producer price of cocoa, and the creation of a separate Oyo state, which farmers declared to be of moment to the politicians rather than themselves.[61]

During the war, grass roots militancy flourished while national labour leaders lost credibility and influence. After the war, faced by a renewed alliance of the rival central labour unions the Adebo Commission increased wages by £2 a month and recommended comparable adjustments in the private sector, when it made its interim award in 1971. The Commissioner of Labour agreed to exempt companies who had increased wages since 1964. This led to a wave of strikes in foreign firms, which forced the employers (anxious for their valuable machinery and vulnerable managers) and the government to give way. Strikes were organized in Lagos by factory-based unions, and in Kano by workers' committees. Leaders of central unions were conspicuous by their absence.[62]

The continued economic importance of petty commodity production maintains the possibilities of economic independence and individual mobility. The common people admire the entrepreneur who has prospered by developing his or her own business, and who continues to live among his or her customers and clients. They admire the generous patron who may assist others to establish themselves, though he or she claims in return their custom, labour-power and loyalties. Entrepreneurial values are two-edged. They lay claim to opportunities for all, and to the assistance of the rich. They unite the common people in opposition to the appropriation of opportunities by the rich at the expense of the poor. People look to their 'brothers' or 'sisters' for security. 'Brothers' or 'sisters' are defined only by context, according to criteria of kinship, workplace, neighbourhood, community of origin, or class. The ethic of brotherhood and sisterhood can promote class as well as ethnic solidarities. It may unite workers, and the urban poor among whom they live and whose values they share.[63]

Class action is not a function of the prevailing ethic. It is the product of the social relations specific to different classes. The ethic of competitive individualism, the search for the generous patron and the ethic of brotherhood are shared among all classes. Resentment of corruption and exploitation by the rich and powerful are general throughout society. But it is industrial workers and cocoa farmers who have engaged in militant class action in defence of their interests and their rights.

Workers share the entrepreneurial ambitions of traders and artisans. Wage employment is necessary to provide for them, and their dependents. It is also a source of savings which can be invested in independent trading or craft activities. Increased wages are a means of escaping wage slavery. Thus entrepreneurial ambitions encourage workers' militancy. In 1971, strikes were concentrated in Lagos and Kano, the main industrial centres at that time. In Zaria and Ibadan, where factories are fewer, and opportunities in self-employment for strangers less, there were few incidents.[64] The social organization of industrial production, the concentration of workers in particular cities and suburbs, and common dependence on wages has brought workers to recognize a community of interest and experience. Wage demands have provided the issue, and strikes and industrial actions the sanctions to enforce their demands. Similarly, common dependence on the government's decisions about crop prices, subordination to government officials, and the appropriation of farmers' resources by urban politicians and their clients, have created a specific form of peasant consciousness. Taxes provided both the issue and the sanction for peasant action. Artisans and traders resent the monopolistic practices of merchants. They compete with one another for custom, and look to patrons to give them access to better trading opportunities. They identify their own interests with the wage, price and tax demands of workers and farmers whose spending provides the main

165

source of their custom. Both urban workers and farmers, in taking action in support of their own class interests, see themselves as fighting for their rights in general, and opposing the injustice of the existing order.

The Udoji Commission drew up a systematic regrading of civil service posts, and a revision of wage and salary levels to take account of dramatic inflation. Wages for the lowest paid workers were doubled. The commission recommended that increases be paid over a year in two instalments. In a desperate attempt to buy back political support, the government decided to pay the award in full in January 1975, with arrears, half of which would be tax free, backdated to April 1974. Consumers could join the government in the indiscriminate spending of oil money. Anomalies in the regrading of posts provoked a series of strikes by professionals, such as doctors, pharmacists and engineers, hospital and university workers, and students, who argued that the new scales discriminated against them in favour of administrators. Workers in the private sector went on strike to secure the extension of the awards and arrears to them. The government was forced to agree to a 30 per cent minimum pay rise, with full arrears, for both sectors. The massive spending spree which followed accentuated inflation, shortages and congestions. Farmers tried to hold up food deliveries, and force down transport costs, increased by the petrol shortage. Far from buying off class antagonisms, the government accentuated them. Farmers, workers and unionists were variously detained, to be released when the government fell in July 1975.

CONCLUSION THE 1975 COUP AND THE POLITICS OF CAPITALISM

On 29 July 1975, field officers who had fought the civil war and in several cases executed the coup of 29 July 1966 removed Gowon and the military governors, who had exercised administrative power for eight or nine years. Colonels and majors organized the coup. Four brigadiers took over the key positions in the government and army: Murtala Muhammed, head of state; Obasanjo, chief of staff, Supreme Headquarters; Danjuma, chief of staff, army; Bisalla, commissioner of defence. All officers above that rank were retired. The head of state and the military governors, with small cliques of civil service advisers and business associates, had decided policies and allocated patronage with scant regard for their military peers, let alone anyone else. The indefinite postponement of civilian rule and the determined retention of office by the governors, perpetuated their personal appropriation of the spoils of office. The authority of the Federal Executive Council, which included Brigadier Muhammed and other officers, were flagrantly overriden by Gowon's appointment of a NNOC general manager. The Udoji payments and port congestion demonstrated the government's ineptness. The coup was arranged in such a way as to avoid any shedding of blood, and to attempt to ensure the solidarity of the officer corps and the army.

The new government realized that the economic development, social stability and international standing of Nigeria required institutional reform and firm and disciplined government. They needed to create a constitutional framework within which conflicts among interests could be managed without threatening the authority of the state and the stability of society. They needed a central state authority capable of deciding on, and implementing, public policies. They needed a programme which could meet popular aspirations. The most obvious feature of the new government has been its capacity to use military authority to decide a number of intractable issues, and to carry out its declared intentions.

Its first step was to establish federal military authority over state governors and civil servants. The new state governors are responsible as serving officers to the chief of staff, Supreme Headquarters. They may be, and have been, transferred or removed. They no longer sit on the Supreme Military Council. Permanent secretaries are excluded from meetings of the federal Executive Council unless specifically invited. Several top federal and state permanent secretaries, including Ayida and Asiodu have been retired.

Measures were taken to discipline the civil service. The government retired 10,000 employees, of whom a well publicized minority held senior police, judicial, academic and administrative posts. Tribunals exposed some amazing abuses, the government suspended certain contracts, and reappropriated certain assets. It set up a Permanent Corrupt Practices Investigation Bureau and a Public Complaints Commission. Such measures could scarcely end collusion between state officials and local and foreign capitalists, as long as the state continues to be the major avenue for private accumulation of money, and the leading allocator of opportunities for profit.

The Gowon regime had failed to reorganize the army after the civil war. As Lt.-Gen. Danjuma declared, '. . . since the civil war, the Nigerian Army has been run as a social service, maintaining and paying an exceedingly large body of men that we do not really need and whom we cannot equip'.[65] At the beginning of 1976, the army announced a cautious policy of demobilization. Senior officers were promoted to generals and brigadiers. In February 1976, an incompetent attempt at a coup failed, but the head of state was assassinated. The coup makers resented the recent promotions, feared demobilization, and allegedly planned to restore Gowon to power. Most of the participants were publicly executed,

167

including Major General Bisalla. Popular support for the actions of the new government and fear of the consequences of any new round of killing within the army account for the bitterness and anger of both the army and the public. Nationalist resentments focused on Britain, where Gowon was exiled.

The new government took action to resolve the constitutional problems with which Gowon had failed to deal. The 1973 population census was rejected in favour of the 1963 figures. A commission was set up to examine petitions for new states. Some 200 proposals were made to draw different boundaries for sharing out oil revenues, jobs and opportunities. The commission recommended the creation of twenty states. The government agreed to, and established, a total of nineteen, and declared that to be the limit. A government proposal for uniform local government throughout the country was turned down, and traditional rulers have been accorded new respect, and allowed an active role in local government. A new federal capital is to be built at Abuja, in the centre of the country. A unitary state has been set up in federal disguise. But it leaves local institutions, patronage and appointments in state hands, and ensures protection at the federal level for the interests of the far north.

On 1 October 1975 a firm timetable was drawn up for a return to civilian rule. A draft constitution has been submitted, and local government elections held, without overt party politics. From the institutions of local government, a constituent assembly is to be elected to consider the draft constitution. Political parties will then be formed for successive state and federal elections, prior to the handover of power on 1 October 1979. The constituent assembly, with its basis in local, indirect elections, supplemented by government nominations, recalls the 1950 General Review of the Constitution. 'Demilitarization' of politics may prove less final than its model, the 'decolonization' of political office.

The draft constitution seeks to combine an effective central executive, capable of directing state policy and arbitrating among conflicting interests, with effective representation for sectional interests. It thus recommends an executive president, whose appointment and powers are hedged with an array of checks and balances which would have pleased Montesquieu himself. Presidents must win a plurality of votes, and one quarter of the votes in each of at least two-thirds of the states, or a majority of votes both nationally and in half of the states. Presidential authority thus requires the support of a broad coalition of state interests. The composition of federal and state governments and their agencies, and the conduct of their affairs, must give due representation to their constituent states and communities, defined as recognizing 'the federal character of Nigeria'.[66] A draft which would have outlawed discrimination by state of origin was dropped.[67] A series of statutory bodies, appointed by the president with legislative approval, will carry out politically sensitive tasks, such as running elections and reviewing revenue allocation, and making politically sensitive appointments. Appointments to defence, police and security councils will not require legislative approval. Nor will ministerial appointments. The draft constitution and the somewhat muted debate which has followed it have been, in the words of the dissenting Minority Report on the Constitution, primarily concerned with 'provisions for the formal and dubious accountability of one set of members of the bourgeois political class to another . . .'.[68]

The Third Plan had announced that finance was no longer a constraint on development, and the Gowon government spent and planned accordingly. Its expenditures rose rapidly to meet its revenues, and its plans assumed a continued increase in oil production and prices, together with a moderate rate of inflation. In May 1975, oil production had fallen back from 2.3 million to 1.6 million barrels a day. Immediately after the coup, the Muhammed government cut prices as a 'gesture of goodwill'. Since then, with demand high, production has risen to 2 million b/d in 1976, and prices, royalties and taxes have been increased. But despite this the companies have cut back exploration and development. In October 1976 Lt.-Gen. Obasanjo promised incentives for exploration, and emphasized the need for good relations with the companies. In April 1976 a government memorandum proposed to merge NNOC and the Oil Ministry into a single Nigerian National Petroleum Company. But no action was taken until twelve months later. Administrators objected to paying oil professionals salaries comparable to their counterparts in the companies, since this would raise the salaries of oil technocrats and hence their status above those of the administrators.

The government is committed to ambitious investments intended to transform oil revenues into productive industries. Long delayed plans for an iron and steel mill, oil refineries and oil pipelines are going ahead. Ambitious schemes for liquefied natural gas, direct reduction steel plants using gas, and a petrochemical industry are planned. The 1976 and 1977 budgets encouraged assembly industries with increased protection for vehicles and other manufactures, and reduced duties on raw materials. Merchant and development banks have been directed, without immediate effect, to use their money for long term loans at low interest for industrial investments. The new Indigenization Decree further expands the scope of Nigerian ownership and shareholding. A new category of businesses requiring 60 per cent Nigerian ownership covers banks, trading companies and a number of industries.

The 1976 Indigenization Decree, like its predecessor, renegotiates the

169

terms of the relations between foreign and local capital. Foreign firms can realize the value of past investments by selling shares, and take new profits from management contracts rather than direct investments. Increased industrial investment will expand their market opportunities. Its success will depend on the expansion of the state sector, and will require an increase in the number of local technocrats and a consequent strengthening of their position within the state. But commerce offers easier and more lucrative profits than production does to private capitalists with access to government favour. A strategy of state-directed industrial expansion may well be undermined by the resulting competition over the commercial opportunities created by state expenditure.

A strategy of industrial development requires control of the labour force. The realization of any ambition to export manufactured goods depends on 'competitive' labour costs. Attempts to establish control have taken three forms: industrial relations legislation, reform of trade unions, and wage controls. In 1976 two new labour decrees created a complex hierarchy of institutions, headed by a National Industrial Relations Court, for enforcing settlements, banned strikes in essential services, and enabled the government to proscribe unions which act to 'disrupt the economy'. This law was soon applied to the bank employees. In December 1975 a Nigerian Labour Congress had eventually been established by appointing 102 national officers and sharing the top positions among the rival centres. In 1976, the government banned foreign labour organizations and set up the Adebiyi Commission[69] to enquire into the activities of the trade unions. In September it appointed an administrator to form a single central labour organization, and in 1977 proposed to establish a single central body with 31 industrial affiliates. By April, thirty-four unions had been listed, and the administrator had drawn up a detailed list of regulations for union elections. In 1977, the government banned a number of leaders from further trade union activity. The White Paper on the Adebiyi report promised to stamp out 'racketeering, abuse of office, personality cult, politicization, conflicts of interest, and similar malpractices', and to submit the power of trade union leaders to 'reasonable and civilized regulation'. A new code of conduct for union leaders prohibits conflicts of interest, 'chronic indebtedness', 'drunkenness', and initially banned participation in politics. A wage freeze was declared until 1 June 1977, after which wage increases were to be limited to 7 per cent in the coming year, despite inflation of over 60 per cent since 1975. In such circumstances, neither proscription, nor regulation, of unions is likely to prevent industrial action by workers.

Despite the need to reduce expenditure, the government has maintained its commitment to universal primary education, and to spending on health, housing and agriculture. Cheap fertilizers and credit are being made available to 'feed the nation'. They may well contribute more to private commerce and government employment than to agricultural production. The proposal of the constitutional committee to abolish the marketing boards, once the main source of state government income and patronage, was rejected. Instead these have been reorganized as federal boards for each commodity.

In international politics the Nigerian government has taken a strong nationalist lead. In October 1975, it was still deploring external encouragement of rivalries in Angola.[70] With the South African intervention, it committed itself decisively to the MPLA, praised Soviet support for African liberation and dismissed the American 'directive'[71] to African heads of state to insist on Soviet and Cuban withdrawal as 'a most intolerable presumption and a flagrant insult on the intelligence of African rulers'.[72] Nigeria plainly intends to continue her leading role in negotiations between developed and underdeveloped countries for new terms of trade and investment.

The Nigerian military government aims to establish the institutional conditions for industrial development and political stability. State investments and state regulation of the economy are intended to promote the development of capitalist production and national independence. Its constitutional measures and proposals attempt to accommodate the politics of sectional competition to the need for central direction of public policy. As Petras and Morley argue, '. . . regulation of foreign capital and promotion of growth and expansion of national bureaucratic and private capital leads to a new historical bloc of classes – in which national and foreign industrial capital collaborate.'[73] However, the capacity of the Nigerian state to achieve this measure of realignment with foreign capital remains doubtful. Technocratic nationalism lacks a firm class base in Nigerian society. Profit-making continues to depend on collaboration with foreign firms and on the favour of the state. The state continues to control access to money, contracts and commercial opportunities. Politics is a struggle for the control of these resources. But these resources are also means by which politics is carried out. The constitutional proposals recognize and accommodate this sort of politics. Politics is assumed to be a business of reconciling divergent interests, pursued by competing elites. Questions of foreign domination, class power and state policy are ignored or evaded. Bourgeois domination, the purpose and foundation of such politics, is taken for granted.

Civilian constitutional rule requires a bourgeoisie in command of productive resources, capable of settling its own affairs peaceably, maintaining the authority of the state, and accommodating the participation in

171

politics of subordinate classes. The production, market, state and moral relations of Nigerian society generate conflicts among competing comprador interests for access to scarce resources, between compradores and technocrats over the direction of state policy, and between the state and the subordinate classes over the terms of their exploitation. Neither the policies of the military government, nor the proposals of the constitution-makers show either the will or the capacity to tackle these sources of political instability. Civilian rule is thus likely to repeat the 'failure of politics', and hence to invite in its turn a fresh demonstration from the military of the 'failure of administration'.

7

Senegal

DONAL B. CRUISE O'BRIEN

Any form of multi-party political life, in a West African state today, is obviously enough of an oddity to arouse at least some curiosity in a student of political affairs in the region. The peculiar circumstances by which new constitutional amendments were adopted (in April 1976) to 're-animate party politics' in Senegal, by providing for the creation of a tripartite political system, should re-awaken even the most jaded observer. The revised constitution decrees that there should henceforth be three political parties in Senegal, each to work within a constitutionally defined ideological framework. The governing Union Progressiste Sénégalaise designates its own ideological position as 'socialist and democratic', leaving an allocated space for one party to its right ('liberal and democratic') and another to its left ('Marxist–Leninist or communist', as the constitution bluntly stipulates).[1] The deliberate (and of course presidentially inspired) creation of a legal communist opposition party, is an oddity not only in West African terms but indeed by any international standards.

Elsewhere in the West African region the political trend over the past fifteen years has of course been moving firmly away from multi-party electoral competition: towards single-party regimes with attendant presidentialist quasi-dictatorships, military coups with consequent soldierly dictatorships. Such changes of regime have on the whole been accompanied by an enduring fragility of political authority with more or less latent communal strife behind an unconvincing institutional façade of national unity. Nor, until very recently, has Senegal itself been such a startling exception to the regional political rule: there may have been no military coups (even attempted), but on the other hand since independence there has been a progressive consolidation of authority under the monopoly auspices of Léopold Senghor's Union Progressiste Sénégalaise. Opposition voices had been more or less stridently raised in the immediate post-independence years, but all parties of opposition had by 1966 either been legally banned or else incorporated in the governing UPS. Ten years later the president seems bent on undoing his good work: how does he imagine that he (or even the country) can afford such a paradoxical luxury?

The presidential teacher sternly refuses to countenance deviation from the ideological principles stipulated for his legalized opponents. As Article Two of the revised national constitution specifies, 'the political parties may be dissolved by decree in a situation where the repeated declarations of their national leaders, the resolutions adopted by their national committees, prove that they do not respect the objectives defined by their statutes, with reference to one of the three specified schools of thought'. So, pupils, you will have only yourselves to blame if you fail to live up to your constitutionally allocated ideology. In effect, President Senghor (with any necessary guidance from the Ministry of the Interior) will decide whether or not you are conducting yourselves like good communists (or, for that matter, liberal democrats) and if necessary take disciplinary measures appropriate to the occasion.

The single-party UPS regime has of course quite effectively mono-polized the exercise of political power over the past decade (and under various names and initials has dominated Senegalese political life for a quarter of a century) but the constitutional revisions of 1976 at least at face value do suggest a quite startling political confidence in the pres-idential palace. The general amnesty which was then also declared for political detainees has reinforced the prevalent impression of presidential confidence: a proud boast indeed, no political prisoners in Senegal. It does remain the case that elections to the National Assembly (scheduled for 1978) are to be by single national list, the party with a national electoral majority taking all parliamentary seats. There may be three parties to contest these elections, but psephologists will be awarded no prizes for correctly forecasting that electoral outcome. The constitution in its revised form does also provide for the prime minister (at present, Abdou Diouf) to succeed automatically to the presidency in case of the present incumbent's death or resignation, and the successor is then to serve out his predecessor's five year electoral mandate (at present, to 1978). The timing of Léopold Senghor's disappearance from the Senegalese political scene is beyond the scope of constitutional provision, but in principle at least a stable succession is assured. Parliamentary or presidential polling, so long successfully manipulated by incumbent authority in Senegal, will no doubt remain faithful to traditional electoral practice.

Prior to the dramatic constitutional revisions of April 1976, it is true that the past few years had already seen the slow and very cautious

174

emergence of one possible alternative party to the UPS, Abdoulaye Wade's Parti Démocratique Sénégalais. The PDS had been legally recognized in 1974, Wade then descending from a political trial balloon designated Club Nation et Développement, a 'policy discussion group' of academics, businessmen, lawyers and civil servants.[2] This club had been reputed to enjoy at least a benevolent neutrality from the presidential palace, and the founder of the PDS, with a habitual circumspection, initially defined the new party's role as 'one of contribution, not opposition'. The PDS newspaper (*Le Démocrate*) has nonetheless been on occasion openly critical both of government policy and of the more flagrantly undemocratic internal procedures of the governing UPS, sufficiently critical indeed to assure the newspaper a wide circulation even among the regime's more uncompromising opponents.

Within the ideological parameters defined by the recent constitutional amendment, President Senghor has made it clear that the PDS is to be to his right, 'liberal and democratic'. Wade apparently would prefer his party to be seen as 'working-class socialist', but he is not disposed to cling to this (or possibly any other) ideological fetish. His party has after all enjoyed a measure of presidential protection, which indeed is sorely needed in the face of many forms of harassment by the UPS cadres. A PDS rally at Kolda in 1975, for example, provoked the local UPS to assault those with the temerity to attend: but, perhaps more surprisingly, an official investigation subsequently ruled that nineteen UPS militants had indeed been guilty of bodily assault, and (light) prison sentences were consequently imposed. The *préfêt* conducting this investigation, as an agent of state administration, would in such circumstances take instructions from the highest government levels. But UPS notables remain most distrustful of the PDS: in January 1976 Wade went so far as to declare that 'the principles of contribution and of opposition are not incompatible' and in June he defiantly proclaimed that 'the PDS will win the elections to the National Assembly in 1978, or whenever they may be held'.[3] Within the UPS, distrust extends not only to the obvious target of a new opposition party, but increasingly to the president himself: after all those years of loyal (if not disinterested) service to the governing party, what is Senghor trying to do? Neither UPS cadres nor indeed any other sources appear to have fully convincing answers to that question.

In its own odd way, Abdoulaye Wade's PDS is a tantalizing enough political case study. But the political intentions of Wade and his friends have been altogether too ambiguous to arouse enthusiasm among Dakar's numerous semi-clandestine oppositionists: the effective result of adhesion to the PDS often being to stake a claim to promotion within the governing UPS hierarchy. And the official PDS programme, although mentioning a need to rectify 'flagrant social inequalities', and 'to organize the peasantry in new ways', scarcely amounts to a stirring or even a plausible manifesto.[4] A party which publicly hesitates between the 'not incompatible' principles of contribution and opposition would indeed appear to invite a membership of temporary ex-UPS malcontents: nothing here, in any case, to stir the hearts of youth or to mobilize the more intransigent oppositional ideals.

It was perhaps partly in consequence of the widespread scepticism aroused by the PDS in opposition circles that President Senghor announced (already in January 1976) his intention to allow the creation of a third political party, to be of Marxist–Leninist ideological affiliation. A communist party (Parti Africain de l'Indépendance) had previously been established in Senegal, as long ago as 1957, but the PAI then enjoyed only three years of legal existence, being banned following violent confrontations at the polls in St Louis in 1960. Abdoulaye Wade himself, in a letter to his (then) friend and founder of the PAI (Mahjmout Diop) had proffered pertinent advice at the moment of the PAI's foundation

> Not only will you have all sorts of difficulties on the internal level – and you should not wilfully look for difficulties – but the strategic position of our country, and Soviet–American competition, mean that the USA will necessarily intervene. Think hard about that, because it is no theory. The goal of a party is essentially – in my opinion – the conquest of power as a prior condition to any realisation of its aims . . .
>
> The national struggle is no mere adventure, and you don't mobilise a people for a hopeless action. Now we have always agreed on the question of independence, although ideology is another matter. I have been saying this for some time, and I repeat, the negroes will be liberated even against their will.[5]

Sound enough for 1957, although international circumstances have changed somewhat in two subsequent decades: perhaps even a Cuban colonization of West Africa could now be envisaged as a (remote) possibility, and Guiné-Bissau has yet to be invaded by the US marines.

Whatever the shifting strategic realities of global *Machtpolitik*, however, Wade's allusion to communist 'difficulties on the internal level' remains altogether pertinent. Mahjmout Diop himself, having returned quietly to Senegal with a presidential pardon in December 1975, after fourteen years of exile, would now no doubt testify to that. The PAI did after a fashion survive those lean years, as a progressively attenuated local clandestine group, but the younger militants of Dakar's Marxist *groupuscules* have come to regard the ageing militants of that party as distinctly *vieux jeu*. And the recently reorganized and (relatively) efficient state police in any case keeps all extreme leftist political intrigue under close enough surveillance.

Mahjmout Diop, re-familiarizing himself with such 'difficulties on the internal level', was slow enough to declare himself willing to take the officially allocated seat to Senghor's (constitutionally extreme) left. In April 1976 he did receive another presidential nudge, having his full political rights restored following a declaration of political amnesty approved by the National Assembly. In August he finally shuffled forward to pick up the presidential gauntlet: following a 'national renovation conference' of his erstwhile associates, a request for the constitutional recognition of the PAI was formally issued – and the necessary recognition then very promptly (within a week) accorded.[6] So now we have it at last, a legal opposition party of plausible Marxist–Leninist credentials (and impeccable antecedence): with the hindsight of November 1976, it seems likely enough that the unfortunate Mahjmout was allowed to return to Senegal only upon condition that he subsequently take that constitutional hot seat.

Although Senegal's revised constitution might appear (to the uninformed outside observer) thus to have catered for a broad enough range of ideological tastes, the presidentially stipulated opposition party programmes, and the presidentially selected legal opposition leadership, do still quite effectively serve to deny any legal status for a very wide range of excluded Senegalese political ambitions. Leopold Senghor's remarkable political career has after all to date been devoted (for nearly three decades past) to the very skilful elimination of rival political groups – by absorption, or if necessary by legalized suppression. Strewn by the wayside of this triumphal progress there have of course been many political casualties, with more or less bitter memories surviving to the present day. One should perhaps itemize the more significant of such losers: (a) erstwhile supporters of Lamine Guèye and the Senegalese branch of the French SFIO, legally amalgamated with Senghor's party (then the Bloc Populaire Sénégalais) in 1958, many of whom still cherish some nostalgia for the golden days when Lamine ruled the coastal municipalities (*communes*); (b) friends and followers of ex-prime minister Mamadou Dia, who was deposed in the constitutional crisis of 1962 and then kept under house arrest until 1974, a group (to its opponents, a clan) now surviving above all in certain sectors of the civil service; (c) the coalition following Cheikh Anta Diop, whose first political party (Bloc des Masses Sénégalaises, 1962–3) did – albeit briefly – pose a serious electoral threat to the government. Much of the BMS leadership was then absorbed to the

177

governing party, but not Cheikh Anta himself: the membership had largely been recruited from the more disgruntled elements of Lamine Guèye's urban clientele; (d) supporters of Abdoulaye Ly and the Parti du Regroupement Africain – Sénégal, uneasily absorbed to the UPS in 1966, Ly himself (like Cheikh Anta Diop) having subsequently raised himself (or been raised) above politics, to a research post at the Institut Fondamental d'Afrique Noire (IFAN) – the research institute as police station.

These various excluded groups, in local parlance *clans* each of which is united above all by personal allegiance to a given leader, may not share very much in the details of a political programme (or, as they say in Senegal, an ideology). But there is one possible overall unifying principle – a shared desire to displace Léopold Senghor. Cheikh Anta Diop would appear to have had something of the sort in mind when he recently applied (February 1976) for legal recognition of a new party, to be entitled Rassemblement National Démocratique. The projected RND was to be 'an alliance of patriots and democrats united under a nationalist programme, without any consideration of class, age, or political origin ... there will be no exclusion' – an open invitation indeed.

Where more exalted, 'ideological' considerations are concerned, Cheikh Anta Diop might perhaps best be designated a cultural nationalist, in his voluminous writings[7] the proponent of an argument whereby the Senegalese Wolof tribe (and other African peoples, no exclusion here either) are shown to be the product of a diaspora from the high negroid civilization of ancient Egypt. The merits of this bitterly contested historical argument are not at issue here, but the projected RND does have its own more immediate historical resonance in the Senegalese political tradition: Galandou Diouf, opposing the local hegemony of Blaise Diagne, already in the 1920s had reduced the relevant principle to a single curt slogan – 'everything against Diagne is ours'. Lamine Guèye, despite his nominal adherence to the (let us say) revisionist Marxist principles of French parliamentary socialism, effectively mobilized the Senegalese (urban) electorate against Galandou Diouf in the 1930s under a similarly elementary organizing principle. The spoils of office, municipal and parliamentary, for such leaders might only become more remote with any fastidious insistence on ideological purity: no exclusion, except for those obstinate individuals who failed to come to terms with the party machine. And for Senghor, considering Cheikh Anta's application to form his new RND coalition, *that* sort of opposition would apparently not do at all. The vacant ideological slot had been presidentially specified as Marxist–Leninist, and Cheikh Anta duly received a stern presidential rebuke (February 1976): 'it is not permissible that a party, essentially the same one, should change its ideology according to political circumstance'.[8] Perhaps only a head of state could permit himself such effrontery: Cheikh Anta has given no public indication of having changed his political beliefs, which remain as far as ever they were from the principles of Marx or Lenin. But of course it is the president who decides what is or is not 'permissible', and for the moment it would seem that the projected RND has no place within Senegal's new constitutional framework. Like Kemal Atatürk, Léopold Senghor will choose his own opposition, but to Turkish authoritarian democracy he can add his own characteristic touch of French academic pedantry. Senegal's first *agrégé en grammaire* firmly intends to teach his recalcitrant pupils the ideological rules of their own party programmes. So Cheikh Anta Diop, suitably chastised, must for the moment return to his (governmentally subsidized) research in history and linguistics: perhaps he would be politically well advised to take up a new academic discipline (the territorial boundaries of scholarly endeavour do seem to be taken with an especial seriousness in Senegalese politics: Cheikh Anta Diop himself rebuffed an invitation (from Abdoulaye Wade) to join the PDS on the stated grounds that 'you are a jurist, and I specialize in other disciplines').[9]

One obvious question, in reviewing these constitutional manoeuvres, remains obstinately salient – why should Léopold Senghor, towards the end of a long political career (much of which has been devoted to a relatively delicate elimination or incorporation of organized opposition to the UPS regime) belatedly seek to undo at least some of an achievement substantially his own? Several explanations have tentatively been advanced, although neither political observers nor actors can claim with any confidence to read the presidential mind. It was suggested, for example, that Senghor aspired to UPS membership of the Second Socialist International (an ambition realized in October 1976), and that European parliamentary socialists welcomed at least a multi-party façade in Senegal (although the French socialists apparently had little initial enthusiasm for such a project: perhaps François Mitterand in particular found it hard to forgive Senghor his French parliamentary Gaullist and Catholic friends of the 1950s). Where Wade's PDS is concerned, there seems some agreement that the intention (at least originally) was to provide for a moderate legal alternative party which might recruit among the government's own employees: in Wade's own words, 'those civil servants didn't belong to any party, legal or illegal; they just didn't care'.[10] Although it should be added that these same functionaries were not at all indifferent to the salary demands put forward by their trade union (as they demonstrated in the national general strike of 1968, and again on a reduced scale in 1969). More than half Senegal's national budget by then had already been allocated to civil service salaries, and (despite a wage freeze applied since independence) their wage claims could not plausibly be based on any notions of national social justice. But if the state's employees are in material terms still clearly a privileged elite, it remains equally clear that their strike action can immobilize the state apparatus. And it took all of President Senghor's formidable skill in negotiation to avert that threat, through a combination of (minor enough) wage concessions, a manipulation of personal and factional rivalries in the union leadership, and ultimately the legal incorporation of all members to a single government controlled trade union with statutory representation (eight seats) in the national parliament. But if the trade union leadership could be divided and/or bought, the membership although quiescent since 1970 retains an acute enough sense of material grievance and political frustration.

In these circumstances it might not be altogether frivolous to suggest that the PDS opposition, with its widely-read newspapers, could be (presidentially) intended to provide at least a harmless distraction for the restive state employees. Abdoulaye Wade's intricate political manoeuvres may not inspire any charismatic devotion, but they have provided a subject of lively enough discussion (and all within the law) for the Dakar elite. Carry on talking: better that than leave the presidency without the means of national adminstration. A novel enough purpose perhaps for a political party, but then Senegal of late has been a land fertile in political novelty. Where the Marxist–Leninist PAI is concerned, possible presidential intentions do of course come fairly readily to mind: a legal communist pary in obvious ways does facilitate the task of police surveillance, even if (for this reason among others) the PAI leadership may not readily recruit much of a mass following.

Due allowance being given to these notionally presidential purposes, one further question does remain. In principle at least, the game has its obvious dangers: and how can Senghor be so confident of his ability to retain control of this legalized opposition? Any attempt to answer this latter question might logically start by considering the military dispositions which to date have protected the regime from the danger of an armed coup d'état. Senghor's government since independence has indeed been periodically threatened by urban rioting, notably at St Louis in 1960, then at Dakar in 1963 and again in the late 1960s, but the regime ever since 1960 has enjoyed a crucial external support in the detachment of French soldiery posted to the nation's capital. This military presence, effectively Léopold Senghor's French praetorian guard, perhaps more than any other single factor explains both the president's political durability and his recent willingness to allow legal indulgence to (at least some

180

ot) his opponents. The French garrison has indeed been substantially reduced since 1960 (nine hundred officially remaining in 1976), but it does remain encamped on the perimeter of Senegal's only international airport and could very promptly be reinforced should need arise.[11] Senegal's own national army has been stationed, by a combination of strategic and political preference, near the nation's borders and far from the nation's capital, so that urban rioters can scarcely yet aspire to organized armed support. This French military presence, although it may not be likely to survive Senghor himself, has for the moment come to be recognized by all local political leaders simply as a fact of Senegalese political life. The same politico-military fact also of course helps to explain the apparent nonchalance of President Senghor in spending such a large part of his time at his second home in Normandy. And it does explain both why the governing UPS has been able to afford a relative weakness of party organization in the capital city and why the president can now permit himself the apparent luxury of legal party opposition (even, if you will, Marxist–Leninist). An African head of state who can spend half the year in France can apparently now also afford himself a great deal by way of Senegalese constitutional experimentation.

The revised constitution of 1976, in providing for a dual opposition, does appear to have been designed (and has certainly been applied) to provide for legal political organization above all in Senegal's larger towns. This may be seen as a tacit acknowledgement of the governing party's relative weakness in an urban setting. The UPS is indeed very effective, in its own clientelistic style, as an instrument of state control across most of rural Senegal: but the UPS leadership, and of course the president himself, must be concerned by this urban weakness. Senegal is after all by now much the most urbanized country in West Africa, with 27 per cent of the population living in centres of more than 50,000 inhabitants.[12] The state's capital, Dakar, has grown to a sprawling city of 800,000 people: from a governmental perspective, Dakar in particular is the major worry. Within the capital city there is of course a very substantial educated elite, most of it in some form of governmental employment, a smaller proportion with managerial posts in French or other commercial concerns, and a now disturbingly large segment (among well qualified school leavers) without any prospect of employment corresponding to educational achievement. In 1975 in Dakar the government, having 'nationalized' the retail bread market, required a secondary school *brevêt* (O level, roughly) as a condition for the allocation of a humble bread kiosk: striking testimony indeed to the crisis of educational overproduction resultant from the combination of a plethora of secondary schools and a stagnant national economy. Senegal's urban elite, since the colonial days of the four coastal communes, has continued to hold aspirations to a French style of life – which an economy still uncomfortably dependent on peanut production can of course scarcely afford. The older generation of the ex-*commune* educated elite (and three of the historic *communes* are now incorporated within the Dakar agglomeration) may enjoy their own discreet nostalgia for the days of Lamine Guèye, although Senghor has not deprived them of their civil service positions. But for their juniors (very often their sons), especially for those with some experience of university education and scant prospect of rapid career advancement, more intransigent political opposition has its evident attractions. In periods of national political stability (the last five years) this would appear a world of futile Paris-styled *gauchisme*, very sketchily organized in semi-clandestine extremist *groupuscules*. But at certain moments of crisis in state authority (the summers of 1968 and 1969, notably) these youthful malcontents have demonstrated a formidable enough capability in raising riot on the streets of Dakar. Whether those of the little groups will adhere to the legal PAI (as the president no doubt desires) is yet to be seen, but there are obvious grounds for scepticism here. (One need only bear in mind the low fashion rating of the French communist party among the militants of the Boulevard St Michel.) As indeed, although on other grounds, there are already proven reasons to doubt the willingness of the daddies of these activists (paradigmatically speaking) to display more than a passing curiosity about the machinations of Abdoulaye Wade's PDS.

The urban deficiencies of the governing party's organization, and the relative strength of urban subversive potential, may in part explain the presidential desire to give a legal status to political organization in the towns. The continuing presence of France's Dakar garrison may also in large measure explain the president's ability to satisfy this constitutional desire. But in reviewing the constitutional initiatives of 1976, reference to this (on the whole discreet, and certainly little publicized) French armed presence can clearly be no more than a starting point to any attempt at a full or politically coherent explanation of the deliberate recreation of party opposition – even under the carefully controlled conditions specified by the revised Article Two. And here, thinking in comparative West African terms, one must I think turn to quite a different perspective, that of the peculiarly coherent communal situation presently emerging in Senegal. There may be no single discernible architect, but this is one new micro-nation genuinely under construction.

In this communal perspective, that of the mass base of political allegiances and of potential antagonisms, the primal significance of a nationally shared adhesion to a hegemonic religion – Islam – should not require emphasis. Differential allegiances to particular saints of three major Sufi brotherhoods (Tijaniyya, Qadiriyya, Mouride) do indeed exist, there is a small Roman Catholic minority (including Leopold Senghor, a neutral figure for the arbitration of occasional inter-Islamic squabbles), and on the state's periphery also a rapidly diminishing minority which has yet to see the light of any universal religion, but for nine-tenths of Senegal's population Islam does provide a basic element of shared communal identity. Muslims may bicker over details of devotional practice, and over many mundane matters, but all believers recognize a single transcendent Book and a single Prophet.

Of more immediate political significance, perhaps, than national quasi-unanimity in religious belief, is the emergence (especially rapid since independence) of an unofficial national language – Wolof – spoken according to recent estimates by some four-fifths of Senegal's population.[13] Tribal ('ethnic') census data have concealed the prodigious dissemination of the Wolof language (the Wolof *ethnie* from 1900 to 1970 consistently accounting for about one-third of total population). But those non-Wolof *ethnies* which are in the process of abandoning their ethnic language (Serer, Fulbe, Mandinka, Diola, etc.) a process especially affecting those tribesmen who migrate to any of Senegal's larger towns, are also effectively in the process of discarding a potential vehicle for minority 'tribalist' political consciousness in favour of a (sometimes admittedly grudging) adhesion to a state-wide socio-linguistic community. Wolof is the preferred linguistic medium for virtually all townsmen; it is the language of African trade, of the schoolyard (though not the schoolroom), and of virtually all inter-ethnic marriages (even if neither partner be Wolof by birth).[14] It does remain above all an unwritten language (discounting a certain limited traditional use of Arabic characters, and more recent attempts to adapt a Latin script, for an as yet esoteric Wolof transliteration).[15] The French language in these circumstances remains the sole language of official documentation, and of formal education, despite the preponderance of Wolof as an oral medium: Senghor's *agrégation* in French grammar, not to speak of his early career at the Ecole Coloniale, will not apparently allow much latitude in presidential thought on the status appropriate to Senegal's native languages. Wolof may proliferate as a national vehicular language in common speech, but the medium of literate authority must for the present remain French.

A partial consequence of this reluctance, at the highest levels of state officialdom, to countenance the adoption of Wolof as a written medium, is that the diffusion of the Wolof language remains substantially unorganized – again discounting recent efforts of a small number of Dakar

Wolof literati (grouped around the newspaper *Kaddu*).[16] But it is perhaps precisely because the process of Wolofization has been so spontaneous, so little organized, that it has provoked virtually no organized popular resistance. Those who speak other Senegalese languages may on occasion be subject to a certain derision (especially among urbanites), as *lakakat* (speakers of the strange and incomprehensible), but among Wolof speakers the *lakakat* are as much pitied as truly scorned. After all, nothing prevents them from learning Wolof language, and thereby abdicating *lakakat* status. Within the Wolof-speaking cultural group, there is a striking absence of fastidiousness where tribal 'origins' are concerned. The variant of Wolof currently being diffused across Senegal is itself a hybrid, 'Dakar Wolof' with its very extensively borrowed French terminology,[17] and for adepts in this urban-generated medium the country purists of the Wolof zone itself (Kayor, Baol, Saloum, etc.) are themselves subject to a certain pity for their failure to keep linguistically up to date. The French colonial policy of cultural assimiliation has thus worked in a mysterious and unintended manner, but in political terms it has apparently served to lay some of the base for a Senegalese national language.

If the linguistic dimension of communal consciousness in these circumstances poses no irreducible difficulties for the Senegalese state, somewhat more serious problems are implicit in the 'regionalist' sentiments which remain keenly enough felt in certain zones on the state's periphery. The largely Tukulor region of northern Senegal (Fleuve) continues to suffer from the decline of the regional capital of St Louis (capital for all of Senegal before independence). The multi-tribal Casamance region of southern Senegal, a potentially rich tropical agricultural zone, suffers from a relative governmental neglect in comparison with the peanut-producing regions to its north. And the sparsely populated eastern region (Oriental), although perhaps in the future a substantial producer of iron ore, has long been virtually ignored in the government's economic plans. But for inhabitants of these peripheral regions, however strong the resentment of a more or less benign governmental neglect, there is a well-established escape route – join the crowd and go to Dakar. To some observers, as to some inhabitants of the relevant regions, this may appear a solution of despair, but it is of course politically significant that economic life in these regions to a substantial extent depends on (very often, meagre enough) cash remittances from the urban centre. And, to return to socio-linguistic considerations, it is also significant both that these urban migrants necessarily learn the Wolof language and that upon return to their native regions they bring back the urban lingo with their cash. For the materially ambitious *lakakat* the message is clear: if you want to rise in life, learn Wolof. It is no coincidence, in the cant phrase, that Wolof should be the talk of the schoolyard. So in communal terms the ground in Senegal is well prepared for relatively non-antagonistic tribal contradictions.

In attempting to assess the precise degree and quality of communal allegiances and antagonisms at a popular level, admittedly a very difficult task for any observer, one is I think well advised to look outside political life, and indeed away from the traditional ethnographic domains of social anthropology (as practised in Senegal). Popular attitudes to sport, and in particular to the most popular sport in Senegal – wrestling – may provide a more relevant measure. Here (very literally) is an arena, not only within which various communal champions display their differential physical prowess, but also (more important for this argument) around which variously communal crowds display allegiances of course to their pre-ferred champions but also by extension to the tribe or region which the champion is held to represent. Wrestling has long been a sport popular in villages across most of Senegal: in the north, for example, a young man sets up a drum in the village square, and the first to knock over the drum has taken up the challenge and thus immediately starts the fight. Village wrestling of this kind does indeed persist, but over the past decade wrestling has also taken on a national dimension: the champions have taken on semi-professional status, and the big crowds and the big money draw the big men to (where else?) Dakar. These crowd-pulling conflicts are indeed wondrously variegated spectacles: the champion, with his retinue of gorgeously apparelled ladies and magicians to cast spells deemed useful to the combat, may be expected to dance, to dress ele-gantly, and to give speeches of proper belligerence. A national wrestling federation does attempt to impose internationally recognized rules for such conflicts, but to date crowd appreciation effectively sets its own heterodox standards. The federation (with French, and American Peace Corps, technical assistance) may be reluctant to accept the punch as a legitimate part of wrestling, and cannot for example see quite how to score the dropping of an opponent on his head,[18] but such internationalist pedantry is unlikely to be allowed to spoil the crowd's fun.

But to return to the political significance of Senegalese wrestling, it is obviously important that there is now a recognized national sport (centred, like so much else, on the capital city) and that champions of the nation's tribes and/or regions can meet without provoking (as it were) even a riot. In the spring of 1975 there was a fight between a gigantic *Casamançais* champion with the improbable name of Double Less and a Dakar Wolof wrestler called Mbaye Guèye, which did occasion some supplementary scuffles in the stadium. The match had been given perhaps

185

somewhat reckless advance publicity by its organizers, as 'Casamance versus Senegal', and President Senghor subsequently felt obliged to make the scarcely convincing public declaration that 'there is no place for regionalism in sport', but qualified observers at the Stade Demba Diop remarked that fighting in the stadium was provoked by those who had bet substantial sums on the (Wolof) loser.[19] Many of these latter punters were swiftly to change allegiances (regionalism indeed has little place in sound betting principles) while *Casamançais* exuberance was subsequently dampened by Double Less's performance outside the wrestling arena proper: he might be big (6' 6''), and a good wrestler (reaching the fifth round in the 1976 Olympic Games), but Mbaye Guèye could out-sing, out-talk, out-dance and out-dress him any time. The Wolof hero still retained his retinue of fine ladies, even after he had suffered the indignity of being dropped on his head at the national stadium. To the extent that the fight might legitimately have been represented as 'Casamance *vs* Senegal' (a notion vehemently repudiated by most *Casamançais* in Dakar) it may thus be said that 'Senegal' did after a fashion eventually triumph. President Senghor may understand anything that needs to be understood in Senegalese political intrigues, but wrestling, and popular reactions to big fights, clearly lie outside his expertise. Yet the manner of the very rapid recent efflorescence of this oddly syncretic national sport should perhaps give heart to anyone engaged in the purposeful construction of a Senegalese nation.

A purposeful, political, dimension to 'nation building' does however also exist in Senegal, as may be discerned from examination of the functioning of the governing Union Progressiste Sénégalaise. The UPS is a remarkably efficient organization in its own unedifying way, a party machine which (unlike any of its opponents, legal or other) does operate across the entire national territory. Not, to be sure, that it is a machine designed for any purpose so imprudent as mass 'mobilization', but it does quite effectively incorporate enough of existing rural leadership (*marabouts*, tribal aristocrats, traders) to make political life difficult or in many areas virtually impossible for organized opposition. And in the bush (*'la brousse'*, a colonial term still prevalent among the Dakar political elite, of whatever ideological coloration) it has not been forgotten that Léopold Senghor was the first national politician to take the trouble even to visit many of the country's rural areas (in the late 1940s and early 1950s, when Senghor solicited votes among the then newly enfranchised rural electorate). UPS patronage machinery still provides an avenue for rural ambition, and a vehicle for the selective distribution of governmental favour (roads, schools, dispensaries, etc) as well as career advancement for trusted rural intermediaries. Material and even some nostalgically ideal considerations thus combine to make the UPS (despite the flimsy appearance of its formally democratic party apparatus) quite a formidable agency of national political power. Factional disputes within the UPS at every level ('clan politics') do furthermore provide for a competitive if not formally a very democratic national political life.[20] Clan politics in this Tammany idiom may still provide a more authentically competitive, and even in its own bizarre manner a more democratic, political framework than the carefully supervised ideological discourse imposed by Senegal's new constitution.

With West African comparisons in mind, the Senegalese state does now appear to have emerged as a uniquely effective political apparatus. The peanut economy may still pose stubborn limitations to any dramatic improvement in the material well-being of the majority of Senegal's citizenry,[21] but economic considerations however dismal should not obscure the extent to which in strictly (perhaps narrowly) political terms we are dealing with a quite remarkable success story. The particular coherence of the Senegalese state, explicable in large measure through the 'mass' social/communal solidarities reviewed above, is also of course a triumph of political leadership. That political guidance since independence has come most obviously from Léopold Senghor, whose skills had been learned initially in Paris under the Third French Republic, directly from his legal guardian Blaise Diagne (Deputy for Senegal in the French parliament, 1914–34), later as a Deputy himself under the Fourth Republic (1945–60). Senghor did prove an apt pupil in this hard school of political manoeuvre and bargaining, as those who have periodically sought to out-manoeuvre him would now readily avow. But it would be wrong for an outside observer in the present context to focus unduly on the redoubtable political mastery of this single personality. A large category of African politicians had accumulated relevant experience in the elected municipal governments of the *communes* over a period of half a century prior to Senegalese independence. And outside the coastal municipalities, another tradition of political leadership, very differently rooted but increasingly in symbiosis with the first, had also long been established in the country's rurally-based Muslim brotherhoods.[22] The saints of these brotherhoods in much of rural Senegal under colonial rule had come to enjoy a near-monopoly of legitimate political authority, and had learned how to use their status as privileged intermediaries in dealing with French power. After 1960, with Senegalese national independence, saints and municipally-trained politicians could each draw on a capacious enough reservoir of relevant political skills: the post-colonial state could thus be conceived as a bizarre but effective fusion of the traditions of

187

the French *municipalité* and of the Muslim *zawiya*. Whatever may be the future changes in national leadership, whether army officers or revolutionary intellectuals for example should displace the present rulers, and whatever the political intentions of a new regime, it will inherit a complex and inherently viable set of political arrangements, by now quite firmly embedded in a genuinely national political culture.

8

Sierra Leone

CHRISTOPHER ALLEN

Little of the standard literature on Sierra Leone is comparative, with the notable exception of Martin Kilson's seminal but dated volume, and Christopher Clapham's recent short monograph, the framework of which is geographically and conceptually too narrow.[1] The remaining general literature tends to rely too much for explanation on idiosyncratic features of Sierra Leone, or on an excessively narrow set of factors, as with the material on local politics discussed below. To avoid these problems while not denying any specificity to Sierra Leone politics, this chapter concentrates on four areas or phenomena which are common to West Africa, and attempts to show to what extent Sierra Leone's experience resembles that of the rest of West Africa (especially the coastal states) and why in some respects it is, or seems, unlike its neighbours.

The four areas are: economic dependency, the growth of authoritarian political behaviour, the role in national politics of local political arenas, and class. Since Sierra Leone is a typical instance of the presence and effect of economic dependency and of the growth of authoritarianism, the account of these phenomena is mainly descriptive. The importance of local political loyalties and alignments and the complexity of their influence on local–central relations in West Africa has had greater attention recently, notably in Ghana with Martin Staniland's entertaining monograph on Yendi, the impressive study of Ahafo politics by John Dunn and Sandy Robertson, and Richard Crook's fine doctorate on Ofinso in Ashanti.[2] Sierra Leone is perhaps a paradigm of the role of local arenas in that they seem to be of more determinant and ubiquitous importance there than in any other coastal West African state (though Northern Nigeria and Upper Volta may prove similar). Why should this be so? And what are its implications for class analysis? Since such analysis is still a minority occupation among Africanists there are few instances of its application to Sierra Leone, and one can do little more than seek to establish that it is not precluded by sketching in outline the nature of

Sierra Leone bourgeoisie, and by examining the apparent absence of class consciousness and other class attributes among workers and peasants.

In such a brief treatment there are inevitably major omissions. The two most significant of these are the lack of a systematic account of Sierra Leone's social structure and of an analysis of the bases of the power and authority of the various post-independence regimes. The former must await the appearance of adequate data; even the 1963 census is poor and unreliable, and there are no substantial accounts of rural differentiation and political economy of the type available for parts of Ghana and Nigeria, for example. I have therefore assumed the existence of a social structure broadly similar to the rest of coastal West Africa and have accounted for the different political behaviour of workers and peasants in Sierra Leone by factors either intrinsic to the country or present there when generally absent elsewhere in West Africa. While political power is not discussed directly each section bears on its analysis, particularly that on local politics; for the stability of Sierra Leone governments has rested to a great degree on their capacity to satisfy both the political leadership of local arenas (notably chiefdoms) and their representatives in the national arenas, which neither of the short-lived Albert Margai and military regimes were able to do.

A POLITICAL CHRONOLOGY[3]

It may help to begin with a brief outline of the political history of Sierra Leone since 1945. Political organization after the Second World War was confined to the small but expanding trade union movement, and to elitist bodies representing the educated and influential among either the Creole community of the Sierra Leone Colony (now the Western Area) or among the hinterland population of the Protectorate, particularly the non-Muslim south. In 1951, with the introduction of an elected African majority on the Legislative Council, the various bodies consolidated into a single party representing Creole interests (and thus doomed to minority status), and the SLPP (Sierra Leone Protectorate, later People's Party), the bulk of whose leadership came from southern, chiefly, families. Since the electorate in the Protectorate then consisted of the members of the District Councils, and thus of chiefs and their allies or clients, the SLPP relied heavily on chiefs both for what rural organization they had, and for mobilizing the electorate.

Reliance on chiefs persisted, deepened by the allocation of credit to them through the District Councils and the provision of political protection to chiefs under attack within their chiefdoms for extensive abuses of the powers of taxation and of allocation of land and labour (discussed

190

more fully in the final section). These abuses underlay (though they did not entirely cause) a widespread outbreak of rural violence in the north in 1955–6, which was also fuelled by the opening to Sierra Leonean diggers of the diamondiferous areas of the east and by the 1955 Freetown strike and riots.[4] This allowed a new Creole-based party, the United Progressive Party (UPP) to gain several northern seats in the 1957–8 election and by-elections, which were the first to be held with universal adult male suffrage. The SLPP was less threatened by this, however, than by a split in its own leadership initiated by Albert Margai, brother of the party's founder and leader, Sir Milton Margai. Albert's party, the People's National Party (PNP), and the UPP played what Cartwright has accurately called 'the game of opposition',[5] yet their existence, and even more that of the Kono Progressive Movement (KPM), based in the diamond areas, illustrated fatal weaknesses in the SLPP. Its reliance on chiefs, and its increasing southern bias, allowed the existence of considerable opposition in the north and east, which finally coalesced in the All Peoples Congress (APC), founded just before independence in 1960, by Siaka Stevens, an ex-minister. The APC brought together a variety of northern politicians from the SLPP, PNP, and UPP, and was allied with the KPM's successor in the 1962 and 1967 elections.

The APC and its Kono ally gained twenty seats (all in the Western Area, North and Kono) of the sixty-two available in 1962, more than any opposition coalition hitherto. The SLPP, itself divided into at least three factions, responded by attacking both opposition parties at the local level while offering inducements to their MPs to change their allegiance. This tactic, already successful with the PNP and UPP, might have greatly undermined the APC but for the death in 1964 of Sir Milton Margai. His brother Albert was appointed the new prime minister (and thus party leader), despite being opposed by the other SLPP factions, particularly the northern leadership under John Karefa-Smart and the eastern MPs. In the process of imposing his authority Albert Margai further antagonized his rivals, and Karefa-Smart joined the APC. Less secure than Sir Milton, Albert soon abandoned his brother's mediatory and co-optative tactics and relied to a far greater degree on force and intrigue.[6] These tactics still further alienated the northern leadership and their electorate, and led to the bulk of eastern MPs favouring Salia Jusu-Sheriff of Kenema for party leader. Attempts to further shore up his position by declaring a republic and a single-party state only drove Creoles and the bulk of the educated population into opposition to the SLPP.

Albert (by now Sir Albert) Margai made considerable efforts to rig the March 1967 elections, but for a variety of reasons failed to do so effectively, allowing the APC with thirty seats to gain the support of the

191

south-eastern MPs and to secure an invitation to form the government. As soon as it became clear to Margai that he could not prevent this (by e.g. bribing APC MPs) he persuaded Brigadier Lansana to declare martial law, as force commander. Lansana was swiftly deposed by the three next most senior officers, who formed a National Reformation Council (NRC). By banning political organizations and activity and carrying out a series of enquiries into the misdeeds of Margai's government, and by governing largely through the administration or by coercion, the NRC were able to retain power briefly. By the end of 1967, however, the APC were training a militia in Guinea and the NRC were losing control of their troops – and what little popular support they had – by policies of economic austerity combined with growing appropriation of privileges for themselves. A conspiracy among junior NCOs, with perhaps some APC involvement, finally overthrew the NRC in April 1968 and, after a brief interregnum, reinstated Siaka Stevens as prime minister.[7]

Stevens at first established a 'national' government incorporating some of the anti-Margai non-APC MPs, something he had intended to do in 1967 in any case. This was only a temporary coalition, however, for the APC quickly sought to decimate the SLPP locally and nationally. Margai's leading supporters were detained on charges arising from the 1967 coups, and some twenty-six SLPP MPs were unseated on petition. A majority of these seats were then won by the APC in an atmosphere of increasing violence, especially in Kono and Kenema. Locally, now that SLPP chiefs and supporters could no longer count on central government support their opponents were able to harass and displace many of them, thus undermining the SLPP's organization. The SLPP's new leadership, Jusu-Sheriff and the veteran M. S. Mustapha, were persecuted and a virtually permanent state of emergency declared, lasting from 1969 to 1975. During this period the SLPP was gradually eliminated, with its candidates bullied into withdrawing in the 1973 'elections' so that the APC collected all eighty-five seats, and with its local leadership steadily drawn into the APC, despite prior records of sometimes vicious hostility to the APC.[8] Sierra Leone is therefore in essence a one-party state, as well as having been a republic with an executive presidency since 1971.

As the APC expanded, the divisions within it became more overt,[9] culminating in the formation in September 1970 of the United Democratic Party (UDP), a largely northern organization led by two Temne ex-ministers. This was banned almost immediately and its leaders detained, though Temne representation in the cabinet was simultaneously increased (and, on the other hand, several prominent former SLPP supporters were given senior appointments in the diplomatic service and public sector). In March 1971, for reasons that have still not been fully described, the northern force commander Brigadier Bangura attempted to overthrow Stevens, but failed and was subsequently executed.[10] These events reinforced the authoritarian trends already shown in the treatment of the SLPP and UDP, and since then the APC has remained a single entity, despite open rivalry between S. I. Koroma, a Freetown-based Temne with a 'radical' reputation, and C. A. Kamara-Taylor, a Limba party boss of long standing. They share with President Stevens the key posts in party and government, and their rivalry in the party proper is reflected in the APC Youth and Women's auxiliaries, where it complicates independent and older divisions.

Opposition outside the APC has increasingly been expressed in violent and conspiratorial forms, with numerous arrests of both civilians and army personnel (including, ironically, the initiator of the 1968 counter coup). In July 1974 there was an attempt by a group of soldiers to assassinate Kamara-Taylor by bombing his house, following which the force commander and commissioner of police were appointed first to parliament and then to the cabinet. Twenty-two soldiers and civilians were sentenced to death for the bombing, and the eight finally executed included ex-Brigadier Lansana, and the two founders of the UDP. Most recently, in January–February 1977, hostility to the government (and dissatisfaction at the growing economic difficulties described below) were expressed in a series of demonstrations. These began at Fourah Bay College outside Freetown, and drew guarded approval from the Sierra Leone Labour Congress, but after APC counter-demonstrations had evolved into rioting, they spread to Freetown and then to Kenema and Bo, with considerable violence shown in their suppression.[11] With the APC's political base contracting again, shown in the dismissals of several ministers and junior ministers in 1976, the prospects for a stable continuance of APC rule seem poor.

ECONOMIC DEPENDENCY[12]

The Sierra Leone economy is classically dependent. The bulk of the population rely on agriculture for a living, while the main non-subsistence economic activities are the production for export of palm oil, coffee, cocoa and minor agricultural items, mining, and government employment. Mining since the war has been dominated by a handful of foreign firms: the Selection Trust in diamonds, William Baird of Glasgow in iron ore, and Alusuisse and a few other firms in bauxite and rutile. These operations, though providing at least three-quarters of the value of exports in the 1960s, yielded well under half – indeed at times barely a fifth – of government revenue. The latter has instead been largely derived from import duties, personal taxes and fees, and agricultural revenues. These last have been out of all proportion to the modest contribution of cash crops to export value, showing a high level of direct and indirect taxation of farmers and leading to declining production trends in most export and even food crops in the postwar period. This pattern of extraction has contributed to persistent balance of payments problems and to an underlying tendency for government revenue to fall in real terms. The economy has therefore been since the early 1960s in a state of actual or incipient crisis in which all measures designed to produce a rough balance of trade together with adequate revenue have proved rapidly self-defeating. Where crises have been averted it has been through the intervention of unplanned external changes such as the devaluation of the pound (sterling).

This can be seen clearly in the Albert Margai period, which began at the ending of the decolonization boom brought about by increased government spending financed from aid, public borrowing, and Currency Board receipts. These sources provided some 29m Leones (2 Leones = £1) in the four years after independence, wholly financing development spending. In the next three years, however, these sources provided only Le 14m, while recurrent public spending rose continually and absorbed the yield from standard revenue sources. Matters were made worse by the continual drain of capital through diamond smuggling, and through corruption. Public spending, and in particular development spending, was financed instead from accumulated reserves. By 1966, 'almost all of the cash balances and disposable foreign assets of the government had been used up',[13] but even these proved insufficient, leading to growing reliance on contractor-finance: under Albert Margai Le 11.5m were borrowed in this fashion as against Le 7m received in aid. The projects so financed cost far more than the original estimates, were often more expensive than alternatives for which aid or private finance were available, and were run at a loss once completed.[14]

Thus by 1967 there was a trade deficit of Le 20m, a similar deficit on current account, rising capital outflows, foreign reserves covering barely two months' imports, debt servicing costs equal to 20 per cent of export earnings, and the diversion of commercial credit from private borrowers to the public sector. All too uncomfortably familiar to British readers, particularly as the crisis was solved in the short run by an International Monetary Fund stabilization programme (in essence a fiscal and monetary package involving large cuts in recurrent spending and a virtual standstill in development spending, plus tight control on the supply of money and credit). Since this involved an inevitable period of economic stagnation or even recession, plus declining real incomes for both wage-

194

earners and farmers, it was not implemented by the Margai government. When it *was* implemented under the military regime, its success depended to a large extent on fortuitous external events which increased public revenues by raising export prices, among other factors.

The 'national' government which succeeded the military regime in 1968, and even more the purely APC government of 1969, thus inherited a position not unlike Albert Margai's in 1964: a balanced budget and trade account due to budgetary conservatism and accidental external features. Politically, the main features of the IMF programme could no more be implemented by the APC government than by Albert Margai's. The need for public spending for private and political ends was as great – if not greater – since the APC government incorporated more factions than had Margai's SLPP government. Furthermore, the basic effects of dependency remained: the same revenue constraints and the same un-balanced reliance on cash crops and minerals. The APC tried to raise revenue by piecemeal, *ad hoc*, measures, some of which had positive effects, as did the fortuitous increase in the world price of coffee and cocoa of 1975–6. More useful still has been the belated decision to pay a reasonable producer price for rice, an important food crop. This has eliminated the need to import rice, which cost Le 23.5m in 1973–4, a tenth of the value of exports.[15]

Spending, however, has risen even faster since the 1970 split in the APC and the imposition of a virtually permanent state of emergency. With aid payments running in cash terms only a little above their levels of ten years before and largely confined to road-building and technical assistance, Stevens like Margai before him has gone for contractor finance. Again the projects are expensive and dubious; again there are cheaper alternatives; and again the resulting indebtedness has helped to wreck the budget. In mid-1971 Sierra Leone's external debts were Le 46m, of which 28 per cent were contractor-finance: much the same as in mid-1963. By mid-1976 total external debts were Le 114m of which 57 per cent were from contractor-financed projects, generating Le 22m in debt-servicing: 25 per cent of revenue and 20 per cent of export earnings. The deficit for 1975/6 was Le 62m, with a forecast for 1976/7 of a Le 104m deficit, less whatever might be raised externally. Debt servicing, according to the June 1976 budget, was to take up 37 per cent of government recurrent spending and 53 per cent of revenue. Reserves fell again to two months imports, and the government has been borrowing massively from foreign firms and on the local market: Le 30m in 1975/6, in an attempt to cover current spending, for revenue was 30 per cent short of commitments.[16]

The government's revenue problems stem only in part from debt servicing and food or oil imports. Since a third of revenue comes from import duties, attempts to cut imports and thus improve the trade balance increase the budgetary deficit. So also does the falling value and level of major exports. During the last two years, Sierra Leone has seen the end of iron-ore mining by William Bairds due to declining profitability, and fluctuations in diamond sales, combined with persistent warnings that the end of significant production is in sight.[17] This is said to be the result of massive past illegal mining financed by diamond dealers who are protected in turn by APC leaders;[18] most of the stones are then smuggled out. Rutile mining has temporarily ceased, and has an uncertain future, and while existing bauxite workings are under no threat and the reserves are huge, further exploitation may be very costly. Agriculture provided only 16 per cent of the value of exports in 1974. To bring about a permanent increase in agricultural export revenue it is necessary to encourage production, which can only be done by raising producer prices – which has to some extent been done already – and by cutting export taxes, making the farmer no longer the most highly taxed Sierra Leonean, but also thereby reducing revenue.

Sierra Leone's recurrent economic crises are the result of its incapacity to control the key elements of its economy, together with three factors arising from the political system: the necessity for politically-inspired public spending, the growth of corruption, and diamond smuggling. The origins of these factors and reasons for their persistence are dealt with in the next and last sections.

AUTHORITARIANISM[19]

Authoritarianism is, as Fanon, Zolberg and others have pointed out, a characteristic of all 'falsely decolonized' African states, of which Sierra Leone is one. Though it owes many of its details to colonial models of government, authoritarianism arises fundamentally from two phenomena: the nature of the decolonization process, and the nature of the incumbent elites and the processes tending to transform them into a bourgeoisie. I shall briefly outline these, in turn.

Adopting an electoral form of decolonization rather than one based on an active struggle for independence brought in its train several consequences in West Africa.[20] *Firstly*, a need to demobilize politically the radical and militant sections of existing parties, which had grown up in the 1940s and which opposed a strategy of compromise with the colonial authorities.[21] *Secondly*, a need to mobilize electorally a vast rural population hitherto largely unmobilized except on a local basis and for brief periods. This entailed relying on the existing holders of rural power and the existing bases of loyalty in rural society, as the party's principal means of mobilization. In Sierra Leone the relevant means were chiefly families, and the chiefs in particular, together with the Poro Society and its analogues, and to a lesser extent Islamic notables.[22] Ethnic loyalties were less important in this early stage, unless one regards the conflict between the Creoles of the colony area and the protectorate political leadership as both important and ethnic in nature, neither of which seems reasonable. These two consequences, though not in themselves necessarily authoritarian developments, did promote such developments by eliminating one source of opposition, and by installing within the party machinery an authoritarian group of rural notables. Indeed in Northern Nigeria the party machinery was scarcely distinguishable from such a group.

In order to retain the support of rural and urban notables, and to justify that support to their subjects, clients or congregations, party leaderships distributed material benefits, or patronage, and began to change their ideology. The latter shift can be seen in a greater stress on the legitimacy of emirs, chiefs, *marabouts*, and the like, against the democratizing, levelling or millenarian attacks of their various subjects, and in the activation of social cleavages arising from tribe, locality, history, religion and other communal divisions. The distribution of material benefits is more mundane, and took two main forms: the selective provision of services or benefits to the electorate, and the allocation to notables of money and other gains, or of preferential opportunities to obtain these, such as official posts or licenses. In Sierra Leone the first can be seen in the southerly bias of development spending, while the second is illustrated by the extensive provision of rural loans to chiefs and their clients, as described by Kilson.[23]

Since political patronage involves the private use of public funds to create political support, it was of great importance to the party leadership to retain office. To the extent that party leaders, their associates, and the key members of the party machine came to rely on state funds for their personal wealth, the necessity to stay in power became still greater. Retention of office in a multiparty system implied the winning of successive elections, ensured by both maintaining party unity and support, and by undermining the opposition. The first of these depended mainly on patronage, at the cost of a growing drain on public resources, and on a developing ideology of unity and of the wastefulness or impropriety of opposition. There were already authoritarian elements in this process, but they entered principally in the methods of containing or undermining opponents. The most common methods included: co-optation of opposition leaders and factions (though this calls for their inclusion in the distribution of patronage); the abandonment or rigging of elections; the banning of parties and the creation of one-party states; and the harassment and destruction of the opposition by local repression, legal intimidation, arrest, exile and even the killing of its leaders. All of these tactics have been used in Sierra Leone since 1951, although Sir Milton Margai could afford to attempt to co-opt most of his opponents and gradually expand party patronage to a greater degree than could Sir Albert.[24]

In this way the nature of decolonization led to authoritarian government. So also did the initial nature of the incumbent elite, which was in all West African states marked (but for a handful of individuals) by high status but little wealth or capital. Patronage, made necessary by the exigencies of party building, gave them access to wealth, and while this was initially widely distributed in return for votes, it rapidly became less and less broadly distributed as the opposition was co-opted or subjected to greater repression. State funds, used at first for party building, were more and more diverted into private hands, becoming a crucial source of the growth of a bourgeoisie marked by a culture of corruption and an economic role complementary and subordinate to foreign capital.[25] As the size and demands of the elite both expanded, and as external sources of revenue such as aid or foreign investment began a relative decline in the 1960s, so less and less revenue was distributed downwards. Wage increases became harder to obtain, rural services were not improved, and producer prices stagnated as did urban employment, while the gap between rich and poor became greater and more conspicuous. Under these conditions mass unrest grew more common, forcing the government into increased repression and into greater reliance on the police and army, thereby creating most of the preconditions for a military coup.

This pattern is amply apparent in the present government's authoritarian behaviour.[26] There has been intensive repression of opposition, against a background of a prolonged state of emergency and continual political violence, both at local and at national levels. Thus in 1968 and 1969, the by-elections were accompanied by considerable intimidation on both sides, while in the north several chiefs were unseated after local rioting. Nationally, there have been at least two attempted coups and major assassination attempts.

At the national level repression has been directed at three sets of targets: prominent opponents, army dissidents, and the media. There have been frequent detentions, arrests and trials of the leading members of all three factions of the SLPP, and of the main leaders of the banned United Democratic Party. Salia Jusu-Sheriff, for example, was detained in November 1968 following violence in the Kenema by-elections; he was

198

charged in February 1969 and again sixteen months later, but never brought to trial. In September 1972 he was again detained and charged in connection with killings in Kailahun, but brought to trial only after a year – and then acquitted. Ibrahim Bash-Taqi and Mohammed Forna of the UDP were detained from October 1970, when the party was banned, until July 1973, and then redetained after the 1974 bombing incident. In July 1975, following a trial, they were executed.

The army was considerably reorganized after the end of the military regime in 1968, with the APC increasing its size and the proportion of the budget spent on it and on the police, and purging it of southern senior officers – by 1971 there was only one left.[27] This was, however, of little avail, since there were attempted coups in October 1970 and March 1971, the latter led by the Temne force commander Brigadier Bangura. Since Bangura's execution in June 1971 army involvement in opposition activity has been limited to individual officers and NCOs, many of whom have been detained or dismissed, notably after the 1974 bombing. Recently the APC have co-opted the force commander and the head of the police into the cabinet in an attempt to forestall any future attempts at military intervention. The media, finally, have also been severely repressed, with the SLPP paper bombed and its staff harassed and frequently detained, while the smaller mimeographed opposition papers so characteristic of Sierra Leone have been banned or – as in Kono – crudely displaced by official APC organs.

The APC have justified repression by claiming that its opponents are responsible for the endemic political violence. While this is partly true, the close relationship between repression and elections casts doubt on the claim, as does the government's failure to prove its case in the courts. Even the treason trials arising from the 1967 coup resulted eventually in the discharge or acquittal of all the accused, while of all the APC's political detainees, only those charged with the 1974 bombing have been convicted. It is, perhaps, in the APC's favour that the most successful prosecutions have been against its own members, for kidnapping, ritual murder, and – most recently – fraud.[28]

Election-rigging has not taken the form favoured by Albert Margai of manipulating the casting or counting of votes, though this may have happened in some of the 1968–9 by-elections in Kono and Kenema. Instead the SLPP, and even some APC dissidents, have been prevented or dissuaded from campaigning, as in many by-elections and in district council elections, or even from standing, as in the 1973 elections when only five of the eighty-five seats were contested, and even those were all won by APC members. As a result many SLPP supporters have thought it prudent and safer to declare for the APC. The journal *West Africa* lists many prominent SLPP ex-MPs and ex-ministers joining the APC since 1973, while in local arenas we can see the adhesion of rural ruling families, like the bulk of the Demby family in Bo, of M. M. Koroma's section of the Kai-Samba clan in Nongowa, and the Quee-Nyagua family in Lower Bambara. All of these were prominent SLPP supporters. M. M. Koroma for example, wishing to deprive his nephew of the chieftaincy, stood in 1967 for the SLPP against the chief's brother Kutubu Kai-Samba, who was an Independent candidate and the MP. In this he was supported by Albert Margai, since Kai-Samba was a prominent opponent of his within the SLPP. Koroma was beaten but reappeared in the 1968 by-election as the APC candidate, only to be beaten again.[29]

The ideology of the APC leadership has duly changed to suit their new circumstances. They now stress their support of both the institution of chieftaincy and its present incumbents. Since 1970 Stevens has repeatedly stated that chiefs are the supreme authority at chiefdom level, and that 'government expects people to respect their chiefs'.[30] There has also been continual propaganda for a one-party state together with attempts by Stevens to justify this and the absence of elections, on two grounds. It is firstly argued that Sierra Leone cannot afford two parties through lack of adequate talent – much of which, it is true, is dead, in detention, or in exile – and secondly that precolonial methods of consultation are superior to electoral methods, and should replace them.[31]

These familiar ideas have been reflected in a series of institutional changes. Parliament has a much lessened role, though there is occasional mild criticism, and the party and its associated organs play the main public initiatory roles, though without any internal democracy. A republican constitution, so unpopular with the APC and its Creole supporters in 1966, was introduced in 1971 and followed immediately by an executive presidency of substantial powers. By the end of 1976, despite great coyness on the part of President Stevens, it was evident that the introduction of a *de jure* one-party state, formalizing the *de facto* version of the past three years, was imminent.

CHIEFDOM ARENAS AND POLITICAL MOBILIZATION

Sierra Leone's first national election, held in 1951, involved mobilizing not the bulk of the rural population as in Ghana or Senegal, but only a few thousand Creoles and the members of the twelve district councils, themselves dominated by chiefs and chiefdom officials. Thus the task of the SLPP was to ensure the political support of the chiefs, rather than that of their subjects. This need was then reinforced by the election to the legislature of as many chiefs as SLPP nominees, and the necessity of a coalition with them if the SLPP were to gain a majority in the legislative council and thus control of the unofficial members of the executive council.

In return the SLPP left the chiefs' local authority untouched, and even enhanced it by providing them free credit and other economic opportunities. There resulted a growing competition for chiefly office and a growing resentment of chiefly abuses, factors which had already led to a series of violent attempts at removal of southern chiefs in the 1940s and early 50s, and which now underlay extensive rioting and destruction of chiefly property in the north-west in 1955–6. There was related rioting in Moyamba at the same time, while other southern areas like Kenema and Kono, though less active than in 1948–52, still showed persistent local violence towards chiefs.

The SLPP leadership were unable to respond by disowning the chiefs; indeed chiefs were now more influential within it than in 1951. Victor Minikin, for example, describes the Kono SLPP branch of this period as a loose and informal group of chiefs, chiefdom officials and influentials, who met usually at District Council meetings; and he quotes a revealing remark by the MP Paul Dunbar: 'there was no reason to organize before an opposition party emerged'.[32] When opposition parties did emerge, or flourish, in the wake of the northern riots, they too were drawn into reliance on chiefly families, for two reasons. They were, firstly, of the same social composition as the SLPP and had essentially similar ambitions and political philosophies. And even had they wanted to pursue a different strategy, the short time they had to organize for the 1957–8 elections and by-elections would itself have forced them to recruit support from the rivals of SLPP-backed chiefs.

At the local level a similar pattern emerged. Just as chiefs whose tenancy was threatened looked to the SLPP for protection, so their rivals for the chieftaincy joined opposition parties in the hope that their national success might lead to deposition in their favour. Where – as in most of the south – opposition parties had little possibility of survival we find chiefly rivals moving into opposing factions in the SLPP, and unsuccessful candidates for chieftaincies emerging as backers of Independent candidates. Thus in Bombali East constituency, the Independent candidate in 1957 was the rival to the SLPP-backed chief Bai Sebora Kamal II. In 1958 he stood again, this time for the newly formed People's National Party, and was joined by a second unsuccessful chieftaincy candidate, standing for the slightly older United Progressive Party.[33]

These early opponents of the SLPP were largely absorbed into it during the pre-independence 'United Front' period, a favourite tactic of Sir Milton Margai. This did nothing, however, to reduce hostility in the north to chiefly abuses, which had continued under SLPP protection. It also tended to emphasize Southern dominance of the cabinet which was in turn reflected in a strongly southern bias in public spending.[34] There were, finally, several prominent politicians left outside the United Front, notably Siaka Stevens, an SLPP founder and minister until 1957, but now a PNP leader. Out of these diverse tendencies, and united mainly by distrust of the governing party, came the All People's Congress.

The APC has often been seen as a radical party, notably by John Cartwright, who argues that it represented the interests and desires of subordinate strata in Sierra Leone.[35] Its leaders were certainly drawn less from the chiefly and educated elites than the SLPP, and included men with a radical reputation and political style. But its attraction for the poor, urban or rural, owed much more to its being the sole opposition party outside Kono, and to its northern bias. In both the 1962 and 1967 elections the APC appealed not so much on a class or populist basis, but on the basis of dissatisfaction with the SLPP, producing in 1967 a coalition uniting conservatve Creoles, radical intellectuals, and rural notables. The new party had but a year to organize for the 1962 elections, and outside Freetown it was obliged to use the same tactics as past opposition parties. Thus it recruited many of its candidates and local supporters from chiefly families or their rivals; and it won most of its seats in the areas most affected by the 1955/6 riots. It did the same in the north in 1967 with similar results, but won the election because of two rather different factors. These were the massive anti-SLPP urban vote due to declining real incomes and northern migration to towns, and the split in the SLPP. This had been caused by Albert Margai's unsuccessful attempts to weaken his rivals in the party through intervention in chieftaincy affairs in their constituencies.[36] The refusal of these men to support Margai after the election made the appointment of Stevens as prime minister inevitable, since he alone could command a majority of ordinary members. In 1962, under Milton Margai, all fourteen Independent MPs had by contrast declared rapidly for the SLPP, giving it a majority.

Events since the restoration of the APC have not weakened the perpetually reproduced importance of local disputes and local arenas, though the direct involvement of the party in such disputes has lessened since 1973. In the north the deposition of chiefs prominent as SLPP supporters has aligned the APC more closely with the new incumbent ruling families. This hold was not shaken by the formation of the UDP in 1970, for though it was clearly a northern party, it was confined to prominent Temnes in Freetown, and had almost no organized rural support willing to show itself in the north at the time of its banning. In the south, the SLPP lost its coercive powers and main sources of patronage, while most of its MPs were unseated through election petitions in 1968. In the subsequent by-elections, their candidates once more relied on chiefly connections and on coalitions based on family or chiefdom solidarity and rivalries, while the APC candidate was often a former Independent or an SLPPer who had failed to gain nomination or election in 1967. As a result many former SLPP seats were lost, though several were retained through the strength of ruling family linkages. Some SLPP chiefs, but by no means all the most prominent, were deposed and replaced by formerly unsuccessful claimants now having APC support. Since 1973, rather than evicting SLPP notables, the APC has encouraged them to join, and they have brought with them their own chiefly coalitions. Thus in both north and south the pre-1967 local basis of political alignment has remained untouched, though it is now perhaps of less significance.

CLASS FACTORS IN SIERRA LEONE POLITICS

Sierra Leone possesses the three main politically influential indigenous classes of modern West Africa: a dependent local bourgeoisie, a working class, and a peasantry, though these terms should not be taken to mean precisely the same social formations as in industrialized societies.[37] The bourgeoisie is weakly developed by comparison to Ghana or Nigeria, but its political behaviour has been essentially similar. This has not been true, however, of the other two classes, despite apparently adequate numbers and the occurrence of major instances of class activity. Before discussing the significance of this, it is necessary to deal with the peculiarities of the Sierra Leone bourgeoisie, and with the topic of corruption.

1. *Corruption and the indigenous bourgeoisie*:[38] One consequence of party building through patronage was a growing diversion of public funds into the hands of individual party leaders, and a declining redistribution of such funds to the lowest levels of the party and the electorate. Corruption of this type is usually combined in West Africa with the diversion of business and commercial opportunities to the elite collectively (as with legal restrictions on trading by non-citizens) or to individual members, usually illegally. Both activities lead to the creation of a dependent bourgeoisie characterized by the accumulation of capital through political power and its reinvestment in ways complementary to the existing patterns of dependency, such as in land or property, trade and transport, agency work and sub-contracting. Such methods create a considerable drain on public funds through direct theft or through the basing of public spending decisions not on economic criteria but on the probability of getting a kickback (the most spectacular example being of course the

203

1975 Nigerian cement deal, which cost around $1,000M, then a fifth of Nigeria's oil revenue).

Sierra Leone cannot match such extravagance, but the various reports on corruption produced under the military and 'national' governments make it clear that leading members of the SLPP, and especially Albert Margai, were deeply involved in corrupt activities, the taking of bribes, the theft or diversion of public funds, and the taking of economically unjustifiable decisions for political and personal ends. Thus the decision to rely on contractor-financed projects arose as much from kickbacks as from the decline in other external sources of revenue. The reports finally show that ministers had reinvested corruptly gained capital, not only in land and property, but also in transport, rice dealing and other forms of trade, construction and cement block making.[39] Unlike Ghana and Nigeria, the effect of this diversion of funds was not to create a substantial bourgeoisie. Indeed it is doubtful if the SLPP leadership sought such an effect, despite the eventual restrictions on non-citizens in the sectors of landownership and trade. What underlay this was the position of the Lebanese and Indians. The African business and commercial stratum of the late colonial period was very small and undercapitalized. In 1949 there were only nine African companies registered in Sierra Leone, with an average share capital of a little over £6,000. By 1956 this number had risen to fifteen companies with average capital of £12,000, but this was still only a quarter of the average capitalization for Lebanese and Indian firms. As a result, Africans controlled only 2 per cent of the import and export trade, compared to 19 per cent by Lebanese and Indians, and 63 per cent by European firms.[40]

The Lebanese in particular were involved in sectors attractive to African businessmen, such as transport, diamond dealing, rice trading, produce buying, textiles and so on. To protect their interests they have given extensive bribes to politicians, made large gifts to both parties, given donations to prominent chiefs, and engaged in many joint ventures with SLPP leaders.[41] We find as a result that their predominance in both produce-buying and diamond dealing, two areas that elsewhere would have become party preserves, actually increases after internal self-government. In 1959 37 per cent of diamond dealing licences were held by non-citizens, and in 1969 70 per cent; similarly in 1962/3 the PMB had ten Lebanese or Indian agents out of a total of twenty-four, but nine out of eighteen by 1969.[42] The SLPP instead placed its leading members in positions where they would enjoy privileged access to capital, credit or bribes, rather than establish them in protected businesses or set them up as capitalist farmers, as in Kenya or Malawi. Even the Industries Board was used more to make loans to SLPPers than to encourage African entrepreneurship, for its average loan by its suspension in 1966 was a little over £700. Sierra Leone Investments, established in 1961 by the UK and Sierra Leone governments to make rather larger loans, was involved in only five enterprises by the time of the coup, and had managed to lose a third of its capital in its first four years of business.[43]

Since 1968 data on corruption has been less available, though there have been persistent rumours of the involvement of ministers, party officials and parastatal management in the illegal mining and smuggling of diamonds. Ibrahim Bash-Taqi, while still at liberty in 1970, asserted that ministers were involved in the theft of Le 9m of diamonds while in transit at Hastings Airport, and while there is no clear proof, the subsequent police investigation, trial and commission of enquiry only confused the issue. The main suspect, a Lebanese diamond dealer and political associate of the president, Henneh Shamel, was deported straight after the trial.[44] There is, on the other hand, plenty of evidence for the redirection of patronage to the APC's supporters, as one might expect: Victor Minikin mentions the re-allocation of mining licences and appointments to Permit Boards, Court Presidencies and posts as government representatives in the diamond separation plants, as examples in Kono District.[45] The Lebanese, though perhaps subject to a higher level of demands for gifts and bribes,[46] appear to occupy the same dominant position within the economy as they did before the military regime. Indeed, although some of its members have changed, the nature and position of the bourgeoisie seems identical to that under the SLPP.

2. *Workers and Politics*: Part of the reason for the relative inactivity of both workers and rural strata lies in their distinctive social situations. Workers in Sierra Leone include a large group of diamond diggers who while being technically employees function rather more as private armies.[47] The remaining workers are neither as numerous nor proportionately as significant as in Ghana or Nigeria or other areas in which workers have played a substantial political role since the war. Important though such factors are, political and institutional factors must also figure in the explanation.

Since 1945 workers, and particularly organized workers, have had a varying influence in West African political life.[48] In the period 1945–52 recent research has shown that they, their ideas and their leaders were an important and perhaps crucial element in the creation of radical sections of the nationalist movement, such as the UPC in Cameroun, or the Nigerian Zikists. The repression of radical nationalism naturally reduced this influence, but equally important was the provision of bargaining machinery and substantial wage increases, and the co-optation of trade union leadership. The former allowed the growth of a successful apolitical 'economist' strategy among trade unionists, largely replacing the older strategy of public confrontation. The latter separated union leaders from rank-and-file pressures and control, and gave them sources of patronage essential to retaining their leadership, through the provision of international funds and party backing. Under these conditions radical influence waned and was expressed feebly, mainly at the level of ideas and in criticism of the union leadership.[49] After independence, there occurred growing hostility to the government among workers, a deepening distrust of their union leaders, and the beginnings of a more sophisticated critique of union co-optation and of the nature of the post-colonial state. These changes are reflected in major strikes and confrontations with government, notably in Nigeria and Senegal.

In Sierra Leone, despite basic similarities to other West African states at the end of the war, we do not find any radicalizing effect of workers on the nationalist movement, which remained in the hands of the educated protectorate elite and the Creole leadership. Sierra Leone had had a much earlier provision of bargaining machinery and co-optation of union leaders than elsewhere.[50] Under the direction of the Labour Officer, Edgar Parry, Wages Boards and Joint Industrial Councils were established from 1946, and union recognition by employers secured, leading to a series of early wage increases in the major industries. Union leaders, apart from enjoying an assured status until then confined to the elite, were protected from their rivals by prohibitions on the formation of competing unions. Patronage was also provided, in that union leaders were able to nominate at least half of the vacancies filled through the Labour Exchange, which all major employers were obliged to use. As a result the turnover of leaders was very low and there were only five strikes in 1946 to 1950. Indeed there were few strikes of any size, and little other proof of industrial militancy, until the 1955 strike and riots in Freetown. By this time the international labour movement was also providing patronage in the form of grants, scholarships and the like, and corruption had made its appearance among union leaders. The 1955 strike arose, however, not from any radical influence but from the combination of sharp increases in food prices resulting from the diamond boom of the early 1950s, and the attempt by government and employers to abuse the bargaining machinery and avoid restoring real wages. The riots and looting that broke out reflected the unpopularity of Lebanese store owners and the scarcity of goods. The stoning of ministers' houses was due to their involvement in denying wage increases or in the hoarding of foodstuffs. Such roles were the direct or indirect result of the SLPP's integration into colonial government. There is, however, no evidence that the rioters' hostility arose from any 'Fanonist' consciousness of this integration, as opposed to its resulting from simple objection to the actions themselves.[51]

Whether in the last decade or so Sierra Leonean workers have begun to follow the same paths as their Senegalese or Nigerian counterparts is hard to say on the scanty evidence available, though the middling size of the labour force, its dispersal over widespread mining operations, and the importance within it of employment in public services rather than in industry, would all militate against this. Certainly union leaders continue to remain in office with ease, to collect international funds, trips and scholarships, and remove union funds.[52] There are hints of the growth of militancy and new ideas; Stevens in 1972 criticized 'the growing practice of trade unionists demanding the dismissal of managerial staff, especially senior African staff'.[53] But without serious research it is impossible to make any reliable judgement.

3. *Rural 'populism'*: Sierra Leone's rural population is both economically stratified and occupationally divided along lines familiar in coastal West Africa. The paucity of readily available socio-economic information makes discussion of class factors difficult, since these are related to the monetization of the economy and the commercialization of agriculture. It is worth emphasizing, however, that, as with workers, Sierra Leone's cash crop farmers are thinner on the ground than in much of coastal West Africa.

Analysis of chiefdom politics has thus far presumed an implicit general model: that political alignment on national issues is explicable in terms of alignment on chiefdom issues, which are essentially parochial in nature. Thus we find Minikin arguing that 'voting was not a matter of expressing any party preference but of supporting the candidate favoured by the chiefdom faction which the voter happened to support', the faction being defined in terms of rivalry for the chieftaincy. It is not necessary, of course, to argue this for *all* 148 chiefdoms to be able to say, as I wish to, that in Sierra Leone chiefdom affairs are unusually important and determinant. The implication in the work of Minikin, Barrows and Tangri that chiefdom affairs and intra-elite rivalries are *all*-important, is far more disputable.[54]

Minikin is concerned with voting alignments, but Barrows and Tangri take the argument further, to deny Kilson's thesis of the primacy of class or sectional interest in rural protest. Kilson asserts that episodes of chiefdom violence since the 1930s include instances of 'virtual peasant revolt against traditional rulers and authority', instigated by 'youngmen', whom he describes as 'adult males in the age range 25–35 years . . . who were increasingly involved and dependent on the modern market . . . small-scale cash-crop farmers . . . independent traders in hinterland towns

207

... and wage-labourers'.[55] Barrows by contrast sees these events as just 'a violent extension of ordinary ruling house competition', and quotes the District Report's judgement that 'behind every youngmen trouble is a group of elders'.[56] More formally and more carefully, Tangri asserts that 'initiated by the fears and ambitions of influential men in opposition factions, often within the context of a widespread malaise, violence has not been popular revolt against the ruling elite. Influential opposition leaders, concerned with corporate and individual interests, have focused on popular discontent mainly to generate support for an attack on the ruling elders from disaffected "youngmen".'[57]

The weakness of this position emerges in examining voting patterns. It cannot fully explain the success of the APC and the Kono-based opposition parties despite considerable repression of their supporters and the safer alternative of standing as or voting for an Independent. It ignores the fact that candidates sought to get the APC nomination and must have believed it of some intrinsic value. And it forces us to argue that chiefs were both widely unpopular and maintained in office only by government support, for otherwise the rivals they had defeated for the chieftaincy could not have been more successful in an election. As John Cartwright says 'if *most* chiefs were estranged from their people, something more than purely local factors was at work'.[58] A second and analogous weakness arises from the disregard of other variables, or their treatment as subordinate functions of chiefdom rivalries. There are several additional sources of political alignment, such as patron–client relations, sex and ethnic loyalties. To take these in reverse order, it is clear that while ethnicity in Sierra Leone may perhaps be seen in terms of chiefdom loyalties and as a political device, a sense of regional deprivation seems to have been an important factor in the 1962 and 1967 voting in Kono and the North. The role of women in rural Sierra Leone politics has been almost completely ignored despite their greater influence within the APC than the SLPP and Rosen's interesting demonstration of economic and sexual antagonisms developing in Kono as a result of diamond mining.[59]

Patron–client relations have been shown to be significant in APC mobilization in Julian Pollock's study of the areas around Makeni in northern Sierra Leone.[60] His patrons, often teachers or traders, were able to perform services for a variety of rural groups (mainly Kilson's 'youngmen'); they operated through non-chiefdom organizations and across chiefdom boundaries; and they were usually opposed to chiefs. They were as likely therefore to consolidate political support as the rivals for the chieftaincy, and it is easier to explain how they could mobilize such support. It is worth noting at this point that while all parties have nominated mainly ruling family members as candidates, there was also a significant group of obvious patrons among both candidates and their nominators, suggesting that parties are well aware of their ability to mobilize support. The APC in particular has relied on teachers, traders and rural businessmen.

The notion of the primacy of chiefdom rivalries is thus plainly over-stated. In particular it distorts the role of rural 'populism'.[61] Tangri argues that the grievances of the 'youngmen' were simply a convenient vehicle for the resolution of conflicts among chiefdom influentials, who were always the initiators of violent protest. Like Barrows he defines 'youngmen' politically rather than sociologically, as 'persons other than those holding positions of authority'; he sees chiefs and their rivals in the same way and not as significant members of a socio-economic elite stratum; and again like Barrows he borrows the interpretations of the colonial administration, despite his remark that 'the channels of com-munication between the government and the population were poorly developed'.[62] Thus his conclusions on the unimportance of conflicts of interest between sections, strata and classes derive less from his evidence than from his initial assumptions. Kilson is also selective and also relies on assumptions, but he does present an account of the genesis of economic conflict between chiefs and cash-croppers, traders, wage-labourers and potential rural patrons, based on the growing importance to chiefs of their involvement in commercial agriculture and related businesses. This is not incompatible with the strong evidence for the role of chiefdom rivalries, does not involve one in arguing that the APC is or was a radical party, and is of greater explanatory power and more valuable for comparative analysis.

It does, however, raise an important problem: if chiefdom violence expresses rural populism and is a form taken by class conflict in at least some cases, and if as the evidence suggests it has become more frequent since 1945, why have we not seen class-influenced movements com-parable to, say, the Agbekoya of Western Nigeria or the Northern Ele-ments Progressive Union in Northern Nigeria? An answer is suggested by an interesting quotation from Victor Minikin: 'the national leaders in Sierra Leone feared the implications of mass participation in politics . . . instead they directed the energies and attention of the people into local-level politics which became a safety-valve preventing the tensions implicit in mass participation from bursting into the national arena'.[63] Ignoring the conspiratorial element in this assertion, what it suggests is that the form taken by expressions of rural class antagonisms has inhibited the development of explicit class consciousness and class organizations. Such forms of political action as the violent deposition of chiefs or voting for an opposition party are not the creation of the subordinate classes employ-

209

ing them, and are open to manipulation by superordinate classes or strata, yet they produce apparent successes and occasional gains, helping to ensure their continued use. Like the workings of rural patron–client relations[64] such mechanisms which contain class antagonism exist elsewhere in West Africa. What makes them particularly prominent in Sierra Leone is the already noted integrity and importance of chiefdom arenas. Unlike most other West African examples, the continual involvement of central authorities in the resolution of local disputes and in particular in chieftaincy disputes has not meant the gradual and partial displacement of local institutions like chieftaincy by such central institutions as the party or administration. The reason lies in the far greater initial degree of reliance on chiefs by the SLPP than say the Convention People's Party of Ghana or the Action Group of Western Nigeria, a reliance that has been maintained and transmitted to opposition parties (though to a lesser degree).[65]

9

Conclusion

JOHN DUNN

The states of the West African littoral have widely different colonial histories and post-colonial experiences. It is unlikely that the full range of disparities between such experiences can be explained in any simple and comprehensive fashion. It is far from clear, for instance, that the varying demerits of colonial rule stand in at all a direct relation to the varying achievements of post-colonial governments. Consider, for example, the three Guineas. Guiné-Bissau contrasts most agreeably with Equatorial Guinea far to the south, western Africa's diminutive but notably horrid answer to Amin's Uganda, though each is a product of the lackadaisical Iberian style of colonialism. Both, too, contrast in many ways with 'Guinée Sékou Touré', a regime with wide initial popular support but always intensely personal in character. Sékou Touré himself battles grimly on, like an eighteenth-century prizefighter increasingly blinded by his own blood. As Bill Johnson shows so eloquently, Touré has chosen his country's political fate for it and he has spread the consequences of his choice very broadly indeed. He has chosen gallantly; but also, and increasingly, he has chosen gratuitously. *C'est magnifique; mais ce n'est pas la politique.* By contrast those who have taken the capitalist way with less resentment have in some cases found its gradients decidedly less steep. Their political theory is plainly more conservative: for forms of dependency let fools contest; what e'er is best administered is best. (And dependency being what it is, best-administered means administered with the minimum of fuss and gratuitous *ressentiment*.) Their political practice by contrast is eminently flexible, entrepreneurial enough indeed to make a friend of a wide variety of hostile occasions. Only their cultural style displays some real rigidity. Léopold Senghor on protracted periods of residence at his Normandy farmhouse, or delivering frosty instruction on how high culture is done to the *nouveaux riches parvenus* of Lagos is a living reminder of days when the Black Arts were largely something practised in Paris or New York. Houphouët-Boigny in ponderous pre-

211

varicatory dialogue with his people[1] has hardly as yet attained a successful routinization of charisma. It is certainly hard to imagine quite this style being politically sustained several decades into the future (and not simply because of the prospective mortality of the protagonists).

It seems natural in the first instance to seek to explain the contrast between Touré's regime and the regimes of Senghor and Houphouët-Boigny by adducing deep historical differences between the societies which they govern. But on the accounts offered here[2] this natural impulse will yield little reward. It is always difficult for political analysts (and especially for Marxist analysts) to decide whether it is politically more urgent or analytically more proper to indict patterns of political choice or to seek to explain them. In the case of these three francophone territories it seems probable that the prospects for social explanation of any great power are too poor to make it rational to eschew much in the way of individual moral judgement. Indeed it is quite possible that the only historically deep and structurally powerful differentiating factor in the explanation of the disparate political experiences of these countries in the post-colonial period as a whole is the most blatant of all political factors at the state level – the sheer territorial and demographic scale of the Federation of Nigeria. The intricate political legacy of Usuman dan Fodio and Lord Lugard[3] is a country as close to being ungovernable as any which one could imagine, a political unit the internally peaceful maintenance of which through time may simply have always been beyond any conceivable political capabilities, a gong-tormented political sea subject at best to the most fitful of calms.

But if political initiative and skill, political lethargy and fecklessness and (largely deplorable) political taste do more to explain most of the differences between these post-colonial histories than is dreamed of in the political science of Professor Bretton,[4] and if the explanatory rewards of the present comparison are less sweeping than some might hope, there are perhaps other types of lesson which we may legitimately draw from it. To see the experiences of these states together is to see much more clearly how much structurally they do have in common. It is to see, for example, not merely *that* they are, but more importantly *why* they are, such easy states to ruin through the exercise of political choice. It is to see how far such internal political stability as they can muster is a product of the extent to which they were ever effectively *stabilized* in the process of decolonization. (Nothing stabilizes like stability or destabilizes like instability.) It is to see the extent to which the state apparatus, an external control structure built by aliens for alien purposes, still stands over against the rest of society. All of these states, as Chris Allen emphasizes, are authoritarian structures and are such by simple inheritance, though

212

some certainly wield the knout far more brutally than do others. All of them possess armed forces with a clear preponderance of the means of violence within their territorial limits, forces which are all too ready to offer themselves as guardians of the rest of society and relatively beyond the means of the rest of society to guard against, should they make the offer. Within such structures, it is unsurprising that the two stablest of the francophone territories, Senegal and the Ivory Coast, should have been those which contrived to retain an external guard against such involuntary internal guardianship. Nor is it surprising that in those countries in which the armed services as a unit have chosen to assume governmental functions on one occasion they have seldom refrained from reassuming them again on a subsequent occasion even where they have actually returned them into civilian hands at all. A more interesting analytical level, though one as yet rather poorly developed,[5] is the role of all of these states as patronage systems, politically interstitial to the relation between these societies and the world economy, drawing resources from monitoring this relation and expending them in maintaining its internal political acceptability. The level of resources available for patronal disbursement is a complex function of this pattern of exchanges, governments with *rentier* incomes from foreign enclave producers – oil companies (Nigeria above all) or mining companies (Guinea and Liberia most particularly) – being better placed to win friends and to influence at least some among their subjects in an intended direction than those governments which must take directly from one set of their subjects or borrow from abroad without detectable collateral in order even to provide for themselves (at the scale to which they have become accustomed), let alone to disburse to others among their subjects. If the politics of patronage implies the routine engineering of lop-sided friendships, what can make even lop-sided friendships most readily acceptable is the handsome disbursing of palpable benefits. But where the supply of such benefits is exceedingly scanty – as in Senegal – it is possible for the talented to eke it out by a more energetic and polished use of charm and social adroitness.[6]

It is certainly unclear as yet (though perhaps Guiné-Bissau *might* in due course make it clear) how these authoritarian structures can be rendered more effectively responsible to their own subjects. Competitive electoral politics has certainly elicited some real communal solidarity at a local level. It is relatively easy to be sardonic about such solidarity from the perspective of universal political values; but in terms of the moral or experiential meaning of political action it is hardly as yet at all clear that it is proper to be so.[7] What is clear, however, is that the *consequences* of this pattern of political involvement (however well-intentioned its participants may be by their own lights – and what other lights are there by

213

which it is possible to be politically well-intentioned?) are very costly. All of these countries display savagely uneven internal development as a direct consequence of the pattern of their incorporation into the world economy. Competitive electoral politics in such conditions consist largely in the mobilization of resentment at uneven development, while one-party regimes which have initially emerged from electoral competition prove to be simply authoritarian governments under another name. Terminating the competition does not necessarily dismantle the organized resentment. Military government in countries (such as Dahomey-Benin) in which territorially consolidated electoral fiefdoms confront one another can readily constitute simply a continuation of such ethnic feuds by other means. The bizarre politics of Dahomey emanate, of course, from a country which is poor as well as ethnically riven. The comparison with Togo and its phosphate revenues makes it apparent how hard it would be to build a stable patronage system through the resources of the Dahomean state.[8] But the same comparison also underlines how small a difference it would in all probability now make to the prospects of such a venture to transfer the phosphate revenues from Lomé to Cotonou.

This is still not a particularly impressive haul to have drawn from the exercise of comparison. Human frailty no doubt explains something of the paucity of such findings. But it may be worth asking in conclusion whether such paucity is not more or less what one should *expect* to find and whether more grandiose hopes are not in some way theoretically misconceived. 'Is a science of comparative politics possible?', asks Macintyre; returning on balance the answer that whether or not it is possible in principle, it is certainly in practice by no means at all probable.[9] What we have tried to offer here (with all due allowance for the variations in the authors' theoretical tastes) is less grandiose than a contribution to a science of comparative politics. It reflects, perhaps at best, a balance between recognizing the rationality of historical process and assessing the openness of history, a balance which can and will be tilted to very different angles by different observers of history but which every observer of history must seek to hold as best he or she can. By setting these seven experiences side by side we can explain (or at least seek to explain) how what did happen in these countries *could* have happened (what about these societies and their historical location made it – broadly – *possible*). We cannot explain why it *did* happen.[10]

The key truth about politics – morally, practically, theoretically – is always that matters could have been different. It is always in political analysis necessary to inquire what would have had to have been different and by how much for other (preferred or less acceptable) outcomes to have ensued. Sometimes the answer to such a question may be simply and exhaustively: different actions by different (or even by the same) leaders. But usually such questions require answers which are either less simple or else confessedly less exhaustive. Thinking about how different matters *could* have been under what conditions is thinking counterfactually. In a world exactly like our own in every respect except that in it kangaroos did not have tails, (so philosophers at least have been led to believe) kangaroos would fall over.[11] West African states, like kangaroos, could certainly in principle be made different (docked, as it were). How different could they be made, as a result of *what* changes? Thinking counterfactually is the central modality of political judgement, just as description in counterfactual depth is the core of social analysis (one reason, though by no means the only reason, why social analysis is so intractable to a positivist methodology). All political scientists must in a metaphorical sense be 'realists' about possible worlds.[12] They do not, of course, need to know the technically correct semantics for possible worlds; but they do need to see clearly what it is that they are attempting to do. (If one does not coherently understand one's own analytical goals, one is relatively unlikely to attain them.) Nor is this simply a matter of academic interest. Counterfactuals for political agency are at the core of the concept of responsible government (and by no means only of the concept of responsible government in the form in which this might, with the withering away of the state and the burgeoning of other putatively better frames of social relations, turn out to be simply a shibboleth of bourgeois capitalism). The ability to determine whom or what to blame when things have gone wrong is a precondition for human rational social cooperation in a world in which things still can go wrong as a result of human action. And a world in which things *can* no longer go wrong as a result of human action will be either a world which is no longer populated by humans or else a world which it is as impossible for us to imagine as it would be preposterous for us to expect or desire. In the meantime (the time of human comprehension) learning what could or could not have been done in the recent past is a prerequisite for deciding rationally what is to be done in the present or near future.

To think counterfactually about political agency is to revel intellectually (if not necessarily emotionally) in the openness of history. But it is certainly not necessarily to blind oneself to the grubby rationality of historical process. The human will is scarcely the master of historical process. There remain, nevertheless, choices for which men can rationally be praised and blamed – in that they chose to act in one way and not in another. It is possible to see rulers as responsible agents, to hold them responsible for their political actions and to *make* them responsible[13] (a semantic relation and not merely a pun) to those whom they rule. It would take an austere structuralist wholly to exempt General Amin from responsibility for the horrors of Uganda today.

It is a causal property of political structures such as the states of West Africa that very drastic consequences for their internal political and social coherence or division follow from the political intentions and skills of very small numbers of persons in the higher offices of the state. Power in patronage systems is vividly personal at their summit, though, as in any social system, its scope is impersonal and causal enough in use. Such causal properties are appropriate objects for a political scientist to seek to identify. But if the causal property which is duly identified is just such a personalization of power at the summit, its very discovery will preclude a very delicate structural explanation of the historical diversity which it generates. It is scarcely necessary to study West African states to identify many feats which lie well beyond the powers of their rulers. But even the minutest comparative study of their structures will not serve to explain the disparities of their political fortunes.

How, then, should we see the performance of West Africa's rulers in the post-colonial period? Sadly, the blame is simpler to allocate than the praise – not necessarily because more blame than praise is due; but simply because the evil that some men have done and are doing forces itself on the most casual of attention. Seeing the ruin that politics can wreak, we may perhaps learn greater respect for its less showy achievements. It may not be able to make a populace healthy, wealthy and wise; but at its worst it can go a long way to sicken, impoverish and bemuse one. Foreigners, over these matters, can only try to the limits of their abilities to help West Africans to see more clearly precisely whom to blame and precisely for what. They are certainly responsible for using their eyes and their minds as well as they can and for reporting honestly the results of their having done so. It would not be difficult for them collectively to surpass their present level of performance. But only the peoples of West Africa can learn how to make their rulers responsible to them. It will scarcely be an easy task.

Notes

CHAPTER 1. COMPARING WEST AFRICAN STATES

1. See e.g. Zbigniew Brzezinski and Samuel K. Huntington, *Political Power USA/USSR* (New York 1964). Paul Hollander, *Soviet and American Society: a comparison* (New York 1973).
2. Robin Luckham, *The Nigerian Military: a sociological analysis of authority and revolt 1960–67* (Cambridge 1971). Richard Sandbrook, *Proletarians and African Capitalism: the Kenya Case 1960–72* (Cambridge 1975). R. D. Grillo, *African Railwaymen: solidarity and opposition in an East African labour force* (Cambridge 1973). Robin Cohen, *Labour and Politics in Nigeria 1945–71* (London 1974). Richard Jeffries, *Class, Power and Ideology in Ghana: the railwaymen of Sekondi-Takoradi* (forthcoming, Cambridge University Press, African Studies Series).
3. Aristide R. Zolberg, *Creating Political Order: the party-states of West Africa* (Chicago 1966).
4. Ken Post, *The New States of West Africa*, 2nd ed. (Harmondsworth pb.ed. 1968).
5. Anton A. Bebler, *Military Rule in Africa: Dahomey, Ghana, Sierra Leone and Mali* (New York 1973). J. M. Lee, *African Armies and Civil Order* (London 1969). Claude E. Welch (ed.), *Soldier and State in Africa: a comparative analysis of military intervention and political change* (Evanston 1970). Ruth First, *The Barrel of a Gun: political power in Africa and the Coup d'Etat* (London 1970). William F. Gutteridge, *Military Regimes in Africa* (London 1975). Dennis Austin and Robin Luckham (eds), *Politicians and Soldiers in Ghana 1966–72* (London 1975). Samuel Decalo, *Coups and Army Rule in Africa: Studies in Military Style* (New Haven 1976).
6. Seymour Martin Lipset, *Political Man: the social bases of politics* (London 1960), chs 2 and 3.
7. *West Africa*, 3,068, 19 April 1976, p. 549, but see now *West Africa*, 3,089, 13 September 1976, p. 1349; 3,090, 20 September 1976, p. 1363; and especially 3,102, 13 December 1976, p. 1891.
8. Basil Davidson in *West Africa*, 3,067, 12 April 1976, pp. 496–7.

9. Perry Anderson, 'Portugal and the end of ultra-colonialism', *New Left Review*, 15 (May–June 1962), 83–102; 16 (July–August 1962), 88–123; 17 (winter 1962), 85–114.

10. John Dunn, *Modern Revolutions: an introduction to the analysis of a political phenomenon* (Cambridge pb. ed. 1972). Franz Schurmann, *Ideology and Organization in Communist China*, 2nd ed (Berkeley, Calif. 1968). Donald Zagoria, Jeffrey Race and Charles Tilly's contributions to John Wilson Lewis (ed.): *Peasant Rebellion and Communist Revolution in Asia* (Stanford, Calif. 1974).

11. M. Crawford Young, 'Rebellion in the Congo', in Robert I. Rotberg and Ali Mazrui (eds), *Protest and Power in Black Africa* (New York 1970), pp. 968–1011. Benoît Verhaegen, *Rébellions au Congo*, 2 vols (Brussels 1966–9). Jean-Claude Willaume, *Patrimonialism and Political Change in the Congo* (Stanford 1972).

12. Basil Davidson, *The Liberation of Guiné* (Harmondsworth pb. ed. 1969), and Davidson's articles in *West Africa*, 1976, issues 3,065–9. Gérard Chaliand, *Lutte armée en Afrique* (Paris 1969). Lars Rudebeck, *Guinea-Bissau: a study of political mobilization* (Uppsala 1974). Rudebeck's study is the most informative and systematic.

13. Julian Pitt-Rivers, *The People of the Sierra* (Chicago pb. ed. 1969), p. 140. Patron-client relations have been much studied by social anthropologists and political scientists in the last fifteen years. See especially the work of James C. Scott, R. Lemarchand, J. D. Powell, Eric Wolf, F. G. Bailey, J. K. Campbell, J. Boissevain. For two interesting brief discussions in an African context see Colin Leys, 'Politics in Kenya: the development of peasant society', *British Journal of Political Science*, 1 (1971), 307–37 and Jean La Fontaine: 'Unstructured social relations: patrons and friends in the African Societies', *West African Journal of Sociology and Political Science*, 1: 1 (October 1975), 51–81.

14. Nicos Poulantzas, *Fascism and Dictatorship* (London 1974). Nicos Poulantzas, 'The capitalist state: a reply to Miliband and Laclau', *New Left Review*, 95 (January–February 1976), 62–83, and see his *Political Power and Social Classes* (London 1973). There have been several attempts of some interest to adapt Marxist theory of the capitalist state to the analysis of post-colonial states. See especially Hamza Alavi, 'The state in post-colonial societies: Pakistan and Bangla Desh', *New Left Review*, 74 (July–August 1972), 58–81. Bruce J. Berman, 'Clientelism and Neocolonialism: Center-Periphery Relations and Political Development in African States', *Studies in Comparative International Development*, 9: 2 (summer 1974), 3–25. John Saul, 'The state in post-colonial societies: Tanzania', in R. Miliband and J. Saville (eds), *The Socialist Register 1975* (London 1975). Geoff Lamb, 'Marxism, Access and the State', *Development and Change*, 6: 2 (April 1975), 119–35. Also the work by Colin Leys cited in note 45 below.

15. Poulantzas, 'The Capitalist State', *New Left Review*, 95 (January–February 1976), 74.

16. Poulantzas, *Fascism and Dictatorship*, p. 305 (but see pp. 316, 322–4, 343).

17. Poulantzas, *Fascism and Dictatorship*, p. 151.

18. Jean Copans, book review in *Review of African Political Economy*, 3 (May–October 1975), 99.

19. Samir Amin, *L'Afrique de l'ouest bloquée: l'économie politique de la colonisation 1880–1970* (Paris 1971). (Trans. as *Neocolonialism in West Africa*, Harmondsworth pb. ed. 1974). *Le Développement inégal: essai sur les formations sociales du capitalisme périphérique* (Paris 1973). Samir Amin (ed.), *Modern Migrations in Western Africa* (London 1974), editor's introduction.

20. Andrzej Krassowski, *Development and the Debt Trap: economic planning and external borrowing in Ghana* (London 1974). Leslie Grayson, 'The role of suppliers' credits in the industrialization of Ghana', *Economic Development and Cultural Change*, 21: 3 (April 1973), 477–99. D. L. Cohen and M. A. Tribe, 'Suppliers' credits in Ghana and Uganda: an aspect of the imperialist system', *Journal of Modern African Studies*, 10: 4 (1972), 525–41.

21. This faith is still apparently shared by some foreign observers: see e.g. *The Times*, Business Section, Commodities, 20 April 1976.

22. But see Michael A. Cohen, *Urban Policy and Political Conflict in Africa: a study of the Ivory Coast* (Chicago 1974), pp. 54, 72–6, 96, 127–8, 132, 135–6.

23. Cf. A. S. P. Woodhouse (ed.), *Puritanism and Liberty* (London 1938), esp. pp. 26–7, 53–4, 57–9. The text of the Putney debates as a whole forms a profoundly instructive ideological complex to set against the issues considered, for example in P. C. Lloyd's *Power and Independence* (London 1974). (See esp. Ireton's query (p. 26), 'I would very fain know what you gentlemen do account the right you have to anything in England – anything of estate, land or goods, that you have, what ground, what right you have to it.' and p. 27, '. . . when I hear men speak of laying aside all engagements to (consider only) that wild or vast notion of what in every man's conception is just or unjust, I am afraid and do tremble at the boundless and endless consequences of it.')

24. See e.g. H. L. van der Laan, *The Lebanese Traders in Sierra Leone* (The Hague 1975). Rita Cruise O'Brien, 'Lebanese entrepreneurs in Senegal: economic integration and the politics of protection', *Cahiers d'Etudes Africaines*, 15: 1 (1975), 95–115; and Cohen, *Urban Policy and Political Conflict*, pp. 128–9.

25. Samir Amin, *L'Afrique de l'ouest bloquée*.

26. See e.g. Elliot J. Berg, 'Structural transformation versus gradualism: recent economic development in Ghana and the Ivory Coast', in Philip Foster and Aristide R. Zolberg (eds), *Ghana and the Ivory Coast: Perspectives on Modernization* (Chicago 1971), pp. 187–230. Michael O'Connor, 'Guinea and the Ivory Coast: contrasts in economic development', *Journal of Modern African Studies*, 10: 3 (1972), 409–26. But of Samir Amin, *Le Développement du capitalisme en Côte d'Ivoire* (Paris 1967).

27. See in addition to works cited in note 26 above, Jon Woronoff, *West Africa Wager: Houphouët versus Nkrumah* (Metuchen, N.J. 1972).
28. Polly Hill, *The Migrant Cocoa Farmers of Southern Ghana: a study of rural capitalism* (Cambridge 1963). Polly Hill, *Studies in Rural Capitalism in West Africa* (Cambridge 1970). Sara S. Berry, *Cocoa, Custom and Socio-economic Change in Rural Western Nigeria* (Oxford 1975). For an illuminating account of the political action of cocoa farmers in Western Nigeria see now C. E. F. Beer, *The Politics of Peasant Groups in Western Nigeria* (Ibadan 1976).
29. Richard Jeffries, *Class, Power and Ideology in Ghana*; P. C. Lloyd, *Power and Independence: urban Africans' perception of social inequality* (London 1974).
30. Richard H. Tawney, *Business and Politics under James I: Lionel Cranfield as Merchant and Minister* (Cambridge 1958). E. P. Thompson, *Whigs and Hunters: the origin of the Black Act* (London 1975).
31. Official reports and other such materials are particularly copious for Ghana and Nigeria. For Ghana see Herbert Werlin, 'The Roots of corruption: the Ghanaian enquiry', *Journal of Modern African Studies*, 10: 2 (1972), 247–66, and Victor T. Le Vine, *Political Corruption: the Ghana Case* (Stanford 1975). For a balanced general survey see James C. Scott, *Comparative Political Corruption* (Englewood Cliffs, N.J. 1972).
32. Fred W. Riggs, *Administration in Developing Countries: the theory of prismatic society* (Boston 1964); and *The Ecology of Public Administration* (New Delhi 1961).
33. See e.g. Edward J. Schumacher, *Politics, Bureaucracy and Rural Development in Senegal* (Berkeley 1975). Robert M. Price, *Society and Bureaucracy in Contemporary Ghana* (Berkeley 1975).
34. Poulantzas, *Fascism and Dictatorship*, p. 239.
35. For a clear statement see Thomas Szentes, '*Status quo* and socialism', in Issa Shivji, *The Silent Class Struggle*, Tanzanian Studies no. 2, (Dar es Salaam 1974), pp. 78–117. Poulantzas, *Political Power and Social Classes*, p. 334.
36. See Dennis Austin and A. Jeyaratnam Wilson (eds), *Ghana and Sri Lanka: a political comparison* (forthcoming). The contrast is particularly salient in the case of trade unions and political parties.
37. See e.g. John Dunn and A. F. Robertson, *Dependence and Opportunity: political change in Ahafo* (Cambridge 1973). And cf. the stimulating analysis by J. D. Y. Peel, 'Inequality and Action: the forms of Ijesha social conflict' (unpublished manuscript).
38. See John Dunn, 'Politics in Asunafo' in Austin and Luckham (eds), *Politicians and Soldiers in Ghana*, pp. 164–213. Martin Staniland, *The Lions of Dagbon: political change in Northern Ghana* (Cambridge 1975). But it is perhaps invidious to pick examples of a point which is indicated by most of the better recent historiography of the colonial period.
39. Henry L. Bretton, *Power and Politics in Africa* (London pb. ed. 1973).
40. Michael Crowder, *West Africa under Colonial Rule* (London 1968). Ruth

220

Schachter Morgenthau, *Political Parties in French-speaking West Africa* (Oxford 1964). Zolberg, *Creating Political Order.*

41. First, *The Barrel of a Gun.* Lee, *African Armies and Civil Order.* Bretton, *Power and Politics in Africa.* Amin, *L'Afrique de l'ouest bloquée.*

42. John P. Mackintosh (ed.), *Nigerian Government and Politics* (London 1966). Frederick A. O. Schwartz Jr, *Nigeria: the tribes, the nation or the race* (Cambridge, Mass. 1965). Luckham, *The Nigerian Military.* K. W. J. Post and Michael Vickers, *Structure and Conflict in Nigeria 1960–66* (London pb. ed. 1973) (or more rewardingly: K. W. J. Post and George D. Jenkins, *The Price of Liberty: personality and politics in Colonial Nigeria,* Cambridge 1973). Robert Melsom and Howard Wolpe (eds), *Nigeria: Modernization and the Politics of Communalism* (East Lansing, Michigan 1971). Howard Wolpe, *Urban Politics in Nigeria: a study of Port Harcourt* (Berkeley 1974).

43. A. G. Hopkins, *An Economic History of West Africa* (London pb. ed. 1973).

44. E. A. Brett, *Colonialism and Underdevelopment in East Africa: the politics of economic change 1919–39* (London pb. ed. 1973).

45. Colin Leys, *Underdevelopment in Kenya: the political economy of neo-colonialism* (London pb. ed. 1975).

46. Amin (ed.), *Modern Migrations,* introduction.

47. G. B. Kay (ed.), *The Political Economy of Colonialism in Ghana* (Cambridge 1972), editor's introduction. Staniland, *The Lions of Dagbon,* ch. 3. Roger G. Thomas, 'Forced labour in British West Africa: the case of the Northern Territories of the Gold Coast 1906–27', *Journal of African History,* 14: 1 (1973), 79–103.

48. Aristide R. Zolberg, *One-Party Government in the Ivory Coast* (Princeton 1964). Martin Staniland, 'Single-party regimes and political change: the P.D.C.I. and Ivory Coast politics' in Colin Leys (ed.), *Politics and Change in Developing Countries* (Cambridge 1969), pp. 135–75. Michael Cohen, *Urban Policy and Political Conflict.*

49. I. A. Akinjogbin: *Dahomey and its Neighbours 1708–1818* (Cambridge 1967). Karl Polanyi, *Dahomey and the Slave Trade: an analysis of an archaic economy* (Seattle 1966). Kwame Yeboa Daaku, *Trade and Politics on the Gold Coast 1600 to 1720; a study of the African reaction to European trade* (Oxford 1970). Ivor Wilks, *Asante in the Nineteenth Century: the structure and evolution of a political order* (Cambridge 1975).

50. See e.g. Dunn and Robertson, *Dependence and Opportunity,* esp. ch. 4. For the importance of seeing the consequences of past political choices in the frame in which current political choices and forces are defined see Paul Brass's helpful study, *Language, Religion, and Politics in North India* (Cambridge 1974).

51. For Northern Nigeria see M. G. Smith, *Government in Zazzau: a study of government in the Hausa Kingdom of Zaria in Northern Nigeria from 1800 to 1950* (London 1960). S. J. Hogben and A. H. M. Kirk-Greene, *The Emirates of Northern Nigeria* (London 1966). I. F. Nicolson, *The Adminis-*

221

tration of Nigeria 1900 to 1960: men, methods, and myths (Oxford 1969). C. S. Whitaker, Jr, *The Politics of Tradition: continuity and change in Northern Nigeria 1946–66* (Princeton 1970). John N. Paden, *Religion and Political Culture in Kano* (Berkeley 1973). For Ghanaian examples see Dunn and Robertson, *Dependence and Opportunity*, and Staniland, *The Lions of Dagbon*.

52. Donal B. Cruise O'Brien, *The Mourides of Senegal: the political and economic organization of an Islamic brotherhood* (Oxford 1971) and *Saints and Politicians: essays in the organisation of a Senegalese peasant society* (Cambridge 1975).

53. Compare the views of J. A. Braimah (J. A. Braimah and J. R Goody, *Salaga: the struggle for power*, London 1967, ch. 22) with that of the Sardauna of Sokoto (Schwartz, *Nigeria, the Tribes, the Nation*, p. 79) and contrast the subsequent political fortunes of the two areas. A similarly distorted pattern of educational access without local employment opportunities and the consequent over-recruitment into the officer corps of the army among Ibos in Nigeria and Ewes in Ghana has had dramatic impact on the national politics of both countries since 1965 (see Luckham, *Nigerian Military*. Austin and Luckham (eds), *Politicians and Soldiers*).

54. Cf. Leys, *Underdevelopment in Kenya, passim* esp. pp. 198–206. Leys does not deny, of course, that ethnic solidarism is a major factor in Kenyan internal politics. But he is unable to throw (or perhaps merely uninterested in throwing) any but the thinnest analytical light on how and why it plays such a major role. Compare the amount of illumination provided on this issue by the less theoretically ambitious study by Geoff Lamb, *Peasant Politics: conflict and development in Murang'a* (Lewes 1974).

CHAPTER 2. GHANA

1. Dennis Austin's *Politics in Ghana* (London 1964) remains the classic account of Ghanaian politics from 1945–60. The years since then have been dealt with in radical fashion by Bob Fitch and Mary Oppenheimer in *Ghana: end of an illusion* (New York 1967), and in more turgid fashion by Trevor Jones in *Ghana's First Republic* (London 1976) and Roger Pinkney in *Ghana under Military Rule* (London 1972). For the real flavour of Ghanaian politics, Maxwell Owusu's *The Uses and Abuses of Political Power* (Chicago 1970), and John Dunn and A. F. Robertson's *Dependence and Opportunity: political change in Ahafo* (Cambridge 1974) cannot be too highly recommended. Dennis Austin and Robin Luckham have usefully collected essays in *Politicians and Soldiers in Ghana* (London 1975) of which John Dunn's essay on Asunafo is the most illuminating.

2. The immediate pre-independence period is dealt with in Austin, *Politics in Ghana* and Rathbone, *The Transfer of Power in Ghana*, University of London, Ph.D. thesis, 1968.

3. See Austin, *Politics in Ghana*, Geoffrey Bing, *Reap the Whirlwind* (London 1968).

4. See especially Richard Jeffries's illuminating London Ph.D. thesis (1974) on the railway and docks and harbour workers of Sekondi-Takoradi, and especially the revised version of this forthcoming in the Cambridge University Press African Studies Series (1978).
5. The best accounts of the 1969 election are to be found in Austin and Luckham (eds) *Politicians and Soldiers in Ghana*.
6. A. G. Hopkins *An Economic History of West Africa* (London 1972).
7. See especially his excellent paper to the Past and Present conference on urbanization, held at University College London in the summer of 1975.
8. *West Africa*, 3,104, 3 January 1977, p. 24.
9. *The Times*, 14 January 1977, p. 10.

Further reading

An exhaustive list of publications on modern Ghana would require too many pages to complete. The basis for any further reading must be the two volumes edited by Birmingham, W., Neustadt, I., and Omaboe, E. N. under the overall title of *A Study of Contemporary Ghana*; vol. 1, *The Economy of Ghana* and vol. 2, *The Social Structure* (London 1966) remain indispensable despite being considerably out of date. Important aspects of Ghanaian social structure are examined in Philip Foster's *Education and Social Change* (London 1965) and Jack Goody (ed.) *Changing Social Structure in Ghana* (London 1975). By far the best attempt to relate the texture of Ghanaian life to political expression is John Dunn and A. F. Robertson's *Dependence and Opportunity: political change in Ahafo* (Cambridge 1974) which despite its limited regional focus has a wider applicability, not least in its methodological originality. Similarly local in focus is Maxwell Owusu's persuasive study of Agona Swedru, *The Uses and Abuses of Political Power: a case study of continuity and change in the politics of Ghana* (Chicago 1970). Dennis Austin's study, *Politics in Ghana 1946–60* (London 1964) remains the most valuable historical account of the rise of mass nationalism. His sensitivity to all things Ghanaian and his apparent delight in them set a high standard which few subsequent scholars have emulated. David Apter's *Ghana in Transition* (New York 1968) is more analytically adventurous than Austin's volume but affords the reader far less information. Bob Fitch and Mary Oppenheimer provide a Marxian reworking of the post-war period in their *Ghana: end of an illusion* (New York 1966) which remains fresher reading than Roger Genoud's *Nationalism and Economic Development in Ghana* (New York 1969). Kwame Nkrumah's own account of his career to 1957, *Ghana: an autobiography* (London 1957) is spirited and free, mercifully, from the jargon-loaded nonsenses of his later literary contributions. The Nkrumah period from 1957 to 1966 is interestingly covered by an 'inside-dopester' Geoffrey Bing in his *Reap the Whirlwind* (London 1968). Both Henry Bretton's *Rise and Fall of Kwame Nkrumah* (London 1966) and Trevor Jones's *Ghana's First Republic (1960–66)* (London 1976) are less entertaining but in their accusatory style provide a useful counterbalance to Bing's pleading. Roger Pinkney's *Ghana under Military Rule 1966–1969* (London 1972) is full of factual material but thin on analysis of that

223

period. With notable exceptions the essays edited by Dennis Austin and Robin Luckham *Politicians and Soldiers in Ghana* (London 1975) are similarly arid.

CHAPTER 3. GUINEA

1. The PDG was, until 1958, merely the Guinean section of the inter-territorial Rassemblement Démocratique Africain. For a while after independence the PDG attempted to claim that it was the only 'true' RDA section but if the initials are ever used now in Guinea they are understood to mean Révolution Démocratique Africaine.

2. Guinea has attempted to Africanize its nomenclatures with the result that Touré's name (for example) is now spelt 'Seku Ture'. I have preserved the established nomenclatures throughout simply for clarity's sake.

3. Touré was probably never a member of the PCF (Parti Communiste Français) though he was, of course, a CGT (Confédération Générale du Travail) member. Among his earliest journalistic efforts was a ringing attack on Sartrean existentialism as a bourgeois deviation in the then approved *L'Humanité* style.

4. Numerous famous blacks have at least attempted to make Guinea their home. Apart from exiles – Djibo Bakary, Nkrumah etc. – such figures have included Harry Belafonte, Stokely Carmichael and Miriam Makeba. A later generation of black militants tended to see more hope in the People's Republic of the Congo (Brazzaville) – see Eldridge Cleaver *et al.*, *Revolution in the Congo* (London 1971).

5. *Maraboutage* is understood to mean the exploitation by *marabouts* (Islamic teachers) of their position for pecuniary or other gain. Guinea is about 70 per cent Moslem.

6. Alfa Yaya of Labé, the greatest chief of the Fouta Djalon, was deposed by the French in 1905, restored in 1910 and then re-exiled in 1911. He died in Mauretania.

7. For a bibliography and discussion of the first seventeen of these volumes see R. W. Johnson, 'Sekou Touré and the Guinean Revolution', *African Affairs*, 69: 277 (1970), 350–65.

8. Guinean delegations normally attend with fraternal status the congresses of the PCF, the Soviet and East European Communist Parties.

9, See R. W. Johnson, 'The P.D.G. and the Mamou "deviation" ' in C. Allen and R. W. Johnson (eds), *African Perspectives* (London 1971).

10. Fédération des Etudiants de l'Afrique Noire Française. A later survey showed that Touré's stand had indeed made him the most admired African leader amongst this group; see J. P. N'Diaye, *Enquête sur les étudiants noirs en France* (Paris 1962).

11. No-one had taken Touré's position seriously enough to anticipate this dramatic declaration. Only one western journalist seems to have been present, Roy MacGregor-Hastie, of the British ITV network, whose editor had confused Guinea with Guyana. *The Times* (London), 6 November 1976.

224

12. The best account is by G. Chaffard, *Les carnets secrets de la décolonisation* (2 vols., Paris 1967), vol. 2, pp. 165–268.
13. It is important to insist on the term 'traumatic' in a strict sense in describing both Touré's break with France and Guinea's love–hate relationship with her since. It seems certain that Touré has, at some level, been the rebellious son at ambivalent grips with a father (particularly while de Gaulle was the French president). For a precise analogy see W. Reich, *The Mass Psychology of Fascism* (Penguin edition, Harmondsworth 1975), pp. 58–9. It is for this reason that it is a mistake to see recurrent Guinean efforts to achieve the restoration of relations with France after 1958, and again after 1965, as implying a move towards the West, or to the right. In fact the resumption of relations with France in 1975 coincided with a sharp turn to the left in Guinea. Cuba's relationship with Spain – despite even greater political differences – shows how lastingly deep-seated such links can be.
14. He was released two years later.
15. The JRDA (Jeunesse de la Révolution Démocratique Africaine – formerly just the RDA youth) is the PDG's youth wing.
16. Guinea had alternately declared herself ready for a reconciliation with France and affected a hostile indifference when one did not take place. When the May Events of 1968 occurred in Paris this pretence was pushed aside, Conakry radio carrying a breathless and continuous account of them.
17. Guinea had broken off diplomatic relations with Britain in 1965 over Rhodesia's UDI. Although relations were later resumed neither country has since actually had an ambassador resident in the other.
18. The Foulah (Peul) people, constituting around a third of the population and inhabiting the central highlands of the Fouta Djalon are strong and conservative Moslems whose loyalty to the PDG has always been in considerable doubt, to say the least.
19. The most thorough external coverage of Guinea is to be found in the Paris-based news magazine, *Jeune Afrique*. Its principal writer on Guinea, M. Siradiou Diallo, is a leader of the anti-Touré Guinean exile movement. He has been sentenced to death in Guinea.
20. A high proportion of Guinea's ambassadors has always consisted of those whose political loyalties were too doubtful for the regime to be keen to have them in Conakry. Not a few ambassadors have been summoned home direct to jail with the result that some have defected on receiving such a summons.
21. Guinea straightforwardly supported North Vietnam and the South Vietnamese NLF against the US – although she took no public position over the Soviet invasion of Czechoslovakia in 1968.
22. Nos. 258–60, 20 October–3 November 1969.
23. The Service de Documentation Extérieure et de Contre-Espionnage.
24. G. Chaffard in *Le Nouvel Observateur*, 20 October 1969, p. 51.
25. See, for example, Chaffard's account of the French intervention in 1964 in Gabon to restore the overthrown President M'Ba in *Le Nouvel Observateur*, 20 October 1969.

26. *Le Monde*, 6–7 March 1966.
27. See R. W. Johnson, 'French Imperialism in Guinea', in R. Owen and B. Sutcliffe (eds) *Studies in the Theory of Imperialism* (London 1972).
28. In the mid-1960s the countries of the eastern bloc were paying Guinea two and one-half times the world market price for her pineapples, for example. Guinean production costs were roughly equal to the free market price and there must be doubt as to whether she could export this crop at all without preferential treatment.
29. In 1973 the value of Guinean food imports was some 4.75 billion francs CFA; in 1975 3 billion CFA. Rapid world inflation in that period makes the real drop much greater. See *West Africa*, 18 October 1976. (My calculations for 1973.)
30. These are agricultural bright spots, relatively efficient and productive, thanks largely to the management of Chinese technical assistants and the Guinean army.
31. He nonetheless turns a blind eye to a great deal of extremely public corruption – none more outrageous than that of his brother, Ismael Touré, the Minister of Economics and Finance. Under Ismael's management Guinea's cigarette factory's entire production was at one point routed to Sierra Leone for hard currency, while smokers in Guinea had, mysteriously, to suffer nicotine starvation. Ismael is also probably the worst offender against the law forbidding ministers to own more than one residence. The State Commission for the Verification of Property, the relevant official body, has never been asked to consider the case of Ismael, for long the leader of the 'hard' (pro-Chinese) faction within the BPN.
32. *Sily* denotes 'elephant' in Soussou and is the emblem of the PDG. It sometimes also colloquially denotes Sekou Touré himself.
33. Probably over 500,000 Guineans live abroad in neighbouring Africa countries. Some have left for political reasons but far more for economic ones. This pattern of migration dates back to well before independence, however. The setttlement of so many Guineans abroad gives the anti-Touré opposition-in-exile a considerable importance.
34. See J. Suret-Canale, 'Touba in Guinea – Holy Place of Islam' in C. Allen and R. W. Johnson (eds) *African Perspectives* (London 1971) – a model analysis of social change in a Guinean rural community.
35. The *almamys* (religious chiefs) of the Fouta Djalon have both died in the 1970s and have not been replaced. There is little doubt, however, that any resistance to the regime within the Fouta will take a Moslem form. It is almost certainly this consideration which prompted Touré to convene a National Islamic Council in 1976, to act as a channel of Moslem support for the regime.
36. In an ill-advised economy drive in 1968 the regime attempted to limit the length of the headscarves worn by most Guinean women. This led to fierce pressures and an eventual climb-down by the regime, but such issues are both rare and hardly the basis for an enlightened feminist consciousness. In

226

recent years Touré has criticized the struggle for women's liberation as a false perspective, saying that it must be merely part of a wider struggle for human liberation.

37. Confédération Nationale des Travailleurs Guinéens and Union Générale des Travailleurs de l'Afrique Noire.

38. At least, this seemed to be one of the minor lessons of the 1970 invasion. Only then did it become clear that, though the Milice had conducted endless public rifle displays, they had neither ammunition nor any actual shooting experience. They acquired both during the invasion and their wild and indiscriminate firing was probably responsible for a majority of the civilian casualties inflicted.

39. *Horoya*, 2,246, 6 November 1976.

40. *Horoya*, 2,246, 6 November 1976, p. 33.

41. *Horoya*, 2,246, 6 November 1976, p. 32.

42. *West Africa*, 13 September 1976.

43. See B. Charles, 'Cadres politiques et administratifs dans la construction nationale en Guinée', *Revue de l'Institut de Sociologie* (Université Libre de Bruxelles), no. 2–3 (1967), 159–67.

44. These four make up the principal members of the standing Commission of Enquiry which interrogates political detainees and obtains confessions from them, including, most recently, that of Telli Diallo. A fifth major figure at such sessions is Lansana Diané, another Malinké member of the BPN, also related to Touré by marriage. The inquisition is normally led by Ismael Touré, seconded by Moussa Diakité, the Minister of the Interior and Security, the Beria to Fodéba Keita's Yezhov. Mamadi Keita, the Minister of Education, is also the editor of *Horoya*, a role which makes him the regime's key ideologist (after Touré). Seydou Keita has recently been appointed as Guinean ambassador in Paris – one embassy that Touré will not trust to an envoy of dubious loyalty.

45. *West Africa*, 3 January 1977.

46. *Horoya*, 2,236, 28 August 1976, p. 29.

47. The most significant French interest remaining in Guinea is that of Péchiney's participation in the Fria consortium – but it is dwarfed by its American, British, German, Swiss and Italian partners.

48. R. Dumont, *False Start in Africa* (London 1966). The Guinean regime is not among M. Dumont's admirers. It has coined the term 'Dumontisme' to denote the sins of foreign experts who make sweeping prescriptions for underdeveloped countries on the basis of a brief visit.

49. In his preface to *La pensée politique de Patrice Lumumba* (Paris 1963), published by Présence Africaine.

50. R. First, *Libya – the Elusive Revolution* (London 1974), pp. 250–2.

51. *Horoya*, 2,246, 6 November 1976, p. 34. It is, however, highly significant that these commissars have limited powers vis-à-vis the federal bureaux of the party and their powerful secretaries. They are not to be placed permanently within the ranks of such bureaux and while they may dismiss regional governors on the spot, they have no such power over the regional

party elites. Their maximum power is to order the closure of debate at a meeting of such a bureau.

Further reading

The literature on post-independence Guinea is thin and unsatisfactory. The best single work is J. Suret-Canale, *La République de Guinée* (Paris 1970) which, however, has very little to say about Guinean politics. C. Rivière, *Mutations Sociales en Guinée* (Paris 1971) contains much useful sociological information. Two books which do deal extensively with Guinean politics are C. A. Diakité, *Guinée enchainée ou le livre noir de Sekou Touré* (Paris 1972) and A. Conde, *Guinée: L'Albanie de l'Afrique ou néo-colonie americaine?* (Paris 1972). As their titles suggest, both are ferociously critical, written by the regime's exiled opponents. Uncritical on the other side is A. Diawara, *Guinée, la marche du peuple* (Dakar 1968), which is little more than fairly brainless propaganda. L. Adamolekun, *Sekou Touré's Guinea* (London 1976) is a useful little book, particularly on the subject of administration. It carefully omits, however, virtually all mention of the Kafkaesque side to Guinean life, which is leaving out a good half of the story. B. Charles, *Guinée* (Atlas des Voyages series, Lausanne 1963) is an older work whose charming photographs and illustrations nonetheless convey the contemporary atmosphere well; the text is impressionistic but interesting. On the economic side the situation Reports of the OECD (1965) and of the IBRD (1967) are extremely detailed, particularly the latter. The first is available without too much difficulty, the latter is less easily so. The OECD has also produced a bibliography on Guinea, now a little dated. A more recent, though select, bibliography, is to be found at the end of Adamolekun's book, *op. cit.*, pp. 237–44. The student of contemporary Guinea must, however, read the press, particularly *Horoya*, *Jeune Afrique*, *West Africa*, and *Le Monde*.

The author did not, unfortunately, have access until after this article was written to Sylvain Soriba Camara, *La Guinée sans la France* (Paris 1976). Camara's work is a substantial, reliable, though somewhat formal account of Franco-Guinean relations from the 1950s to about 1970. It is a valuable addition to the literature.

CHAPTER 4. IVORY COAST

1. F. N. Amon d'Aby, *La Côte d'Ivoire dans la cité africaine* (Paris 1951), p. 76.
2. Aristide R. Zolberg, *One-party Government in the Ivory Coast*, rev. ed. (Princeton 1969), pp. 23–4.
3. The time-lag in the colonial penetration of the Ivory Coast as compared to other West African countries is suggested by the fact that in 1916, one year before French military conquest of the Ivory Coast was completed, Senegal had already elected an African deputy to the French National Assembly. *Ibid.*, p. 18.
4. Ivory Coast, *Programme d'action économique et sociale* (Imprimerie du Government, Abidjan 1933), p. 25 and pp. 30–1.

5. Ruth Schachter Morgenthau and Thomas Hodgkin, 'French-speaking Africa in transition', *International Conciliation*, 528 (May 1960), 411–12.
6. Ruth Schachter Morgenthau, *Political Parties in French-speaking West Africa* (Oxford 1964), p. 177.
7. Zolberg, *One-Party Government in the Ivory Coast*, p. 67.
8. For a more detailed account of redefinition of interests during the period of political decolonization, see: Bonnie Campbell, 'French Economic Interests in West Africa and Changes in the French Union with Special Reference to the Ivory Coast 1946–1956' (Master's Thesis, University of Sussex, 1970).
9. Hubert Fréchou, 'Les plantations européennes en Côte d'Ivoire', reprint of Ph.D. thesis (Institut des Hautes Etudes de Dakar, Dept. of Geography) No. 3, 1955. Fréchou's thesis presents an excellent historical summary of the emergence of the African planters, pp. 187–207.
10. Morgenthau, *Political Parties in French-speaking West Africa*, p. 169.
11. Samba Seytane 'Les classes sociales et les dirigeants politiques de l'Ouest Africain', *Partisans*, no. 29–30 (May–June 1968), 58. Table is from Raymond Barbé, *Les classes sociales en Afrique Noire* (1964) and Ivory Coast, *Rapport annuel du Ministère de l'Agriculture* (1960).
12. Samir Amin, *Le développement du capitalisme en Côte d'Ivoire*, (Paris, 1967), p. 107.
13. *Ibid.*, p. 277.
14. Morgenthau, *Political Parties in French-speaking West Africa*, p. 215.
15. The characterization of the Ivorian planter group by Samir Amin as a 'véritable bourgeoisie de planteurs' (*Le developpement du capitalisme en Côte d'Ivoire*, p. 277) appears justified by the fact that they possessed their own autonomous basis of production in spite of the fact that the realization of the surplus which they produced depended upon their integration into the world market. This particular situation of a dependent–dominant local group is central to the explanation of the seemingly contradictory policies followed at times by the Ivorian ruling class.
16. *Ibid.*, p. 278.
17. Morgenthau, *Political Parties in French-speaking West Africa*, p. 178.
18. Jean Suret-Canale, *Afrique Noire. De la colonisation aux indépendances 1945–1960* (Paris 1972), p. 61.
19. A more detailed account of this process is given by Jean Suret-Canale in the first chapter of the volume on this subject. *Ibid.*, pp. 9–72.
20. Morgenthau and Hodgkin, 'French-speaking Africa in transition', pp. 413–14.
21. Suret-Canale, *Afrique Noire. De la colonisation aux indépendances 1945–1960*, pp. 101–2.
22. For a full description and an evalution of the role of these institutions, see *Ibid.*, ch. ii, section 2.
23. Campbell, 'French Economic Interests in West Africa'.
24. Pierre Soudet, 'Les plans d'investissement d'Outre-mer', *Revue d'Economie Politique* (1952) p. 819. Among the many bodies created were

229

the: Compagnie Française pour le Développement de Fibres Textiles; Bureau Central d'Etudes pour l'Equipement d'Outre-Mer; Centre Technique Forestier Tropical.

25. *Ibid.*, p. 820.
26. P. F. Gonidec, 'L'évolution des territoires d'Outre-mer depuis 1946', *Revue juridique et politique de l'Union française,* 3 (July–September 1957 Paris), 441–2.
27. Suret-Canale, *Afrique Noire*, p. 121.
28. 'En effet les Caisses de Stabilisation des Prix du café et du cacao, conçues à l'origine comme un instrument de stabilisation, assumèrent rapidement une fonction différente: celle de percevoir des revenus au profit des gouvernements coloniaux.' Georges H. Lawson, 'La Côte d'Ivoire: 1960–1970. Croissance et diversification sans africanisation', in *L'Afrique de l'indépendance politique à l'indépendance économique* (eds. F. Maspéro and Presses Universitaires de Grenoble, Paris 1975), p. 209.
29. Leonard Barnes, *African Renaissance,* ch. 13, 'Expansion without growth: Ivory Coast' (London 1969), p. 170.
30. Elliot J. Berg, 'The economic basis of political choice in French West Africa', in *American Political Science Review*, 54 (1960), 398–9.
31. For a more detailed analysis of the colonial trading network, see: Claude Roire, 'Les grandes compagnies commerciales et le marché africain', *Revue française d'Etudes politiques africaines*, 64 (April 1971); Suret-Canale, *L'Afrique Noire. De la colonisation aux indépendances*, ch. IV. section 1 pp. 305–19; Georges Ngango, *Les investissements d'origine extérieure en Afrique Noire francophone: statut et incidence sur le développement* (Paris 1973).
32. See the graphic table in G. Mevungu, 'Côte d'Ivoire, Mirage et Réalites', *Tam-Tam*, *Revue des Etudiants Catholiques Africains*, no. 3–4 (June–September 1966), 22. Similar details appear in a recent book published by the same author under his real name rather than a pseudonym: Georges Ngango, *Les investissements d'origine extérieure en Afrique Noire francophone* (Paris 1973), p. 385. Index of the interests affiliated to SCOA:

ADC – Ateliers du Canet
AF – L'Africaine Française
AFRICAUTO – Compagnie Africaine pour l'Automobile
BI – Banque de l'Indochine
BRACODI – Société des Brasseries de la Côte d'Ivoire
BUP – Banque de l'Union Parisienne
CAP – Chantiers et Ateliers de Provence
CCP – Compagnie des Caoutchoucs du Pakidie
CECACI – Compagnie d'Exploitations Commerciales et Automobile
CEGEDUR – Compagnie Générale du Duraluminium et du Cuivre
CFAO – Compagnie Française de l'Afrique Occidentale
CEGEPAR – Compagnie Générale de Participations et d'Entreprises
CFCI – Compagnie Française de la Côte
CIMAG – Société des Grands Magasins de la Côte d'Ivoire

COFIMER – Compagnie Financière pour l'Outre-Mer
CL – Crédit Lyonnais
CNF – Compagnie du Niger Français
LA COTIVOIRIENNE – Société Africaine de Vente à Crédit
ICODI – Société des Impressions sur tissus de Côte d'Ivoire
IVOIRAL – Compagnie Ivoirienne de l'Aluminium
SAGA – Société Anonyme de Gérance et d'Armement
SCOA – Société Commerciale Ouest Africaine
SEDCI – Société d'Etudes pour le Developpement de la Côte d'Ivoire
SERIA – Société d'Etudes et de Réalisations Industrielles d'Abidjan
SFA – Société Forestière d'Azingo
SFCE – Société Française du Commerce Européen
SFGP – Société Financière de Gérance et de Participations
SICAB – Société Immobilière Cocody-Abidjan
SICOACI – Société Immobilière et Commerciale de l'Ouest Africain–Côte d'Ivoire
SIDECO – Société Ivoirienne de Distribution Economique
SIH – Société Ivoirienne d'Habillement
SIPCA – Société Industrielle de produits chimiques et aromatiques
SIPEC – Société Ivoirienne de peintures et de colorants
SHO – Société Commerciale, Industrielle et Agricole du Haut-Ogooué
SNF – Société Niger-France
SOAEM–COTE D'IVOIRE – Société Ouest Africaine d'Entreprises Maritimes – Côte d'Ivoire
SOBOCI – Société des Boissons Hygiéniques de Côte d'Ivoire
SOHICO – Société Hôtelière et Immobilière Cocody-Abidjan
SOVINCI – Société des Vins de la Côte d'Ivoire
TRANSCAP-COTE D'IVOIRE – Société Eurafricaine de Voyages de transit et de camionnage portuaire – Côte d'Ivoire
UFIDA – Union Financière pour le Développement de l'Afrique
UNACI – Union Africaine pour le Commerce et l'Industrie de la Côte d'Ivoire
UNIPAR – Union des Participants et d'Entreprises

33. Zofia Dobrska, 'Economic development of the Ivory Coast from the winning of independence', *Africana Bulletin* 5 (Warsaw 1966), 29. Shortly before independence major investments had been made in the harbour of Abidjan and the electric power station in Bia – two projects which created 'reserves of growth' for future directly productive activities.
34. Suret-Canale, *Afrique Noire. De la colonisation aux indépendances*, p. 140 (our translation).
35. Guy Delaporte, *Quinze années bien remplies au Service du Pays*, Information Service, Caisse de Stabilisation de Côte d'Ivoire, May 1970, p. 10 (our translation).
36. Judith Marshall, 'The state of ambivalence: right and left options in Ghana', *Review of African Political Economy* 5 (January–April 1976), 52.
37. An official publication of the Caisse de Stabilisation dated 1970 states that

231

the Caisse de stabilisation des Prix du Café has operated under favourable conditions above all because of the tariff protection which it has received on the protected markets of the franc zone – 20 per cent duties were imposed against coffee from foreign countries as of 1965. It has benefited as well from the progressive increase in the world market price of coffee which took place between 1955 and 1958. Guy Delaporte, *Quinze années bien remplies au Service du Pays*, p. 3.

38. Dobrska, 'Economic development of the Ivory Coast', p. 16.
39. *Ibid.*, p. 17.
40. *Fraternité* (Abidjan), 6 May 1960.
41. Guy Caire, 'Idéologie du développement et développement de l'idéologie', *Revue Tiers-Monde*, 15: 57 (January–March 1974 Paris) 6 (our translation).
42. Colin Leys, 'The "overdeveloped" post colonial state: a re-evaluation', *Review of African Political Economy*, 5 (January–April 1976 London), 44. Quoted from Nicos Poulantzas, *Political Power and Social Classes*.
43. This is the argumentation advanced for example by Michael Cohen, *Urban Policy and Political Conflict in Africa; a study of the Ivory Coast* (Chicago 1974), p. 60.
44. Gilbert Compte, 'Un rapport du F.M.I. remet en question le "miracle ivorien" ', *Le Monde Diplomatique* (March 1972 Paris) p. 14.
45. Colin Leys, 'The "overdeveloped" post-colonial state', p. 44.
46. With reference to the first Ivorian Assembly elected in 1957, A. Zolberg writes: 'After the elections, the Assembly established for itself and for the government the highest salary scale in all of French West Africa, with an average annual expenditure of $10,000 for each assemblyman and $12,000 for each minister.' Zolberg, *One-Party Government in the Ivory Coast*, pp. 192–3.
47. Teresa Hayter, *French Aid* (London 1966), p. 80.
48. Georges Lawson, 'La Côte d'Ivoire: 1960–1970. Croissance et diversification sans africanisation', p. 207.
49. Ivory Coast, Ministère des Affaires Economiques et Financières, Direction des Affaires Economiques et des Relations Economiques Extérieures, Arrêté No. 7758, Annexe I, 29 November 1969.
50. A discussion of these measures as they apply to the various aspects of cotton textile imports appears in ch. VIII of: Bonnie Campbell, 'The Social, Political and Economic Consequences of French Private Investment in the Ivory Coast 1960–1970. A Case Study of Cotton and Textile Production', Ph.D. Thesis, University of Sussex 1974.
51. Ivory Coast, Ministère du Plan, *La Côte d'Ivoire en chiffres,* Edition 1976 (Paris 1976) p. 71.
52. The intervention of the French forces in West Africa in order to bolster the newly-created governments began even before the formal granting of political independence: in 1960 and 1961 in the Cameroon where the French forces helped restore order to maintain the government of President Ahidjo; in 1960 in Congo-Brazzaville during the massacres of Poto-Poto;

in Gabon in September 1960; in Chad in March 1963; Niger in December 1963; Mauritania in 1961; a second time in Gabon in February 1964 . . .

53. In the mid-1960s there were approximately ten bases in 'French-speaking' Africa and Madagascar – the four major ones being: Djibouti, Dakar, Diego-Suarez and Fort-Lamy. These were complemented by six other secondary ones at Bou-Sfer, Port-Bouët, Douala, Bangui, Niamey and Libreville. A. Lacroix, 'Problèmes de défense en Afrique Noire francophone et coopération militaire francophone', Mémoire du Centre de Hautes Etudes sur l'Afrique et l'Asie Modernes (CHEAM), no. 3,995, March 1965.

54. As M. Ligot states writing of these military agreements: 'les accords de défense font partie d'un ensemble de liens qui fondent par leur caractère multiple et global, une coopération essentiellement politique des Etats intéressés et créent entre eux une communauté de destin. Il y a là plus qu'une alliance militaire, car la coopération va de pair avec une certaine harmonisation de la vie diplomatique et, dans certains cas, avec l'existence d'institutions politiques communes.'
'La Coopération Militaire dans les Accords passés entre la France et les Etats Africains et Malgaches d'Expression Française', *Revue Politique et Juridique d'Outre-Mer* (October–December 1963), p. 517.

55. Morgenthau, *Political Parties in French-speaking West Africa*, p. 185.

56. Cohen, *Urban Policy and Political Conflict in Africa*, p. 23.

57. Morgenthau, *Political Parties in French-speaking West Africa*, p. 211.

58. Martin Staniland, 'Single-party regimes and political change: the P.D.C.I. and Ivory Coast politics', in *Politics and Change in Developing Countries*, Colin Leys ed. (Cambridge 1969), p. 149.

59. Zolberg, *One-Party Government in the Ivory Coast*, p. 318.

60. Staniland, 'Single-party regimes and political change', p. 165. (Speech of President Yacé, opening of the National Assembly, 27 April 1967.)

61. Semi-bi Zan, 'Le Parti Démocratique de Côte d'Ivoire', *Revue française d'études politiques africaines*, 8e Année, 94 (October 1973), 71 (our translation).

62. Georges Lawson, 'La Côte d'Ivoire: 1960–1970. Croissance et diversification sans africanisation', p. 211.

63. Ivory Coast, *La Côte d'Ivoire en chiffres*, Edition 1976, pp. 74–5.

64. 'La prolifération d'entreprises et d'organismes publics autonomes soulève, par ailleurs, des problèmes. Au nombre d'environ vingt-cinq, l'Etat leur a assigné des tâches précises de développement. Il leur accorde des fonds sans que leur situation financière et leur programme fassent l'objets d'un examen approfondis. C'est ainsi qu'une grande partie des investissements publics ne répond pas à ces critères d'investissements rationals.' Gilbert Compte, 'Un rapport du F.M.I. remet en question le "miracle ivoirien" ', *Le Monde Diplomatique* (March 1972), p. 14.

65. Ivory Coast, *La Côte d'Ivoire en chiffres*, Edition 1976, p. 73 (our translation).

66. Cohen, *Urban Policy and Political Conflict in Africa*, p. 62.

67. *Ibid.*, p. 62.
68. *Ibid.*, p. 43.
69. *Ibid.*, p. 62.
70. *Ibid.*, p. 33.
71. The divisive nature of ethnicity is at times used as an instrument by the ruling class to minimize the impact of cross-ethnic protest movements. The revival of ethnic differences can in fact occasionally be seen as a specific policy of those in power. Hence after the protest movements of 1969, in an attempt to break apart the cross-ethnic character of the movement, the army divided those who were sent to agricultural training camps in the interior of the country for 're-education' on ethnic lines. *Ibid.*, p. 106. Also, Semi-bi Zan, 'Le Parti Démocratique de Côte d'Ivoire', pp. 72–3.
72. Cohen, *Urban Policy and Political Conflict in Africa*, p. 69.
73. Samir Amin, *Neo-Colonialism in West Africa* (Harmondsworth 1973), pp. 50–1.
74. Ivory Coast, *La Côte d'Ivoire en chiffres*, Edition 1976, p. 37 (our translation).
75. 'The inflow of immigrants, notably from Mossi in Upper Volta, whose numbers increased from 100,000 in 1950 to 950,000 in 1965, supplies most of the labour for the plantation areas and new urban activities. The foreign African population in 1965 made up a quarter of the country's total; 25–40 per cent of the active male labour force, more than 60 per cent of urban workers outside the public service; and half to two thirds of the labour force in rural plantation areas.' Amin, *Neo-Colonialism in West Africa*, p. 52.
76. This position has been analysed with reference to the Second Plan of Economic Development of the Ivory Coast 1971–5. See Bonnie Campbell, 'L'Idéologie de la croissance. Une analyse du Plan quinquennal de Développement 1971–1975 de la Côte d'Ivoire', *Canadian Journal of African Studies*, x, 2 (1976).
77. Ivory Coast, Ministère du Plan, *Deuxième Esquisse du Plan Quinquennal de Développement 1971–1975* (June 1970 Abidjan), pp. 15–16.
78. Leonard Barnes, 'Expansion without growth: Ivory Coast', in *African Renaissance*, Leonard Barnes ed. (London 1969), p. 174.
79. Georges Lawson, 'La Côte d'Ivoire: 1960–1970. Croissance et diversification sans africanisation', p. 227 (our translation).
80. Ivory Coast, *Deuxième Esquisse du Plan Quinquennal 1971–1975*, p. 26 (our translation).
81. René Charbonneau, *Marchés Tropicaux*, no. 1068 (30 April 1966), pp. 1224–5. Quoted by Leonard Barnes, 'Expansion without growth', p. 176 (our translation).
82. Leonard Barnes, 'Expansion without growth', p. 176.
83. Ivory Coast, *Deuxième Esquisse du Plan Quinquennal 1971–1975*, p. 11.
84. *Ibid.*, p. 12 (our translation).
85. On the basis of his analysis Lawson writes with regard to the impact of agricultural changes: '. . . ces changements ont probablement modifié la répartition des revenus aux dépens des petits paysans.' Georges Lawson,

'La Côte d'Ivoire: 1960–1970. Croissance et diversification sans african-isation', p. 225.

86. 'Ainsi le Plan de Développement 1960–1970 prévoit que 12% en moyenne de la formation de capital seront alloués à l'agriculture et plus de 35% a l'industrie. Une telle disparité n'était pas prévue au départ, mais il devint clair vers la fin de la décennie que le moteur de la croissance devait être l'industrialisation et non la diversification agricole.' *Ibid.*, p. 221.

87. Ivory Coast, Ministère du Plan, *La Côte d'Ivoire en chiffres*, Edition 1976, p. 38.

88. This critical bias against the encouragement of industries based on the processing of locally produced raw materials is particularly striking in the case of textiles in the Ivory Coast where in the early 1970s all raw materials could theoretically be produced locally but in which industrial imports in fact represented 61 per cent of the resources used by the branch.

89. The description of Ivorian industrial concessions granted under the Code is now conditioned by the following footnote: 'Cette loi de 1959 n'apparait plus actuellement adaptée aux conditions économiques ivoiriennes et cer-taines modifications sont envisagées, donnant à l'Administration la pos-sibilité d'établir cas par cas une formule de dégrèvements adaptée à chaque création nouvelle. Les premiers bénéficiaires de la loi de 1959 régrettent de voir disparaître brutalement des avantages importants à l'échéance de leur délai d'agrément; c'est pourquoi il est envisagé d'introduire une dégres-sivité des avantages, acheminant peu à peu l'entreprise vers les conditions de fonctionnement du droit commun.' Ivory Coast, Bureau de Développe-ment Industriel (BDI), *La Côte d'Ivoire industrielle* (Abidjan 1972), p. 48.

90. Amin, *Le développement du capitalisme en Côte d'Ivoire*, p. 261. Because of the liberalism of Ivorian tax regulations, the transfers effected by large private companies are estimated as representing 40 per cent of gross earnings, or 1.6 billion FCA in 1950 (in constant 1965 value), and 11 billion in 1965.

91. 'Les repatriements de bénéfices, salaires etc. . . . se sont élevés, pour la seule année 1969 à 27,800,000,000 CFA'. *Lettre Africaine* (20e année Nouvelle série, No. L.A. 36/70, 22 September 1970), p. 2. This figure requires upward adjustment on the one hand because capital outflows do not take account of practices such as over-invoicing and transfer pricing, and on the other hand because the French notion of gross profits does not take account of the distribution of dividends to shareholders.

92. The Ivorian balance of payment position has evolved as follows over the period 1964 to 1973: (Billions francs CFA)

Year	Balance	Year	Balance
1964	+4,4	1969	+ 9,5
1965	+4,5	1970	+ 9,6
1966	+3,1	1971	− 3,2
1967	−6,3	1972	−18,9
1968	+8,7	1973	−2,3

Ivory Coast, *La Côte d'Ivoire en Chiffres*, Edition 1976, p. 57.

93. Lawson, 'La Côte d'Ivoire: 1960–1970. Croissance et diversification sans africanisation', p. 221.
94. *Ibid.*, p. 222.
95. Pathé Diagne, *Pour l'unité ouest-africaine. Micro-Etats et intégration économique* (Paris 1972), p. 155 (our translation).
96. Lawson, 'La Côte d'Ivoire: 1960–1970. Croissance et diversification sans africanisation', p. 228 (our translation).
97. With regard to the country's dependence on food imports during the period 1950–65, S. Amin writes: 'the food deficit, made up by imports of grain and rice, rose from the equivalent of 27,000 tons of rice in 1950 to 92,000 tons in 1965; making up at that time 75 per cent of the consumption in the towns and 14 per cent of that in the country'. Amin, *Neo-Colonialism in West Africa*, p. 52.

    More recently, according to the Five-Year Plan (1971–5) imports of agricultural and food products were expected to increase in current value terms from 23,703 million CFA in 1970 to 26,318 in 1975 and 38,748 million in 1980. The government's anticipation of continuing basic food imports is clearly suggested by the recent adoption by the Chamber of Commerce of the Ivory Coast of a new 'Règlementation des Importations de Riz en Côte d'Ivoire.' Ivory Coast, Chambre de Commerce de Côte d'Ivoire, Bulletin Mensuel, no. 7 and 8, July–August 1975, pp. 47–56. In 1974 the country imported 178,629 tons of wheat and 119,193 tons of rice. *Ibid.*, p. 22.
98. Amin, *Le développement du capitalisme en Côte d'Ivoire*, pp. 276–7 (our translation).
99. Gilbert Compte, 'Un rapport du F.M.I. remet en question le "miracle ivoirien" ', p. 14 (our translation).
100. The minimum Ivorian agricultural wage was raised in July 1968 to 231 francs CFA per eight hour day. This rate, however, was not imposed on the plantation sector. Similarly when a 5 per cent increase in wage rates took place in August 1974, this increase did not apply to agricultural workers of the plantation sector whose wage increases were to be dependent on the establishment of export crop and notably coffee crop prices. *Marchés Tropicaux et Méditerranéens*, xxx, 1,506 (20 September 1974), 2657.
101. Zolberg, *One-Party Government in the Ivory Coast*, p. 362.
102. Cohen, *Urban Policy and Political Conflict in Africa*, p. 41. Cohen emphasizes the extent to which foreign participation in the labour force is increasingly seen in relation to unemployment.
103. Lawson, 'La Côte d'Ivoire: 1960–1970. Croissance et diversification sans africanisation', p. 227.
104. Campbell, 'The Social, Political and Economic Consequences of French Private Investment in the Ivory Coast', ch. vii.
105. Cohen, *Urban Policy and Political Conflict in Africa*, p. 216.
106. Ivory Coast, *Deuxième Esquisse du Plan Quinquennal de Développement, 1971–1975*, p. 32.
107. In spite of increased foreign financing, the Ivory Coast became a net

exporter of capital in 1968 and 1969. Lawson, 'La Côte d'Ivoire: 1960–1970. Croissance et diversification sans africanisation', p. 226.

108. For the 1963 and 1965 figures, Amin, *Le développement du capitalisme en Côte d'Ivoire*, p. 166.
109. Cohen, *Urban Policy and Political Conflict in Africa*, p. 39.
110. Amin, *Le développement du capitalisme en Côte d'Ivoire*, p. 39.
111. *Ibid.*, p. 194 (our translation).
112. *Ibid.*, p. 174. This displacement applies particularly to textiles and construction.
113. Ivory Coast, *Deuxième Esquisse du Plan Quinquennal de Développement 1971–1975*, p. 17.
114. Amin, *Le développement du capitalisme en Côte d'Ivoire*, p. 194.
115. The conclusions of an inquiry into salaried urban labour carried out in 1971 by the Ivorian Ministère de l'Enseignement Technique et de la Formation Professionnelle, whose findings were not released publicly.
116. Amin, *Le développement du capitalisme en Côte d'Ivoire*, p. 194. On 1 January 1970 the minimum industrial wage (*Salaire minimum industriel garanti*, SMIG) was raised 25 per cent to 58.30 francs CFA per hour. It was increased by 25 per cent on 1 August 1973 to 73 FCFA; on 1 February 1974 to 87.60 CFA and finally on 1 August 1974, it was increased by 5 per cent. Ivory Coast, *VIe Congrès du Parti Démocratique de Côte d'Ivoire, 15–16–17 octobre 1975* (Abidjan 1976), p. 91 (our translation).
117. 'The European share of higher-level jobs in the economy is about 90 per cent, thereby shutting off the highest standards of living to all but a few Africans. The 1965 employment study found that of 510 private businesses in eighteen major industrial activities, only thirteen had African directors.' Cohen, *Urban Policy and Political Conflict in Africa*, p. 54.
118. Amin, *Le développement du capitalisme en Côte d'Ivoire*, pp. 154–5 and p. 172.
119. Cohen, *Urban Policy and Political Conflict in Africa*, p. 39.
120. *Ibid.*, p. 77.
121. This orientation of Ivorian participation in local economic activities is very well illustrated by the creation in June 1970 of the Abidjan stock exchange, or Bourse de Valeurs. The Ivorian government's purchase of a block of shares (as for example was done in a tobacco factory) which are sold to Ivorians, 'valeurs nominales', allows for participation in local profits and an increasing number of shares in Ivorian hands without entailing control in local economic activities.
122. Pathé Diagne, *Pour l'unité ouest-africaine. Micro-Etats et intégration économique,* p. 32 (our translation).
123. *Ibid.* (our translation).
124. *Ibid.* (our translation).
125. *Ibid.* p. 34 (our translation).
126. Although not in official documents, it is nonetheless not difficult to find examples of local initiatives which have been blocked by the withholding of funds to protect already established foreign interests. In the Ivory Coast

one example concerns the case of an Ivorian initiative to set up a fruit juice and canning factory for export for which funds were not made available because of the implications the project had for established foreign interests.

127. Cohen, *Urban Policy and Political Conflict in Africa*, p. 227.

128. Zolberg, *One-Party Government in the Ivory Coast*, regarding youth, pp. 306–9, regarding the unions, pp. 296–305.

129. The events in 1963 were described in the French press as conspiracies, one occurring in January and the second in September. In seven months eight ministers were arrested and only three former ministers retained their posts after the ministerial reshuffle of September 1963. Philippe Decreane: 'La Côte d'Ivoire sous le Signe de l'Expansion', *Le Monde*, August 1964, pp. 1 and 4. Among those arrested during these events was the president of the Ivorian Supreme Court, Mr Ernest Boka, whose death shortly after imprisonment was reported as suicide. A certain number of those imprisoned were held at Yamoussoukro – and not released until 1970 when a general pardon was issued on the celebration of ten years since the signing of political independence.

130. Zolberg, *One-Party Government in the Ivory Coast*, p. 355.

131. Semi bi-Zan, 'Le Parti Démocratique de Côte d'Ivoire', p. 71.

132. Cohen, *Urban Policy and Political Conflict in Africa*, p. 191.

133. *Ibid.*, p. 143.

134. *Ibid.*, p. 157.

135. Ivory Coast, *VIe Congrès du Parti Démocratique de Côte d'Ivoire, 15–16–17 octobre 1975*, p. 175 (our translation).

136. *Ibid.*, p. 180.

137. An important exception in this regard is the series of studies entitled: 'Opinions et attitudes des paysans et ouvriers ivoiriens face au développment', prepared by the Institut d'Ethno-Sociologie of the University of Abidjan for the Ministry of the Plan in 1970–2.

138. Christian Coulon, 'Factions, Elections et Idéologie au Sénégal', Paper presented at the (May 17–18, 1976) Table Ronde Sur les Elections Non-Concurrentielles, Rapport no. 5 (April 1976), Fondation Nationale des Sciences Politiques (our translation). An interesting parallel exists in this regard between the role of factional politics which Coulon describes and the multi-party system. Senegal is a case in point.

Further reading

Ruth Schachter Morgenthau, *Political Parties in French-speaking West Africa*, (Oxford 1964), xxxii + 445 pages. See Part Five, 'Planters and politicians in the Ivory Coast', pp. 166–218. Provides a useful historical background to the origins of the PDCI and politics in the Ivory Coast over the period 1946 to 1960.

Jean Suret-Canale, *Afrique Noire. De la colonisation aux indépendances 1945–1960* (Paris 1972) 430 pages. An excellent account of metropolitan relations and economic interests not only in the Ivory Coast but in all of

French colonial Africa. Traces the evolution of these relations during the crucial period of political decolonization 1945–60.

Samir Amin, *Le développment du capitalisme en Côte d'Ivoire* (Paris 1967). By far the most complete and important volume available on the Ivory Coast. Examines the nature of the Ivorian political economy especially over the period 1950–65, and the socio-economic and political consequences of foreign control over 'development' in the Ivory Coast.

Samir Amin, *Neo-Colonialism in West Africa* (Penguin African Library, Harmondsworth 1973), 298 pages. See ch. 2, especially part 2, 'The contemporary miracle: the Ivory Coast 1950–65'. An English translation of some of the major points of *Le développement du capitalisme en Côte d'Ivoire*. The book is a translation of Samir Amin, *L'Afrique de l'Ouest bloquée* (Paris 1971).

Michael A. Cohen, *Urban Policy and Political Conflict in Africa: A Study of the Ivory Coast* (Chicago 1974), 262 pages. Through an analysis of Ivorian urban policy, the book examines the question of inequality and its social, economic and political consequences in the Ivory Coast.

Martin Staniland, 'Single-party regimes and political change: the PDCI and Ivory Coast politics', in Colin Leys (ed.), *Politics and Change in Developing Countries* (Cambridge 1969). See pp. 135–75. Provides a brief résumé of the evolution of the PDCI from 1946 to 1967 and describes its internal organization and relations at the local level with the administration.

Aristide R. Zolberg, *One-Party Government in the Ivory Coast* (Princeton 1969, revised edition), 400 pages. Provides a rather uncritical and descriptive presentation of the origins of the PDCI, the process of decolonization, the emergence of a single-party system, and Ivorian politics to 1964, updated in the revised edition by the addition of a chapter to 1967.

Bonnie Campbell, 'l'Idéologie de la croissance. Une analyse du Plan quinquennal de Développement 1971–1975 de la Côte d'Ivoire,' in *Canadian Journal of African Studies*, 10: 2 (1976).

CHAPTER 5. LIBERIA

I wish to acknowledge the assistance of the Social Science Research Council, London, for meeting the expenses of study visits to Liberia in 1969 and 1973.

1. The provisional total shown by the 1974 census was 1,496,000 (*West Africa*, 1 July 1974, p. 805).
2. United Nations, *Yearbook of National Accounts Statistics. 1974* (3 vols., New York 1975), vol. 3, pp. 3–4.
3. C. Clapham, *Liberia and Sierra Leone: an essay in comparative politics*, African Studies Series, no. 20 (Cambridge 1976), p. 48.
4. Republic of Liberia, *1962 Census of Population: summary report for Liberia* (Monrovia 1964), pp. 9, 13.
5. J. G. Liebenow, *Liberia: the evolution of privilege* (Ithaca 1969), p. 139.
6. T. Wreh, *The Love of Liberty . . . : the rule of President William V. S.*

Tubman in Liberia 1944–1971 (London 1976), pp. 75–9, claims that the alleged plot was framed by the security agencies.

7. United Nations, *Statistical Yearbook 1974* (New York 1975), pp. 67–8.
8. See M. Lowenkopf, *Politics in Liberia: the conservative road to development* (Stanford 1976), pp. 141–7.
9. *Ibid.*, p. 131.
10. Republic of Liberia, *Quarterly Statistical Bulletin of Liberia (summary for 1972)* (Monrovia 1973), p. 79.
11. Republic of Liberia, *The Budget of the Government of Liberia for the fiscal period January 1 to December 31, 1975* (Monrovia 1975), p. xiv.
12. Lowenkopf, *Politics in Liberia*, p. 132.
13. Clapham, *Liberia and Sierra Leone*, p. 91.
14. For the role of chiefs, see Clapham, *Liberia and Sierra Leone*, pp. 73–86.
15. See S. P. Huntington, *Political Order in Changing Societies* (New Haven 1968), pp. 72–8.
16. See Wreh, *The Love of Liberty . . .*, pp. 102–6.
17. *Ibid.*, pp. 107–12; Lowenkopf, *Politics in Liberia*, pp. 164–6; *West Africa*, 8 March 1976, p. 295.
18. R. L. Clower *et al.*, *Growth without Development: an economic survey of Liberia* (Evanston 1966), p. 24; Clapham, *Liberia and Sierra Leone*, p. 134; *Budget of Liberia for 1975*, p. x.
19. *Quarterly Statistical Bulletin for 1972*, pp. 53, 76.
20. Clapham, *Liberia and Sierra Leone*, pp. 115–17.
21. *Ibid.*, pp. 110–11.

Further reading

There are two general studies of politics and social and economic change in Liberia, J. G. Liebenow, *Liberia: The Evolution of Privilege* (Cornell 1969), and M. Lowenkopf, *Politics in Liberia: The Conservative Road to Development* (Stanford 1976); Liebenow is somewhat more critical, Lowenkopf more up to date, but both may be recommended. Both tend to ignore hinterland politics, which is discussed, though briefly, in my *Liberia and Sierra Leone: An Essay in Comparative Politics* (Cambridge 1976). The economy is most fully examined in R. L. Clower *et al.*, *Growth without Development: An Economic Survey of Liberia* (Evanston 1966), any critical bias in which is more than compensated for in L. P. Beleky, 'The development of Liberia', *Journal of Modern African Studies*, 11 (1973), 43–60.

CHAPTER 6. NIGERIA

1. J. B. Sykes (ed.), *Concise Oxford Dictionary*, 6th ed. (Oxford 1976), pp. 854–5.
2. K. Marx and F. Engels, *The German Ideology. Collected works* (London 1976), 5: 46.

3. D. Ricardo, *On the Principles of Political Economy and Taxation* (Harmondsworth 1971), p. 49.
4. M. Weber, *Theory of Social and Economic Organization* (New York 1947), pp. 278–9.
5. *Report of the Constitution Drafting Committee* (Lagos 1976), 1: v.
6. *Report of the Constitution Drafting Committee*, 1: v.
7. *Report of the Constitution Drafting Committee*, 1: vi.
8. E. Durkheim, *The Division of Labour in Society*, (New York 1964).
9. *Report of the Constitution Drafting Committee*, 1: xiii.
10. *Report of the Constitution Drafting Committee*, 1: xiii.
11. The fallacy in this view is exposed by J. F. Weeks, 'Imbalance between the centre and periphery and the employment crisis in Kenya', in I. Oxaal, T. Barnett and D. Booth (eds), *Beyond the Sociology of Development* (London 1975).
12. *German Ideology*. *Collected Works*, 5: 47.
13. As in N. Poulantzas, *Political Power and Social Classes* (New Left Books, 1973). But compare N. Poulantzas, 'The capitalist state; a reply to Miliband and Laclau', *New Left Review*, 95 (1976), 74, which defines the state as a 'relation', but without appearing to grasp the implication that the state can only be specified empirically. Our own understanding of the state is indebted to the work of Philip Corrigan. See P. R. D. Corrigan, H. Ramsay and D. Sayer, 'The state as a relation of production', Conference of the British Sociological Association, 1977, and *Socialist Construction and Marxist Theory* (London 1978).
14. M. Weber, 'Class, status, Party', *From Max Weber. Essays in Sociology* (New York 1948), p. 189.
15. J. D. Y. Peel, 'Inequality and action. The forms of Ijesha social conflict', Conference on Inequality in Africa, Social Science Research Council, New York 1977, to be published in a book edited by Sara Berry.
16. A term of Portuguese origin, used in China to refer to the agents of foreign business houses. Nigerian Youth Congress, *The Crisis and the People* (Lagos n.d.? 1962), pp. 4–7.
17. J. I. Tseayo, 'The Emirate system and Tiv reaction to "pagan" status in Northern Nigeria', in G. Williams (ed.), *Nigeria: Economy and Society* (London 1976), pp. 78–81.
18. *Report of the Tribunal appointed to enquire into allegations on the Official Conduct of the Premier of, and certain persons holding Ministerial and other Public Offices in the Eastern Region of Nigeria*, Cmd. 51 (London 1957). (The Foster Sutton Report). Cf. O. Osoba, 'Ideological trends in the Nigerian national liberation movement and the problems of national identity, solidarity and motivation, 1934–1965', *Ibadan*, 27 (1969).
19. K. W. J. Post and G. Jenkins, *The Price of Liberty: Personality and Politics in Colonial Nigeria* (Cambridge 1973), pp. 351–93.
20. Action Group, *Democratic Socialism. Being the Manifesto of the Action Group of Nigeria* (Lagos 1960). Its 'socialism' was a matter of supporting local against foreign capitalism. See pp. 7–8.

21. A. H. M. Kirk-Greene (ed.), *Crisis and Conflict in Nigeria. A Documentary Sourcebook, 1966–69* (Oxford 1971), 1: 197.
22. Kirk-Greene, *Crisis and Conflict,* 1: 213.
23. Kirk-Greene, *Crisis and Conflict,* 1: 244.
24. B. J. Dudley, *Instability and Political Order, Politics and Crisis in Nigeria* (Ibadan 1973), p. 75.
25. For the label, and a critique, see N. Girvan, 'The development of dependency economics in the Caribbean and Latin America: Review and comparison'. *Social and Economic Studies,* 22 (1973).
26. International Bank for Reconstruction and Development, *The Economic Development of Nigeria* (Baltimore 1955), p. 27. Cf. S. O. Osoba, 'Ideology and planning for national economic development 1946–72' in M. Tukur and T. Olagunju (eds), *Nigeria in Search of a Viable Polity* (Zaria, n.d. ?1972).
27. *The Economic Development of Nigeria,* p. 30.
28. J. F. Weeks, 'The political economy of labor transfer', *Science and Society,* 35 (1971).
29. J. F. Weeks, 'Employment, growth and foreign domination in underdeveloped countries', *Review of Radical Political Economics,* 4 (1972).
30. *Report of the Advisory Committee on Aids to African Businessmen* (Lagos 1959).
31. Cited F. A. Baptiste, 'The Relations between the Western Region and the Federal Government of Nigeria' (M.A. thesis, University of Manchester, 1965).
32. As recognized by the title of the book by its main author: W. F. Stolper, *Planning without Facts: Lessons in Resource Allocation from Nigeria's Development* (Cambridge, Mass. 1966).
33. *Report of the Commission of Enquiry into the Disorders in the Eastern Provinces of Nigeria,* Col. 256 (London 1950) (The Fitzgerald Report).
34. Kirk-Greene, *Crisis and Conflict,* 1: 125.
35. C.E.F. Beer, *The Politics of Peasant Groups in Western Nigeria* (Ibadan 1976), 219–22; J. A. Atanda, 'The Iseyin-Okeiho Rising of 1916', *Journal of the Historical Society of Nigeria,* 4 (1969); A. Afigbo, *The Warrant Chiefs* (London 1972).
36. For a biography of Adelabu, see Post and Jenkins, *The Price of Liberty*.
37. R. L. Sklar, *Nigerian Political Parties* (Princeton 1963), pp. 284–320, 474–80.
38. P. Waterman, 'Conservatism amongst Nigerian workers', in Williams (ed.), *Nigeria*, p. 182.
39. *The Price of Liberty,* p. 440; K. W. J. Post and M. Vickers, *Structure and Conflict in Nigeria, 1960–66* (London 1973), p. 233.
40. V. I. Lenin, *Imperialism, the Highest Stage of Capitalism. A Popular Outline* (Moscow n.d.), p. 109.
41. Lenin, *Imperialism*, p. 108.
42. Sir Frank McFadzean, Chairman of Shell, preface to their 1976 *Annual Report, Financial Times*, 14 May 1976.

43. *West Africa*, 22 July 1967, cited J. de St Jorre, *The Nigerian Civil War*, p. 179.

44. T. Turner, 'The Nigerian Cement Racket', *Africa Guide 1977* (Great Chesterford 1976).

45. Mr Romanoff, Soviet Ambassador to Nigeria, 1969, cited S. Cronje, *The World and Nigeria, The Diplomatic History of the Biafran War, 1967–70* (London 1972), p. 240.

46. Cited G. Williams, 'Nigeria: a political economy', in Williams (ed.), *Nigeria*, p. 53.

47. A. Ayida, 'The Nigerian Revolution, 1966–76', Presidential Address to Nigerian Economic Society (Ibadan 1973).

48. Decree 18 April 1971. Explanatory note.

49. Cf. P. C. Asiodu, 'Aspects of Nigerian oil policy, 1971–1975. A refutation of Terisa Turner's article . . .' in the *Lagoon Echo* of January–March 1977 (Lagos, mimeo, 1977), reprinted in *Lagoon Echo*, March–April 1977.

50. T. Turner, 'The transfer of oil technology and the Nigerian state', *Development and Change*, 7 (1976), 'Two refineries: a comparative study of technology transfer to the Nigerian refining industry', *World Development*, 5 (1977).

51. *Second and Final Report of the Wages and Salaries Review Commission, 1970–71* (Lagos 1971). (Adebo Report). *Public Service Review Commission: Main Report* (Lagos 1974). (Udoji Report.)

52. *The Public Service of Nigeria: Government Views on the Report of the Public Service Commission* (Lagos 1974), p. 5. Cf. *White Paper on the Second and Final Report of the Wages and Salaries Review Commission, 1970–71* (Lagos 1971), p. 11.

53. P. Collins, 'The state and dependent capitalist development. The Nigerian experience', *Journal of Commonwealth and Comparative Political Studies* (forthcoming).

54. G. Williams, 'Rural underdevelopment', in E. O. Akeredolu-Ale (ed.), *Social Development in Nigeria, Readings on Policy and Research* (Ibadan forthcoming), 'Taking the part of peasants: Rural development strategy in Nigeria and Tanzania', P. C. W. Gutkind and I. Wallerstein (eds), *The Political Economy of Contemporary Africa* (Beverly Hills 1976).

55. *Enquiry into the Cost of Living and the Control of the Cost of Living in the Colony and Protectorate of Nigeria*. Col. 204 (London 1946). (Tudor Davies Report.)

56. P. Waterman, 'The Nigerian state and the control of labor: the case of the Lagos cargo-handling industry', P. Collins (ed.), *Administration for Development in Nigeria* (Ibadan forthcoming).

57. O. Nduka, 'Colonial education and Nigerian society', in Williams (ed.), *Nigeria*.

58. 'Development objectives', in A. A. Ayida and H. M. A. Onitiri (eds), *Reconstruction and Development in Nigeria* (Ibadan 1971), p. 7.

59. *First Report of the Wages and Salaries Review Commission, 1970* (Lagos 1970), p. 11.

60. 'Ecuador: oil up for grabs', *NACLA Latin America and Empire Report*, 9: 8 (1975), p. 35.
61. C. E. F. Beer, *Politics of Peasant Groups*, pp. 160–7, 179–205, 219–23, 241–55; C. E. F. Beer and G. Williams, 'The politics of the Ibadan peasantry', in Williams (ed.), *Nigeria*. G. Williams, 'Political consciousness amongst the Ibadan poor' in E. de Kadt and G. Williams (eds), *Sociology and Development* (London 1974).
62. A. Peace, 'Industrial conflict in Nigeria', in de Kadt and Williams (eds), *Sociology and Development*; Peace, 'The Lagos proletariat: labour aristocrats or populist militants', and P. Lubeck, 'Unions, workers and consciousness in Kano, Nigeria: a view from below', in R. Sandbrook and R. Cohen (eds), *The Development of an African Working Class* (London 1975).
63. A. Peace, 'Social change at Agege' (Ph.D. thesis, University of Sussex, 1973).
64. D. Remy, 'Economic security and industrial unionism: a Nigerian case study', Sandbrook and Cohen (eds), *Development of an African Working Class*.
65. January 1976, cited *The Times*, Nigeria Supplement, 22 August 1976.
66. *Report of the Constitution Drafting Committee*, 1: ix.
67. *Report of the Constitution Drafting Committee*, 2: 158.
68. *Minority Report* (Y. B. Usman and S. O. Osoba), (Zaria 1977).
69. Report of the Tribunal of Inquiry into the Activities of Trade Unions (Lagos 1977) (Adebiyi Report). See P. Waterman, 'Industrial relations and the control of labour protest in Nigeria' (The Hague, Institute of Social Studies, 1977), to which I am indebted.
70. Col. J. N. Garba, Commissioner for External Affairs, to the General Assembly of the United Nations, 7 October 1975. *Nigerian Bulletin on Foreign Affairs*. 5: 3 and 4 (1975), p. 65.
71. Federal Government. Statement of (sic!) Angola, 6 January 1976. *Nigerian Bulletin on Foreign Affairs*, 6: 1 (1976), p. 2.
72. Gen. Murtala Muhammed, to the Extraordinary Summit Conference of the Organization of African Unity, 11 January 1976, in *Nigerian Bulletin on Foreign Affairs*, 6: 1 (1976), p. 10.
73. J. Petras and M. Morley, 'The Venezuelan development "model" and U.S. policy', *Development and Change*, 7 (1976).

We are grateful to Paul Clough, Bill Johnson, Pepe Roberts, Peter Waterman and Gillian Williams for helpful comments.

Further Reading

The following major studies have provided sources for this analysis. Articles are cited in the footnotes.

J. S. Coleman, *Nigeria, Background to Nationalism* (Los Angeles 1958).
R. L. Sklar, *Nigerian Political Parties* (Princeton 1963).

K. W. J. Post, *The Nigerian Federal Election of 1959* (London 1963).

J. P. Mackintosh *et al.*, *Nigerian Government and Politics* (London 1966).

K. W. J. Post and M. Vickers, *Structure and Conflict in Nigeria 1960–66* (London 1973).

R. Melson and H. Wolpe (eds), *Nigeria: Modernization and the Politics of Communalism* (East Lansing 1972).

A. H. M. Kirk-Greene (ed.), *Crisis and Conflict in Nigeria. A Documentary Sourcebook, 1966–69* (Oxford 1971), 2 vols.

H. Miners, *The Nigerian Army, 1956–66* (London 1971).

R. Luckham, *The Nigerian military* (Cambridge 1971).

R. First, *The Barrel of a Gun* (London 1970).

S. K. Panter-Brick (ed.), *Nigerian Politics and Military Rule: Prelude to the Civil War* (London 1970).

B. J. Dudley, *Instability and Political Order* (Ibadan 1973).

J. de St. Jorre, *The Nigerian Civil War* (London 1972).

C. S. Whittaker, *The Politics of Tradition, Continuity and Change in Northern Nigeria, 1946–66* (Princeton 1970).

B. J. Dudley, *Parties and Politics in Northern Nigeria* (London 1968).

P. Baker, *Urbanization and Political Change. The Politics of Lagos, 1917–1967* (Berkeley 1974).

K. W. J. Post and G. Jenkins, *The Price of Liberty* (Cambridge 1973).

R. Cohen, *Labour and Politics in Nigeria, 1945–71* (London 1974).

R. Sandbrook and R. Cohen, (eds), *The Development of an African Working Class* (London 1975).

C. E. F. Beer, *The Politics of Peasant Groups in Western Nigeria* (Ibadan 1976).

T. Turner, *The Political Economy of Nigerian Oil* (London forthcoming).

T. Turner, *State Capitalism and Public Oil* (London forthcoming).

G. Williams, (ed.), *Nigeria: Economy and Society* (London 1976).

CHAPTER 7. SENEGAL

1. *Journal Officiel de la République du Sénégal*, 10 April 1976. Loi No. 76–26, Loi No. 76–27, for details of the constitutional amendments.

2. See *Club Nation et Développement du Senegal* (Paris 1972).

3. See P. Biairnes in *Le Monde*, 31 January 1976, also *West Africa*, 5 July 1976.

4. On the PDS programme, see *Jeune Afrique*, 27 February 1976, p. 36 (article on the party's congress at Kaolack), also *Jeune Afrique* of 30 January 1976.

5. Wade to Diop, letter dated Besançon 29 September 1957, carbon copy of which shown to me in 1967 by Abdoulaye Wade, in Dakar.

6. Official recognition of the PAI reported in *Jeune Afrique*, 27 August 1976.

7. C. A. Diop, *Nations nègres et culture* (Paris 1955, revised 1964); *Antériorité des civilisations nègres. Mythe ou vérité historique?* (Paris 1967); many articles by the same author over the years, especially in the *Bulletin de l'Institut Fondamental d'Afrique Noire*.

8. Senghor's rebuke reported in *Jeune Afrique*, 27 February 1976.

9. Both Abdoulaye Wade and Cheikh Anta Diop were interviewed at some length by the present writer in the course of a four month research visit to Senegal, January–April 1975. Much background information for the present article was collected at that time, through a range of interviews, observation, and pertinent documentation.

10. From an interview with A. Wade, Dakar, March 1975.

11. 27,800 French soldiers were posted in Senegal at the time of independence (1960). 6,600 remained in 1965 and 900 (officially) in 1976. 1960–5 figures in Rita Cruise O'Brien, *White Society in Black Africa. The French of Senegal* (London 1972), p. 124.

12. Senegal's urbanization statistics from the 1970–1 sample census, République du Sénégal. Direction de la Statistique, *Enquête démographique nationale, 1970–1. Résultats définitifs*, the definitive results of which have yet to be fully published.

13. See above all F. Wioland, *Enquête sur les langues parlées au Sénégal par les élèves de l'enseignement primaire. Etude statistique.* Centre de Linguistique Appliquée de Dakar (CLAD). This study is based on a national questionnaire survey among pupils in all Senegalese primary schools. The essential findings are usefully summarized in CLAD, *L'Expansion du Wolof au Sénégal*, Dakar, n.d. (14 pages).

14. On mixed marriages, Wioland, *Enquête sur les langues parlées au Sénégal*, *passim*.

15. The notion of the adoption of a standardized orthography for Wolof originated with researchers in CLAD and is a matter under continuing review from the presidential palace.

16. The *Kaddu* group, currently in some disarray, is animated by the writer and film-maker Ousmane Sembène.

17. See F. Dumont, *Les Emprunts du Wolof au Français*, Dakar, CLAD, 1973.

18. Interviews with Phil Lu, Peace Corps wrestling coach, Dakar, 1975 and London, October 1976. Lu and a French technical assistant (Jean Marc Rochez) have largely been responsible for codification of rules.

19. On the Big Fight (23 February 1975), crowd reactions were reported to me at the time in Dakar. For Senghor's improbable statement, *Le Soleil* (Dakar), 25 February 1975.

20. See Donal B. Cruise O'Brien, *Saints and Politicians. Essays in the Organisation of a Senegalese Peasant Society* (Cambridge 1975), pp. 149–86.

21. For the most up-to-date overall assessment, see International Bank for Reconstruction and Development, *Senegal. Tradition, Diversification and Economic Development,* Washington D.C., World Bank, 1974. A critical evaluation of Senegal's post-independence economic performance will be provided in Donal Cruise O'Brien, 'The Politics of a Monocrop Economy: Ruling Class and Peasantry in Senegal, 1960–1976' (forthcoming).

22. See Donal B. Cruise O'Brien, *The Mourides of Senegal* (Oxford 1971), also *Saints and Politicians* and 'A versatile charisma: the Mouride brother-

hood 1967–1975', *European Journal of Sociology* (1977). Also L. Behrman, *Muslim Brotherhoods and Politics in Senegal* (Cambridge, Mass. 1970).

Further reading

Useful, although dated, general introductions in: W. Foltz, 'Senegal' in J. Coleman and J. Rosberg (eds) *Political Parties and National Integration in Tropical Africa* (Berkeley and L.A. 1964); R. Schachter Morgenthau 'Citizens and Subjects in Senegal' in *Political Parties in French-speaking West Africa* (Oxford 1964).

A more recent general appraisal in: Donal B. Cruise O'Brien, *Saints and Politicians. Essays in the Organisation of a Senegalese Peasant Society* (Cambridge 1975).

On early political history: (rural) M. Klein, *Islam and Imperialism in Senegal. Sine-Saloum 1847–1914* (Edinburgh 1968); (urban) W. Johnson, *The Emergence of Black Politics in Senegal* (Stanford 1971).

On politics 1945–1960: K. Robinson 'Senegal' in W. J. M. Mackenzie and Robinson (eds) *Five Elections in Africa* (Oxford 1960).

On post-independence politics: F. Zuccarelli, *Un parti politique africain, l'Union Progressive Sénégalaise* (Paris 1970) (semi-official but useful); J. L. Balans, C. Coulon, J. M. Gastellu, *Autonomie Locale et Intégration Nationale au Sénégal* (Paris 1975) (on three rural localities); E. Schumacher, *Politics, Bureaucracy and Rural Development in Senegal* (Berkeley and Los Angeles 1975) (on the mechanisms of national administration); C. Cottingham, 'Political consolidation and centre-local relations in Senegal' in *Canadian Journal of African Studies*, IV, 1, 1970 (factionalism in a small town).

On important aspects of social organization: Donal B. Cruise O'Brien, *The Mourides of Senegal the Political and Economic Organization of an Islamic Brotherhood* (Oxford 1971) (Senegal's major brotherhood, for the *zawiya* model); Rita Cruise O'Brien, *White Society in Black Africa. The French of Senegal* (London 1972) (for the *municipalité* model).

CHAPTER 8. SIERRA LEONE

1. M. Kilson, *Political Change in a West African State* (Cambridge, Mass. 1966); C. Clapham, *Liberia and Sierra Leone* (Cambridge 1976). Other general works include J. Cartwright, *Politics in Sierra Leone 1947–67* (Toronto 1970); V. E. King, 'The search for political stability in Sierra Leone 1960–72', Ph.D. thesis, Manchester University 1975; C. Allen, 'Sierra Leone politics since Independence', *African Affairs*, 67 (1968), 305–29; T. S. Cox, *Civil–Military Relations in Sierra Leone* (Cambridge, Mass. 1976); R. Simpson, 'Ethnic conflict in Sierra Leone', in V. A. Olorunsola (ed.), *The Politics of Cultural Sub-Nationalism in Africa* (Garden City, N.Y. 1972), pp. 153–88.

2. M. Staniland, *The Lions of Dagbon* (Cambridge 1975); J. Dunn and A. F.

Robertson, *Dependence and Opportunity: Political Change in Ahafo* (Cambridge 1973); R. Crook, 'Local-central relations in Ashanti', Ph.D. thesis, London 1977.

3. In doing so I have drawn particularly on Clapham, *Liberia and Sierra Leone*, pp. 13–16, and on Allen, 'Sierra Leone politics'.

4. L. Van der Laan, *The Sierra Leone Diamonds* (London 1965).

5. Cartwright, *Politics in Sierra Leone*, pp. 103–22.

6. Though it should not be forgotten that Sir Milton used force frequently, and that many of the tendencies that predominated under Albert Margai had their origins under his brother, notably southern bias and the appointment of Margai supporters to senior civil service posts (see Allen, 'Sierra Leone politics', pp. 308–14).

7. The coup and the NRC period are best described in Cox, *Civil–Military Relations*, with additional detail in *West Africa*, 27 April 1968, 4 May 1968 and 10 September 1976, and in *Africa Confidential 1967*, no. 7, pp. 1–3.

8. E.g. Paul Dunbar, M.P. (discussed in V. Minikin, 'Local politics in Kono district 1945–70', Ph.D. thesis, Birmingham University 1971) and Paramount Chief Yumkella of Kambia.

9. This period is described, but not really analysed, in King, 'Political stability', ch. 4.

10. See *ibid.*, pp. 258–63, and *West Africa*, 2–23 April 1971.

11. *West Africa*, 7 and 14 February 1977.

12. The main accounts of the Sierra Leone economy I have used are R. G. Saylor, *The Economic System of Sierra Leone* (Durham, N.C. 1966); F. A. N. Lisk, 'The political economy of Sierra Leone 1961–71', Ph.D. thesis, Birmingham University 1971; J. L. Collier, 'Economic welfare or economic independence as a central problem of development: the case of Sierra Leone 1951–70', Ph.D. thesis, Johns Hopkins University 1974; and J. F. S. Levi, *African Agriculture: Economic Action and Reaction in Sierra Leone* (Slough 1976). Economic data is taken from Sierra Leone, *Annual Statistical Digest*, Bank of Sierra Leone, *Annual Report* and *Economic Review*. For recent data see *African Development*, April 1976, pp. 371–402, and subsequent issues; and Economist Intelligence Unit, *Quarterly Economic Review: Ghana, Sierra Leone, Gambia, Liberia*.

13. Lisk, 'Political economy', p. 100.

14. Lisk, 'Political economy', pp. 101–20; Collier, 'Economic welfare', pp. 496–506; *West Africa*, 12 April 1970.

15. Levi, *African Agriculture*, pp. 141–6, and 'African agriculture misunderstood: policy in Sierra Leone', *Food Research Institute Studies*, 13: 3 (1974), 239–61; *African Development*, April 1976, p. 391.

16. A. Rake, 'Hard times for Sierra Leone economy', *African Development*, April 1976, p. 380; *Quarterly Economic Review: Ghana, Sierra Leone ...*, 1976/3.

17. *African Development*, April 1976, pp. 383–5 and 387–9; *West Africa*, 3 November 1975. Diamond prices rose substantially, however, in 1976, giving a large increase in revenue from diamonds in that year.

248

18. Minikin, 'Local politics in Kono', pp. 352–3, 424–9; N. O. Leighton, 'The Lebanese middleman in Sierra Leone', Ph.D. thesis, Indiana University 1971, pp. 283–5; Clapham, *Liberia and Sierra Leone*, pp. 111–13, is more non-committal.
19. F. Fanon, *The Wretched of the Earth* (London 1965); A. Zolberg, 'The structure of political conflict in the new states of tropical Africa', *American Political Science Review*, 68 (1966), 70–87; S. P. Huntington, *Political Order in Changing Societies* (New Haven 1968). See also Donal Cruise O'Brien, 'Modernization, order and the erosion of a democratic ideal', *Journal of Development Studies*, 8: 4 (1972), 351–78.
20. This section generalizes broadly about West African politics, drawing on material cited in the other chapters in this volume; see also my bibliographical guides in P. C. W. Gutkind and I. Wallerstein (eds), *The Political Economy of Contemporary Africa* (Beverly Hills 1976) and P. C. W. Gutkind and P. Waterman (eds), *African Social Studies* (London 1977).
21. See e.g. R. Joseph, 'Radical nationalism in Cameroun: the case of the UPC', D.Phil. thesis, Oxford University, 1973, and my forthcoming article, 'West African labour and radical nationalism 1944–52'.
22. On Poro, see Kilson, *Political Change*, pp. 256–8, and K. Little, 'The political function of the Poro', *Africa*, 35: 4 (1965), 349–65 and 36: 1 (1966), 62–72.
23. Kilson, *Political Change*, ch. 13.
24. See Minikin, 'Local politics in Kono', chaps. 5 and 6; Cartwright, *Politics in Sierra Leone*, chs. 7–13.
25. See for example, Ghana, B. Beckman, *Organising the Farmers* (Uppsala 1976), and V. Levine, *Political Corruption* (Stanford 1975).
26. This section draws on *West Africa*, 1968–77; Clapham, *Liberia and Sierra Leone*; King, 'Political stability'; and the local politics sources below.
27. Cox, *Civil–military relations*, ch. 4.
28. See *West Africa*, 22 March 1959 and 3 May 1969 (kidnapping); 26 February 1973 and 3 December 1973 (ritual murder); 15 November 1976 (fraud).
29. On these families see W. L. Barrows, *Grassroots Politics in Sierra Leone* (New York 1976), esp. ch. 5.
30. *Ibid.*, pp. 235, 242; *West Africa*, 7 October 1974.
31. *West Africa*, 15 April 1974; 15 December 1975; 3 May 1976.
32. Minikin, 'Local politics in Kono', p. 321.
33. V. Minikin and P. K. Mitchell, 'Demography and politics in Kenema and Makeni, Sierra Leone', *Pan-African Journal*, 4: 1 (1971), 29–30.
34. Allen, 'Sierra Leone politics', p. 306; J. B. Riddell, *The Spatial Dynamics of Modernization in Sierra Leone* (Evanston, Illinois 1970).
35. J. Cartwright, 'Party competition in a developing nation', *Journal of Commonwealth Political Studies*, 10: 1 (1972), 71–90; F. M. Hayward, 'The development of a radical political organization in the bush', *Canadian Journal of African Studies*, 6: 1 (1972), 1–28.

36. See e.g. Barrows, *Grassroots Politics*, ch. 5 and p. 234; Minikin, 'Local politics in Kono', pp. 311–15 and 354–7.

37. For material on this topic, see Gutkind and Wallerstein, *Political Economy of Contemporary Africa*, pp. 296–8; and for a debate on Nigerian data, see P. C. Lloyd, *Power and Independence* (London 1975) and J. Y. D. Peel, 'Inequality and action: the forms of Ijesha social conflict', paper delivered to the Conference on Inequality in Africa, Mount Kisco, New York 1976.

38. Thie social category has often been incorporated in the literature into the larger category 'petty bourgeoisie', due to the former's modest ownership of property and intermediate status between foreign capital and indigenous subordinate classes. Such a usage seems to me misleading in most West African states, though less so in Sierra Leone where there is no large-scale ownership of capital or property by Africans. For further discussion see C. Leys, 'The "over-developed" post-colonial state: a re-revaluation', *Review of African Political Economy* 5 (1976), 39–48 and G. Williams, 'There is no theory of petty bourgeois politics', *Ibid.*, 6 (1976), 84–9. For Kilson's analysis, see *Political Change*, pp. 79–93.

39. Collier, 'Economic welfare', pp. 388–90, Leighton, 'Lebanese middleman', pp. 267–75. For the official enquiries see particularly, Sierra Leone, *Report of the Forster Commission of Inquiry on Assets of Ex-Ministers and Ex-Deputy Ministers* (Freetown 1968), and *Report of the Beoku-Betts Commission of Inquiry into the Sierra Leone Produce Marketing Board* (Freetown 1968).

40. N. A. Cox-George, *African Participation in Commerce*, pp. 14–15; Sierra Leone, *An Economic Survey of Sierra Leone 1949* (Freetown 1951), p. 24. Further data on the Lebanese can be found in H. L. van der Laan, *The Lebanese Traders in Sierra Leone* (The Hague 1975).

41. Leighton, 'Lebanese middleman', pp. 274–85; Collier, 'Economic welfare', pp. 288–90.

42. Collier, 'Economic welfare', pp. 449, 517.

43. Saylor, *Economic System*, pp. 155–6; Collier, 'Economic welfare', pp. 523–4; see also S. L. Bangura, 'Hard hit by western recession', *African Development*, April 1976, p. 382, for continuation of this phenomenon.

44. See M. Harbottle, *The Knave of Diamonds* (London 1976); *West Africa*, 22 November 1969–28 February 1970; 27 June 1970; 30 June 1972; 11 August 1972; and for other instances of corruption, *African Development*, Nov. 1 1976, pp. 1235–6 and December 1976, p. 1367; *West Africa*, 5 August 1974 and 10 March 1975.

45. Minikin, 'Local politics in Kono', pp. 417–18.

46. D. Rosen, 'Diamonds, diggers and chiefs: the politics of fragmentation in a West African society', Ph.D. thesis, University of Illinois 1973, pp. 131–2.

47. *Ibid.*, ch. 4; Minikin, 'Local politics in Kono', pp. 352–3; van der Laan, *The Sierra Leone Diamonds*, ch. 4; *West Africa*, 21 and 28 February 1969.

48. See note 20 above; and R. Sandbrook and R. Cohen (eds), *The Development of an African Working Class* (London 1975); R. Jeffries, 'The politics of trade unionism in Ghana', Ph.D. thesis, London University 1974.

49. See e.g. C. H. Allen, 'Union-party relationships in francophone West Africa', in Sandbrook and Cohen (eds), *Development of an African Working Class*.

50. H. E. Conway, 'Industrial relations in Sierra Leone', Ph.D. thesis, London University, 1968; F. A. N. Lisk, 'Industrial relations in Sierra Leone', M.Sc. thesis, University of Belfast, 1970, esp. ch. 4.

51. For the 1955 strike, see Conway, 'Industrial relations', ch. 6; Sierra Leone, *Report of the Commission of Inquiry into the Strike and Riots in Freetown, Sierra Leone, during February 1955* (Freetown 1955). For Fanonist ideas among workers in Ghana at the same period, see Jeffries, 'Trade unionism in Ghana', esp. pp. 67–87.

52. See e.g. Sierra Leone, *Report of the Commission of Inquiry into the Administration and Conduct of the Sierra Leone Artisan and Allied Workers Union 1965–68* (Freetown 1970), and *Report of the Faulkner Commission of Inquiry into the Finance and Administration of the Transport and General Workers' Union* (Freetown 1970).

53. *West Africa*, 4 February 1972; for the significance of similar events in Tanzania see I. Shivji, *Class Struggles in Tanzania* (London 1976), chs. 12–13.

54. See W. Barrows, *Grassroots Politics* and 'Local-level politics in Sierra Leone: alliances in Kenema district', Ph.D. thesis, Yale University 1971, ch. 7; V. Minikin, 'Local politics in Kono', and 'Some comments on "Party competition in a developing nation" ', *Journal of Commonwealth Political Studies*, 11: 3 (1973), 265–71, and 'Indirect political participation in two Sierra Leone chiefdoms', *Journal of Modern African Studies*, 11: 1 (1973), 129–35; R. K. Tangri 'Conflict and violence in contemporary Sierra Leone chiefdoms', *Journal of Modern African Studies*, 14: 2 (1976), 311–21.

55. Kilson, *Political Change*, pp. 60, 180 (and in general pp. 60–4, 179–89).

56. Barrows, 'Local-level politics', pp. 316–17.

57. Tangri, 'Conflict and violence', p. 320.

58. J. Cartwright, 'A rejoinder', *Journal of Commonwealth Political Studies*, 11: 3 (1973), p. 276.

59. Rosen, 'Diamonds, diggers and chiefs', pp. 149–99; Minikin, 'Local politics in Kono', pp. 404–5; see also K. Little, *African Women in Towns* (Cambridge 1974), *passim* and F. C. Steady, 'The structure and function of women's voluntary associations in Freetown', D.Phil. thesis, Oxford University 1973.

60. J. Pollock, 'Influence, authority and economic opportunity in a modern West African community', Ph.D. thesis, Edinburgh 1970. See also F. I. Khuri, 'The influential men and the exercise of influence in Magburaka, Sierra Leone', Ph.D. thesis, University of Oregon 1964.

61. 'Populism' is a vague term, which is used here in the senses mentioned by John Saul in 'On African populism', pp. 152–79 of G. Arrighi and J. S Saul *Essays on the Political Economy of Africa* (New York 1973).

62. Tangri, 'Conflict and violence', pp. 313, 319–20.

63. Minikin, 'Indirect political participation', p. 129.

64. See H. Alavi, 'Peasant classes and primordial loyalties', *Journal of Peasant Studies*, 1: 1 (1973), 23–62.
65. Comparison might be made with the emirate system in Northern Nigeria and with the Mouride areas of Senegal; see C. S. Whitaker, *The Politics of Tradition* (Princeton 1970); D. C. O'Brien, *Saints and Politicians* (Cambridge 1975), especially ch. 4; A. U. Jalingo, 'The failure of radical politics in Northern Nigeria', M.Sc. dissertation, Edinburgh University 1975.

CHAPTER 9. CONCLUSION

1. Michael A. Cohen, *Urban Policy and Political Conflict in Africa: A Study of the Ivory Coast* (Chicago 1974), chapter 6.
2. See the chapters by O'Brien, Campbell and Johnson above.
3. S. J. Hogben and A. H. M. Kirk-Greene, *The Emirates of Northern Nigeria* (London 1966). I. F. Nicolson, *The Administration of Nigeria 1900–1960. Men, Methods and Myths* (Oxford 1969). C. S. Whitaker Jr, *the Politics of Tradition* (Princeton 1970).
4. Cf. Henry L. Bretton, *Power and Politics in Africa* (London 1973).
5. But for an illuminating beginning in respect to Senegal see Donal Cruise O'Brien, *Saints and Politicians; Essays in the Organisation of a Senegalese Peasant Society* (Cambridge 1975).
6. See especially O'Brien, *Saints and Politicians*, ch. 6.
7. See John Dunn, 'Politics in Asunafo' in Dennis Austin and Robin Luckham (eds), *Politicians and Soldiers in Ghana 1966–1972* (London 1975), pp. 164–213; and John Dunn and A. F. Robertson, *Dependence and Opportunity. Political Change in Ahafo* (Cambridge 1973), especially ch. 8.
8. See e.g. Samuel Decalo, *Coups and Army Rule in Africa* (New Haven 1976), chs. 2 and 3, especially pp. 90–1. For a helpful brief survey of Dahomean politics see Dov Ronen, *Dahomey Between Tradition and Modernity* (Ithaca N.Y. 1975).
9. Alasdair Macintyre, *Against the Self-Images of the Age. Essays on Ideology and Philosophy* (London 1971). ch. 22.
10. Cf. John Dunn, 'The eligible and the elect: Arminian thoughts on the social determination of Ahafo leaders', in W. H. Morris-Jones (ed.), *The Making of Politicians: Studies from Africa and Asia* (Institute of Commonwealth Studies, *Commonwealth Papers*. xx, London 1976), pp. 49–65.
11. David Lewis, *Counterfactuals* (Oxford 1973), p. 1.
12. See Lewis, *Counterfactuals*, esp. pp. 85 and 65–77, 84–95.
13. For a firm statement see John Plamenatz, *Democracy and Illusion. An Examination of Certain Aspects of Modern Democratic Theory* (London 1973), esp. ch. 7.

INDEX

Abidjan 44, 51, 86–7, 90, 92, 101, 104, 106, 231
Abuja 168
Aburi meeting 155
Accra 24, 26, 42
Acheampong, General 29, 32
Action Group (AG) 139–43, 145, 149, 152, 210, 241
Adamolekun, L. 228
Adebiyi Commission 170, 244
Adebo Commission 160, 164, 243
Adelabu, Adegoke 151–2, 242
Afigbo, A. 242
Agbekoya 209
Agni 90
Akan 28
Akinjogbin, I. 221
Akintola, Chief 142
Alavi, H. 218, 252
Alfa Yaya 38, 224
Algeria 36, 39, 41, 58, 60, 80
Alioune Dramé 43–4, 57
All People's Congress (APC) 191–3, 195–6, 199, 200, 202–3, 205, 208–9
Allen, Christopher 189–210, 212, 247–9, 251
Alusuisse 194
Americo-Liberians 119–23, 125, 129–30
Amin, General 211, 215
Amin, S. 11, 219, 221, 229, 234–7, 239
Amon d'Aby, F. N. 228
Anderson, P. 218
Angola 6, 60, 65, 171, 244
Anlo Youth Association 28
Anoma, Joseph 89
Apter, D. 223
Ashanti (Asante) 19, 20, 28, 189
Asiodu, Philip 160, 167, 243
Assamoi, Alphonse 89
Asunafo 220, 222

Atanda, J. A. 242
Austin, D. 217, 220, 222–4
Awolowo, Chief 142, 144–5, 149, 154–5, 157
Ayida, Allison 159, 162, 243
Azikiwe, Dr 143, 151

Bai Sebora Kamal 201
Bailey, F. G. 218
Baird, William 193, 196
Baker, P. 245
Balans, J. L. 247
Bandama 98
Bangura, Brigadier 193, 199
Bangura, S. L. 250
Banjo, Colonel 155
banks 79, 138, 147, 153, 159, 161, 169; World Bank 146–7
Baoulé 71
Baptiste, F. A. 242
Barbé, R. 229
Barnes, L. 230, 234
Barrows, W. 207–9, 249–51
Bash-Taqi, Ibrahim 199, 205
bauxite 47–8, 59, 60, 193, 196
Bebler, A. 217
Beckman, B. 249
Beer, C. E. F. 220, 242, 244–5
Behrman, L. 247
Beleky, L. P. 240
Ben Bella 36
Bengaly Camara 52, 57
Benin 2
Berg, E. J. 219, 230
Berman, B. J. 218
Berry, S. 219
Biafra 152, 154–6, 163–4
Biairnes, P. 245
Bika, Ernest 238
Bing, G. 222–3

Biobaku, Dr S. 142
Birmingham, W. 223
Bisalla, Major-General 166, 168
Bissau 44
Bo 193, 200
Boissevain, J. 218
Bokassa, Emperor 3
Boké 48
Bong County 124; Bong Mining
    Company 127
Bonny 155
Bouaké 90
Boussac 78
Braimah, J. A. 222
Brass, P. R. 221
Brett, E. A. 17, 221
Bretton, H. 16, 212, 220, 221, 223, 252
Brzezinski, Z. 217
Busia, Dr Kofi 13, 27–9

Cabral, Amilcar 6, 43, 51
Caire, G. 232
Camara, S. S. 228
Cameroons 4, 205, 232
Campbell, Bonnie 66–116, 229, 232,
    234, 236, 239
Campbell, J. K. 218
Cape Verde Islands 6
capitalism 2–8, 11–14, 16–19, 26, 32–4,
    38, 60–1, 63, 66–116, 130–72, 198,
    203–4, 211, 213–15, 229
capital outflows 12, 82, 84, 97–9, 114,
    194–6, 235
Cartwright, J. 191, 202, 208, 247–9, 251
Casamance 184–6
cement 156, 163, 204
Central African Republic 3
Chaffard, G. 45, 225
Chaliand, G. 218
Charbonneau, R. 95, 234
Charles, B. 227–8
chiefs; Native Authorities 37, 50, 53, 56,
    69, 70, 73, 124, 128, 140,144, 146,
    151, 164, 168, 190, 192, 197, 198,
    200–4, 207–10, 226
civil servants; bureaucrats; state
    bureaucracy 14, 15, 28, 29, 31, 32, 43,
    61, 63, 64, 67, 70, 83, 87–9, 103, 106,
    109–12, 114–15, 123, 138–9, 142,
    144–6, 150, 153–61, 163–7, 169, 175,
    179–82, 205
Clapham, Christopher 117–31, 189,
    239–40, 247–9
Cleaver, E. 224
clientage 9, 25, 124, 129, 137, 139, 141,
    143, 146, 148–9, 151, 156, 165, 168,

181, 186, 190, 197–8, 202–3, 205–6,
    208–10, 213, 216, 218
Clough, P. 244
Clower, R. L. 240
cocoa; cocoa farmers 11, 29–33, 69, 70,
    72, 77, 79, 80, 83, 84, 93–5, 102–4,
    140, 143, 151, 164–5, 193, 195, 220,
    230
coffee 46, 68–70, 72, 77, 79, 80, 83, 84,
    94, 95, 102–4, 128, 193, 195, 230,
    232, 236
Cohen, D. L. 219
Cohen, M. L. 89, 91, 108, 219, 221,
    232–4, 236–9, 252
Cohen, R. 217, 245, 250
Coleman, J. S. 245
collectivization 55, 56
Collier, J. L. 248, 250
Collins, P. 243
colons 37, 41, 69
Compagnie Française de l'Afrique
    Occidentale (CFAO) 78, 127
Compte, G. 101, 232–3, 236
Conakry 36–8, 40–5, 54–6, 58, 59, 64
Conde, A. 228
Convention People's Party (CPP) 22–30,
    210
Conway, H. E. 251
Copans, J. 219
Corrigan, P. 241
Cotonou 214
Cottingham, C. 247
Coulon, C. 238
counterfactuals 214–16
Cox, T. S. 247–9
Cox-George, N. A. 250
Creoles 190, 191, 197, 200, 202, 206
Cronje, S. 243
Crook, R. 189, 248
Crowder, M. 17, 220
Cruise O'Brien, Donal 173–88, 222,
    246–7, 249, 252
Cruise O'Brien, Rita 219, 246–7

Daaku, K. Y. 221
Dahomey/Benin 5, 18, 19, 85, 214, 252
Dakar 44, 45, 51, 175–6, 180–6, 233
Danjuma, Lt-General 166–7
Danquah, Dr 24
Davidson, B. 217–18
Decalo, S. 217, 252
decolonization 19, 23, 71, 73, 75, 76, 84,
    138, 141, 151, 168, 194, 196, 198, 212
Decreane, P. 238
Delaporte, G. 231–2
Delco 128

Demby family 200
Dennis, Cecil 121
Dennis, William 121
DeShield, McKinley 122
Dia, Mamadou 177
Diagne, Blaise 178, 187
Diagne, Pathé 236–7
Diakité, C. A. 228
diamonds 191, 193–4, 196, 204–6, 208, 248
Diawandou Barry 57
Diawara, A. 228
Dina Commission 159
Diop, Cheikh Anta 177–9, 245–6
Diop, Mahjmout 176–7
Diouf, Abdou 174
Diouf, Galandou 178
dioulas 49
Dobrska, Z. 231–2
drought 3, 4
Dudley, B. J. 146, 242, 245
Dumont, F. 246
Dumont, R. 61
Dunbar, Paul 201, 248
Dunn, John 1–21, 189, 211–16, 218, 220–3, 247, 252
Durkheim, E. 241

Egypt 155, 178
elections; electorate 20, 22, 23, 26–8, 30, 46, 50, 53, 58, 89, 91, 139–40, 143, 152, 168–9, 173–5, 186, 190–1, 196–203, 207, 213–14
Elima 68
Enugu 150
Ewe 27, 28, 222

factory workers; urban wage-workers; industrial workers 13, 31–3, 90, 106–8, 152, 162, 164–6, 170, 190, 203, 205–7
Fahnbulleh, Henry 126
Fajuyi, Brigadier 144
Fanon, Frantz 196, 206, 249, 251
Fante 28
Firestone Rubber Company 118, 127–8
First, R. 62, 217, 221, 227, 245
Fitch, B. 222–3
Foccart, Jacques 45–6
Foltz, W. 247
Fonds d'Investissement pour le Développement Économique et Sociale (FIDES) 75, 79
Forna, Mohammed 199
Foster, P. 223
Foulahs; Foulah Plot 44, 46, 49, 58, 59, 225

Fouta Djalon 45, 47, 49, 50, 53, 55, 65, 224–6
Fréchou, H. 229
Freetown 191, 193, 202, 206

Ga Shifimo Kpee 24
Gabon 155, 255, 233
Galbraith, J. K. 10
Gambia 5, 117
Garba, Colonel J. N. 244
Gastellu, J. M. 247
Gaulle, Charles de 37, 39–42, 44, 45
Gbedemah, Komla 27, 28
Genoud, R. 223
Ghana 2, 11–13, 16, 18, 20, 22–35, 42, 60, 80, 92, 117–18, 122, 155, 189–90, 200, 203–5, 210, 222–4, 251
Girvan, N. 242
Giscard d'Estaing, President 40, 43, 44
Gold Coast *see* Ghana
Gonidec, P. F. 230
Goody, J. R. 222–3
Gowon, General 13, 145, 156–8, 160, 166–9
Grayson, L. 219
Greene, James E. 121
Grillo, R. 217
groundnuts; peanuts 11, 182, 184, 187
Guèye, Lamine 177–8, 182
Guinea 4, 36–65, 124, 126, 211, 213, 224–8
Guinea, Equatorial 211
Guiné-Bissau 4–7, 11, 13, 15, 42, 65, 176, 211, 213
Gutkind, P. C. W. 249–50
Gutteridge, W. 217

Harbottle, M. 250
Harper 121
Harrley, John 25, 27
Hart, K. 31, 33
Hausa 143, 145, 155; Hausa-Fulani emirates 19, 158
Hayter, T. 232
Hayward, F. M. 249
Hill, Polly 220
Hodgkin, T. 229
Hogben, S. J. 221, 252
Hollander, P. 217
Hopkins, A. G. 30, 221, 223
Houphouët-Boigny, Félix 13, 40, 45, 71, 73, 74, 82, 85, 87, 103, 112–13, 211–12
Huntington, S. 217, 240, 249

Ibadan 150–2, 164–5

255

Ibo (Igbo) 28, 140, 142–6, 155, 157, 222
Ibrahima Barry 57
Ifeajuna, Major 155
indigenization 12, 98, 99, 103, 105,
   108–11, 113, 115, 128, 139, 157, 161,
   169, 203–4
International Monetary Fund
   (IMF) 194–5
Ireton, Henry 12, 219
iron 47, 118, 126–8, 130, 159–60, 169,
   184, 193, 196
Ironsi, Major-General 144, 157
Islam; Moslems 3, 37, 140, 182–3,
   187–8, 190, 197, 224, 226
Ivory Coast 7, 11, 12, 18, 41–4, 60,
   66–117, 121, 127, 155, 162, 213,
   228–39

Jalingo, A. U. 252
Jeffries, R. 217, 220, 223, 250–1
Jenkins, G. D. 221, 241–2, 245
Johnson, R. W. 36–65, 211, 224, 226,
   244
Johnson, Wesley 247
Jones, T. 222–3
Joseph, R. 249
Jusu-Sheriff, Salia 191–2, 198–9

Kaduna 143, 146
Kainji dam 147
Kai-Samba clan 200; Kutubu
   Kai-Samba 200
Kaman Diabi, Colonel 46
Kamara-Taylor, C. A. 193
Kankan 38
Kano 140, 164–5; Kano People's Party
   (KPP) 151
Kano, Aminu 157
Karefa-Smart, John 191
Kay, G. 221
Keita, Fodéba 57, 227
Keita, Mamadi 58, 227
Keita, Modibo 36, 42
Keita, N'Famara 57
Keita, Seydou 58, 227
Kenema 191–3, 198–9, 201
Kennedy, President 41
Kenya 204
Khuri, F. I. 251
King, V. E. 247–9
Kilson, M. 189, 197, 207–9, 249–51
Kirk-Greene, A. H. M. 221, 242, 252
Klein, M. 247
Kolda 175
Kono 191–2, 199, 201–2, 205, 208;
   Kono Progressive Movement 191

Koroma, S. I. 193, 200
Krassowski, A. 219
Kru 125

Laan, H. L. van der 219, 248, 250
labour, forced 69–73, 75, 87, 128, 133
Lacroix, A. 233
LaFontaine, J. 218
Lagos 140, 142, 145, 149, 154, 156,
   164–5
Lamb, G. 218, 222
Lamco 127
Lansana, Béavogui 57
Lansana, Brigadier 192–3
Lawson, G. 104, 230, 232–4, 236–7
Lebanese 12, 112, 128, 138, 204–6
Lee, J. M. 217, 221
Leighton, N. O. 249–50
Lemarchand, R. 218
Lenin, V. I. 242
Lennox-Boyd, Alex 141
Levi, J. R. 248
Le Vine, V. 220, 249
Lewis, D. 252
Leys, C. 17, 83, 218, 221–2, 232, 250
Liberia 2, 3, 5, 44, 117–31, 213
Libya 60, 62
Liebenow, J. G. 239–40
Ligot, M. 233
Limba 193
Lipset, S. M. 2, 217
Lisk, F. A. 248, 251
Little, K. 249, 251
Lloyd, P. C. 219–20, 250
Lofa County 124–5
Loma 125
Lomé 214; Lomé Convention 43, 162
Lowenkopf, M. 123, 240
Lubeck, P. 244
Luckham, R. 217, 221–2, 245
Lugard, Lord 212
Lumumba, Patrice 36, 38, 62, 149,
   227
Ly, Abdoulaye 178

McFadzean, Sir Frank 242
Mackintosh, J. P. 221, 245
Macintyre, Alasdair 214, 252
Macpherson Constitution 140
Maiyegun League 150–5
Malawi 204
Mali 2, 36, 42, 52, 102
Malinké 57–8, 90, 227
Mamady Kaba 52
Mao Tse-Tung 38, 51, 63, 64
Marampa 128

Margai, Sir Albert 190–2, 194–5,
  198–200, 202, 204, 248
Margai, Sir Milton 191, 198, 201–2, 248
market, world *see* capitalism
Marshall, J. 231
Marx, Karl 136, 179, 240
Marxism; Marxist theory of the
  state 9–11, 14, 15, 37, 38, 60, 62,
  132–8, 176, 177, 178, 180, 181, 212,
  218, 223
Massemba-Débat, President 36
Mauretania 3, 4, 38, 117, 233
Melsom, R. 221, 245
Mesurado Group 127
Middle Belt 141
Mikoyan 41
military, the; military regimes; armies;
  military coups etc. 1, 2, 24–7, 29, 43,
  52, 62–4, 85, 86, 88, 112, 114, 125–7,
  129, 131, 143–6, 149, 152–6, 158–9,
  163–4, 166–8, 171–3, 180–2, 188, 190,
  192, 193, 195, 198–9, 204–5, 213–14,
  226, 228, 232–3, 246
miners 13, 31, 150
Miners, N. 245
Minikin, V. 201, 205, 207, 209, 248–51
Mitchell, P. K. 249
Monrovia 121, 123
Morgan Commission 152
Morgenthau, R. S. 17, 73, 221, 229, 233,
  238, 247
Morley, M. 171, 244
Mossi 234
Mouride Brotherhood 20, 183, 247, 252
Moussa Diakité 58, 227
Moyamba 201
Mozambique 6, 65
Muhammed, General Murtala 155,
  166–7, 169, 244
multinational corporations 12, 60, 127,
  153–4, 156–7, 159, 163
Mustapha, M. S. 192

Nasser, President 36, 65
National Alliance of Liberals
  (NAL) 27–8
National Council of Nigeria and the
  Cameroons (NCNC) 140–3, 149,
  151–2
National Liberation Council (NLC) 25–7
National Liberation Movement
  (NLM) 22–4, 26, 28
National Redemption Council
  (NRC) 29–30
N'Diaye, J. 224
Nduka, O. 243

Neustadt, I. 223
Ngango, G (G. Mevungu) 230
Nicolson, I. F. 221, 252
Niger 85, 102, 233
Nigeria 4, 5, 11–13, 16–20, 98, 99, 122,
  126, 132–73, 190, 203–7, 210, 212–13,
  222
Nigeria, Northern 19, 20, 139–41,
  143–6, 154, 158, 168, 189, 197, 252
Nigerian civil war 16, 17
Nigerian National Democratic Party
  (NNDP) 142–3, 157
Nigerian National Oil Company
  (NNOC) 160–1, 166, 169
Njoku, Dr 142
Nkrumah, Kwame 13, 16, 22, 24, 25, 27,
  29, 32, 36, 38, 42, 51, 58, 223–4
Northern Elements Progressive Union
  (NEPU) 140, 142, 151, 209
Northern People's Congress
  (NPC) 139–44
Nyerere, Julius 36
Nzeogwu, Major 149

Obasanjo, General 166, 169
O'Connor, M. 219
Offinso 189
oil 5, 11, 30, 126, 137, 142, 145, 147,
  149, 152–3, 156–60, 163–4, 166,
  168–9, 196, 213
Ojukwu, Lt-Colonel 145, 155
Olympio, Sylvanus 125
Omaboe, E. N. 223
Onitiri, H. M. 243
O.P.E.C. 153, 160
Oppenheimer, M. 222–3
Ore 155
Osoba, O. 241–2, 244
Owusu, M. 222–3
Oyo 141, 157, 164

Paden, J. N. 222
PAIGC 5–7, 42–3
palm oil 46, 76–8, 94, 95, 101, 109, 128
Panter-Brick, S. 245
Parry, E. 206
Parti Africain de l'Indépendance
  (PAI) 176–7, 180, 182
Parti Communiste Français (PCF) 37,
  182, 224
Parti Démocratique de Guinée
  (PDG) 36–40, 45, 48–58, 61–5, 224,
  227–8
Parti Démocratique de la Côte d'Ivoire
  (PDCI) 73, 86, 87, 90, 91, 111–12,
  238–9

257

Index

Parti Démocratique Sénégalais
 (PDS) 175–6, 179–80, 182
patronage see clientage
Peace, A. 244
Péchiney 227
Peel, J. D. Y. 137, 241, 250
People's National Party (PNP) 191,
 201–2
Petras, J. 171, 244
Pinkney, R. 222–3
Pitt-Rivers, J. 218
Plamenatz, J. 252
Polanyi, K. 221
Pollock, J. 208, 251
Poro Society 197, 249
Port Harcourt 156
Portugal 6, 7, 41–3, 45, 46, 65, 162
Post, K. W. J. 2, 152, 217, 221, 241–2,
 245
Poulantzas, N. 9–11, 67, 218–20, 232,
 241
Powell, J. D. 218
Price, R. M. 220
Progress Party (PP) 13, 27–9

Quee-Nyagua family 200

Race, J. 218
railway workers 13, 24, 52
Rake, A. 248
Rassemblement Démocratique Africain
 (RDA) 73, 224
Rathbone, Richard 22–35, 222
Remy, D. 244
Ricardo, D. 241
Richards Constitution 51
Riddell, J. B. 249
Riggs, F. W. 220
Rivière, C. 228
Roberts, P. 244
Robertson, A. F. 189, 220–3, 248, 252
Robinson, K. 247
Roire, C. 230
Ronen, D. 252
Rosen, D. 208, 250–1
rubber 76, 94, 103, 118, 126–7
Rudebeck, L. 218
Rusk, Dean 155
Russia (USSR) 41, 46, 49, 56, 60–5,
 149, 155, 171, 176
rutile 193, 196

Sahara; Sahel 3, 4, 93, 102, 122, 149
Saifoulaye Diallo 57
St Jorre, J. de 243, 245
St Louis 176, 180

Sallah, E. K. 29
Saller, R. 81
Sandbrook, R. 217, 245, 250
San Pedro 98
Saul, J. 218, 251
Savundra, Dr 27
Saylor, R. 248, 250
Schumacher, E. 220, 247
Schurmann, F. 218
Schwartz, F. A. 221–2
Scott, J. C. 218, 220
Sekondi-Takoradi 24, 222
Sembène, Ousmane 246
Senegal 4, 18, 20, 41–4, 60, 69, 74, 92,
 122, 128, 173–88, 200, 206–7, 213,
 228, 246
Senghor, Léopold 40, 173–83, 186–7,
 211–12, 246
Sénoufo 90
Seytane, S. 229
Shamel, Henneh 205
Shell Oil 138, 156–7, 160
Sherman, Charles B. 121
Shivji, I. 251
Sierra Leone 117–18, 122, 124, 127–8,
 189–210
Sierra Leone People's Party (SLPP)
 190–3, 195, 198–204, 206, 208, 210
Simpson, R. 247
Sklar, R. 151, 242, 245
Smith, M. G. 221
Société Commerciale de l'Ouest Africain
 (SCOA) 79, 230
Solod, Ambassador 41
Soudet, P. 229
sport 58, 59, 185–6
Sri Lanka 16
Stalin, Joseph 62–5
Staniland, M. 189, 220–2, 233, 239, 247
state, colonial 2, 3, 5–7, 16, 18–20, 23,
 27, 30, 31, 53, 54, 67–79, 88, 92, 109,
 117–19, 138, 140–1, 148, 150–1, 196,
 206, 209, 211–12, 228
state, post-colonial; neo-colonial etc. 6,
 7, 14–17, 19, 30–4, 47–9, 55, 56, 60,
 61, 66–116, 117–19, 122, 126, 128–30,
 132–72, 184, 187–8, 196, 206, 211–16,
 218
Steady, F. 251
Stevens, President Siaka 191–3, 195,
 200, 202, 205, 207
Stolper, W. 242
Suret-Canale, J. 226, 228–31, 238–9
Syndicat Agricole Africain (SAA) 70,
 71, 73, 87, 89
Szentes, T. 220

Tangri, R. 207–9, 251
Tanzania 36, 37, 155, 251
Tawney, R. H. 14, 220
Telli Diallo 43, 44, 46, 57, 227
Temne 192–3, 199, 202
Thomas, R. G. 221
Thompson, E. P. 14, 220
Tilly, C. 218
Tiv, 141, 143, 145, 152
Togo 28, 125, 214
Togoland Congress 28
Tolbert, Stephen 121
Tolbert William 117, 120–4, 126–7
Touré, Andrée 58
Touré, Ismael 57, 58, 226–7
Touré, Sékou 36–54, 56–9, 61–5,
    211–12, 224–8
Treichville 103
'tribalism'; ethnicity, ethnic associations
    etc 16, 18, 20, 21, 24, 27, 28, 90, 91,
    111, 125, 129, 134, 136, 141–2, 152,
    163, 173, 183, 185, 197, 208, 214,
    222, 234
Tribe, M. A. 219
True Whig Party 117, 121–2
Tseayo, J. I. 241
Tshombe, M. 42
Tubman, Shad 121
Tubman, William V. S. 117, 120–4, 127
Tudor Davies Commission 161, 243
Tukolor 184
Turner, Terisa 132–72, 243, 245
Twi 28

Udoji Commission 160–1, 166–7, 244
Uganda 211, 215
Uneven development 18, 19, 214
Union Progressiste Sénégalaise
    (UPS) 173–6, 178–9, 181, 186–7 (and
    see Bloc Populaire Sénégalais 177)
unions; trade unions, trade unionists,
    strikes etc 22, 24, 37, 46, 51, 52, 63,
    86, 90, 91, 111–12, 148, 150–2, 161–4,
    166, 170, 179–80, 190, 206–7, 220
United Africa Company (UAC) 127,
    138, 150
United Democratic Party (UDP) 192–3,
    198–9
United Party (UP) 24, 26, 27
United Progressive Party (UPP) 191,
    201
United States (USA) 41, 42, 44, 47, 48,
    60, 118, 120, 123, 127, 129, 145,
    149–50, 157, 176, 225, 227

Upper Volta 102, 189, 234
urbanization 31–3, 181, 183–4, 202
Usman, Y. B. 244

Vai 126
Verhaegen, B. 218
Vickers, M. 221, 242, 245
Volta Region 27, 28

Wade, Abdoulaye 175–6, 179–80, 182,
    245–6
Wallerstein, I. 249–50
Waterman, P. 242, 244
Weber, Max 133, 241
Weeks, J. F. 241–2
Welch, C. E. 217
Werlin, H. 220
Whitaker, C. S. 222, 245, 252
Wilks, I. 221
Willaume, J. C. 218
Williams, Allen 121
Williams, Edwin 121
Williams, Gavin 132–72, 243–5, 250
Williams, Gillian 244
Willink Commission 141
Wilson, A. Jeyaratnam 220
Wioland, F. 246
Wolf, E. 218
Wolof 178, 183–6
Wolpe, H. 221, 245
women 37, 38, 51, 52, 64, 193, 208,
    226–7
Woronoff, J. 220
Wreh, T. 239–40

Yacé, Philippe 87, 91
Yamani, Sheikh 137
Yamoussoukro 238
Yendi 189
Yoruba 141, 142, 152, 155, 157
Young, Crawford 218
youth movements; youth protests 51, 52,
    64, 176, 182, 193, 208–9
Yumkella, Chief 248

Zagoria, D. 218
Zaire 6, 36
Zambia 155
Zan, Semi-bi 233–4, 238
Zaria 165
Zikist movement 151, 205
Zolberg, A. 17, 196, 217, 221, 228–9,
    232–3, 236, 238–9, 249
Zuccarelli, F. 247